THE GREATEST TREASON

A novel by Fiorentino Ferri

"The last temptation is the greatest treason
To do the right thing for the wrong reason."
[TS. Eliot]

Foreword

The characters portrayed in this story are fictitious as are the Italian villages in which they play out their destinies. Any resemblance to actual people or places is purely coincidental.

The events and incidents contained in the story are based on fact and hearsay assimilated during boyhood when my Father and Uncle returned to Scotland following their release from Internment Camps in Newfoundland and The Isle of Man respectively and shared what they knew about the sinking of the Arandora Star in which my grandfather died. This was followed by a four-year sojourn in Italy to an area which had witnessed ferocious artillery and hand-to-hand exchanges between the German Army of Occupation and the Allied Army of Liberation.   Attached to the latter were Moroccan Regiments (*Les Goumiers*) from the Free French Army. Having routed the Germans, they subsequently ran amok, looting, burning, raping and killing men, women and children wherever and whenever they found them.

(F.F.)

To my beloved Zio Ettore

Who is Sylvia? What is she,
That all our swains commend her?
Holy, fair, and wise is she;
The heaven such grace did lend her,
That she might admired be.

**(His favourite Song from Shakespeare's *Two
Gentlemen from Verona, music* by Franz Schubert)**

Acknowledgements

My thanks to Grace M and Sergio C for their comments on the Kindle Edition (now withdrawn) of *The Greatest Treason.* They drew my attention to the necessity of retelling my story to a readership which might or might not have a working knowledge not only of Italian and Latin but also a knowledge of Italian, British and Irish History during the first half of the last century (See Appendix Two).

Thanks are overdue to Ronnie S (former Latin Examiner with the SQA) for his Letter in Latin which appears in my story's dramatic dénouement and in-part on the front cover.

And a special word of thanks to Stefano M for his kind assistance in setting the required PDF format for publication.

Cover Designs and Graphics by Stefano Martine(z)

Preface

After two hours of discussion with his friend, Charles Andre, His Holiness, Pope Pius X11th, had good reason to be satisfied with the agreement they had reached.

French Colonial Forces in Italy would be repatriated. In return, he would make an interim appointment to the vacant bishopric of Venafro to resolve local difficulties regarding Church land requisitioned for the French Military Cemetery and to determine the credibility of the French Commander's alleged responsibility for atrocities committed in that area.

The detailed Report he had studied before his meeting with Charles Andre De Gaulle seemed to be fair and objective:

"In May 1944, three Goumier Regiments, under the name Corps de Montagne, formed the vanguard of the French Expeditionary Corps attack through the Aurunci Mountains during Operation Diadem, the fourth Battle of Monte Cassino. These Goumiers Marocains were commanded by General Augustin Guillaume.

"Their value lay in the fact that they were light, highly mobile mountain troops who could penetrate the steepest terrain in fighting order with a minimum of logistical support. The Goumiers' manoeuvre is today viewed by military experts as the critical victory that opened up the way to Rome for the Allies who had come to a complete stalemate against the German Gustav Line[1].

"Relevant comments by the Allied commander, U.S. General Mark Clark, are as follows:

'In spite of stiffening enemy resistance, the 2nd Moroccan Division penetrated the Gustav Line in less than two days.

"The knife-wielding Goumiers swarmed over the hills, particularly at night, and General Juin's entire force showed aggressiveness hour after hour that the Germans could not withstand.

"Cerasola, San Giorgio, Mt. D'Oro, Ausonia and Esperia among others were seized in one of the most brilliant and daring advances of the war in Southern Italy.

"For this performance, which was to be a key to the success of the entire drive on Rome, I shall always be a grateful admirer of General Juin and his magnificent French Expeditionary Corps."

However, what roused Papa Pacelli's greatest concern was the confidential letter he received that day from his Nuncio in Paris, Monsignor Angelo Giuseppe Roncalli[1]. In the main, this letter was devoted to what was termed *Le Marocchinate*- Moroccan Atrocities.

Monsignor Roncalli's figures shocked the Pope: "*.... more than 7,000 people raped by Goumiers: rape against women, children and men, including priests. The mayor of Esperia, in the Province of Frosinone, reports that in his town 700 women out of 2,500 inhabitants were raped and that some had died as a result. Those men who tried to protect wives and daughters were brutally murdered. The number of men killed has been estimated at 800.*"

Angelo Giuseppe Roncalli's letter finished with a statement which horrified Pius X11th:

"It is alleged that General Alphonse Juin told his Goumiers before the battle, which outflanked the German defence in the Liri Valley and broke the Gustav Line: For fifty hours you will be the absolute masters of what you will find beyond the enemy lines. Nobody will punish you for what you will do, nobody will ask you to account for what you might do."

Papa Pacelli could not undo the atrocities committed by the Goumiers. But, as soldiers of the French Liberation Army, he agreed with General De Gaulle that the dead were entitled to proper military burial, as were the soldiers of the German forces.

The problem was that Charles Andre wanted them buried in the area where they had committed most atrocities, which, as chance would have it, was in the far-flung Diocese of Venafro in the Molise Region of Southern Italy.

If he were to keep his side of the bargain with the General, a man of intellect, youthful ambition, intelligence, ingenuity and diplomacy would be required to fill the vacant bishopric of Venafro. According to Monsignor Roncalli, Cataldo Pantaleone, his Private Secretary, was the perfect choice to fill this position.

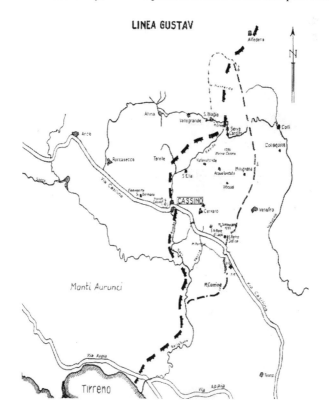

Prologue

The Glasgow Herald, July 4th 1940

British Liner torpedoed off the Irish Coast. German and Italian enemy aliens on board. Nazis panic and rush the lifeboats. Survivors' tell graphic stories.

About 700 survivors of the British liner Arandora Star (15,501 tons), which was torpedoed and sunk off the West Coast of Ireland by a German submarine when carrying 1,500 German and Italian enemy aliens to be interned in the Antipodes, were landed at a Scottish port yesterday. The vessel also had on board British soldiers acting as guards to the aliens and a crew of about 300.

After being struck the liner went down, taking with her many German and Italian victims of the U-boat attack.

A large number of those on board were asleep at the time, and there was panic, particularly among the Germans, when they were aroused by the terrific crash. There was a rush, which seriously hampered the launching of the lifeboats.

In interviews with British survivors yesterday it emerged that great hostility was shown by the Italians to the Germans, not only because of the torpedoing of the liner without warning but also because of the Nazis' ruthless conduct in attempting to rush the lifeboats.

Before the disaster constant vigilance had to be maintained to keep the Italians and Germans from coming to blows.

No estimate of the total casualties is yet possible, but the Italians, most of whom were traders in this country and were interned when Italy entered the war, appear to have been the worst sufferers.

It is hoped that more survivors may yet be landed.

The Arandora Star was owned by Frederick Leyland and Co., Ltd. She was built at Birkenhead in 1926 by Cammell Laird and Co. and reconstructed in 1929 at a cost of £200,000 as a luxury cruiser. This brought her total passenger complement to 360."

Glasgow Herald, 24th May 1941

U BOAT ACE LOST

Commander Who Torpedoed HMS Royal Oak

The German High Command communiqué yesterday said that U-47 Commander Gunther Prien, one of Germany's most decorated submarine commanders, is missing and, must be regarded as dead'.

Prien described in the communiqué as 'the hero of Scapa Flow' was decorated by Hitler with the Knight's Cross with Oak Leaves of the Iron Cross Order.

It is he who sank the Royal Oak at anchorage in Scapa Flow on 14th October 1939 with a loss of 834 lives and also the Arandora Star in which hundreds of German and Italian internees perished on July 2nd, 1940.

Chapter One

Six years had elapsed. In that time, twenty-one-year-old Giovanni Bartolomeo had suffered a series of bereavements which included his father, brother, sister and aunt. It was therefore by no means surprising that the harrowing manner of their deaths had perturbed his sensibilities.

Now, on the last stage of a two thousand miles deliverance from post-war Scotland to Italy, where he hoped to start a new life in the tranquillity of his father's ancestral village, depression made way to panic. Michele Verrecchia, alias *Michele il Brigante,* was the man whose driving evoked in Giovanni elemental instincts of survival.

The rattle-trap motor coach was hurtling to its destination deep in the heart of the Mainarde Mountains, on a road which was little more than a gravel track. Running on bald tyres, the ramshackle bus slid and dragged itself around a series of hairpin bends with apparent disregard for its nine passengers, twelve hens and four pigs.

Only Giovanni seemed concerned with the probability of crashing down the mountainside which beckoned below. His fellow passengers appeared to have every confidence in Michele's ability to get them home in one piece.

Suddenly, the bus skidded to a halt on a passing-place overlooking a vertiginous precipice. Clouds of steam were rising and hissing from the bonnet. Giovanni, who knew little or nothing about combustion engines, logically concluded that water was needed. From the Driver's lack of concern, Giovanni assumed that a water supply was near at hand.

Having finished his cigarette at leisure, Michele reached up to a string luggage rack hanging loosely above the open doorway and pulled down an empty beer crate, which, in a former life had been home to fifteen half-litre bottles of Birra Peroni.

"Let's go Gentlemen!" ordered Michele waving the crate above his head like a piece of balsa wood. "While the ladies' turn a blind eye, we'll do what has to done and be on our way before you can say *Fuck Giuseppe Garibaldi*." With scarcely a glance at Giovanni, Michele and his four cronies stepped off the bus.

Through the windscreen, Giovanni saw five heads disappearing as the bonnet was raised. Seconds later, the noise of clucking hens and grunting pigs was interrupted by a loud escape of steam and obscenities, followed by the clanking of a radiator cap against the engine case.

Giovanni smiled. God alone knew when he had last had occasion to do so as images flashed through his mind of five men taking it in turns to empty their bladders into the radiator.

Once on their way again, Giovanni's thoughts switched from radiators to his brother whose body had been in Police Custody. He reflected on the bus journey from Glasgow to Newcastle where he identified it in the Municipal Mortuary and escorted it to Glasgow for the funeral. A funeral which took place on the day he graduated *in absentia* from the University of Glasgow with a first-class degree in Latin and Greek.

After which came his irrevocable decision to leave the country he held responsible for wiping out his family. To begin what he hoped would be a new life in Italy as soon as international rail links had been re-established.

In an attempt to regain a modicum of composure, Giovanni's thoughts interchanged words from his favourite hymns and prayers. His supplications were interrupted by a clutch of cypress trees signalling the location of the Cemetery where his sister and aunt were buried. The self-control he had mustered disintegrated in an instant. Fellow passengers, aware of the fate which had befallen his relatives, left him to his grief.

11

A sharp bend catapulted the bus into the hamlet of Mottazella. Despite his distress, Giovanni recalled that after the next hairpin bend, he would see Milignano again for the first time in ten years.

Chapter Two

Milignano

In the early evening light, Giovanni expected to see signs of the artillery battles between the Germans and the Allied Armies of Liberation. But nothing on the scale of the devastation he saw when Michele's bus sped to its terminal.

Milignano looked like the set of a war zone in Rome's Cinecittà[1]: pitted tracks and pathways, truncated trees, fields dotted with craters and outlines of ruined and roofless houses. Apart from a few wisps of smoke, there were no signs of life.

When Michele switched off the engine, Giovanni became aware of the silence. Compared to the bustle of market-day activity, barking dogs, braying donkeys, ringing bells, lowing cattle and crying babies which had greeted him on his first visit to Milignano, when Italy was cocking a snoot at the League of Nations[2].

Giovanni watched *Michele il Brigante* rescue his two suitcases hidden under sacks of flour and bundles of artichokes tied to a steel ladder which ran along the roof of the bus and down to its rear bumper.

Michele Verrecchia, driver, black marketeer, general handyman and oracle of gossip, seemed to have surrendered his customary curiosity to the silence of the bleak surroundings. In reality, Michele was thinking of how easy it had been to get his old adversary's son to part with one hundred AM lire[3] for a ten lire bus ride from Venafro. He had never got the better of Silvio Bartolomeo, physically or commercially. His milksop son was another matter.

It would only be a matter of time before he got his hands on the rest of the hard currency he knew young Bartolomeo had in his money belt. Hard currency, even if issued by the Allied Military Authority was always preferable to the edible tariffs he bartered from the locals for transport and jack-of-all-trades services. (hence his nickname as an incorrigible brigand).

Stench wafted from the rubbish strewn on either side of Milignano's main street, nothing more than an uneven pathway stretching from the Campo Sportivo up to Piazza Santa Maria Maggiore.

Giovanni remembered what Milignano looked like when he saw it for the first time: a picturesque village in an unspoiled setting of olive groves, fields dotted with sheep and cattle and houses rising from the volcanic rock of the Pantano Hills at the foot of the Southern Apennines.

It was to this earthly paradise that Silvio Bartolomeo had sent his thirteen-year-old daughter Lucrezia for safety on June 7th, 1940. Three days before Italy's Prime Minister, Benito Mussolini declared war on France and Great Britain. Three years later, Silvio's beloved Milignano had become a battleground for ferocious exchanges between the German Armies of Occupation and the Allied Armies of Liberation.

In the gathering gloom, the silence was broken by angry exchanges when Michele's passengers challenged his demands for flour and artichokes in lieu of cash for carriage and transport services rendered. The Bartolomeo boy's welfare was no concern of theirs. He was Don Pietro's problem and would have to wait where he stood until somebody arrived to claim him like a piece of lost property.

Disoriented by ruined houses and rubble, Giovanni had no idea where the family home was. He regretted not asking Michele for directions before he and his passengers abandoned him at the bus terminus. He decided to walk to the Church of Santa Maria Maggiore where, in the continuing absence of Don Pietro, he hoped to find someone who might know where Silvio

Bartolomeo's house was and if it was habitable.

Lugging his cases, Giovanni trudged up the track. He could see smoke rising here and there from damaged rooftops. He met no one as he passed the ruined houses and spotted no faces peering from shutters clinging precariously to damaged lintels.

Facing him, when he reached the piazza, was the unscathed façade of the Santa Maria Maggiore Church. Sited at the top of a semi-circular flight of concrete steps, the Church looked like an abandoned fortress.

To its left, a First World War Memorial to Milignano's fallen and to its right, contiguous to the Church's facade, the ruins of three partially demolished tenement blocks. Remarkably the middle tenement's ground floor, which Giovanni remembered was the Post Office, was undamaged, its doorway partially obscured by the branches of a scarred lime tree planted at the centre of the piazza one hundred and sixty years earlier.

The tree was a historic reminder of Milignano's feudal past when it was subject to the patronage of La Duchessa Miranda Caracciolo. She was the sister of Admiral Francesco Caracciolo, hanged by Admiral Lord Nelson at the request of the Bourbon King of Naples. At the time, Nelson's flagship HMS Victory was berthed in The Bay of Naples to facilitate his dalliances with the British Ambassador's wife, Lady Jane Hamilton [1].

As Giovanni approached the Post Office, he noticed that its doorway, flanked by boarded windows, was open. Scrambling over the rubble, Giovanni ventured inside.

A smell of damp, dust and body odour assailed him. Two flickering candles in brass holders were propped on the counter providing what light there was until, in theory, electric power was restored later that evening.

Perched between the candlesticks was the source of the noxious odour: an enormous woman shrouded in a wrap-around black overall. Giovanni recognised the small head bristling with grey hair: Ornella Muti, Post Mistress, friend and fellow spinster of his Aunt Bianchina. La Muti had no idea who Giovanni was.

"Porca polenta! My Post Office is closed for business at this time of the day. Santo Cielo. you must be an ass … thinking it could be open. Tomorrow is Sunday. So come back on Monday morning. Not that I care a damn one way or another. But for now, you can take your arse out of here."

Since Giovanni made no attempt to leave, la Muti rose to her feet and leaned between the two candlesticks, her large bosom heaving and spreading over the counter as she did so. "Deaf as well as dumb? We are C-L-O-S-E-D," La Muti spelt the word 'closed' slowly and deliberately, to emphasise the intruder's perceived stupidity.

Giovanni held his ground. As his father was wont to say: barking dogs don't bite. "I would like information about the Bartolomeo house. I need to know if it's still standing.... and if it's habitable"

La Muti said nothing while considering her response to what she felt were intrusive questions. Her hostility was beginning to unnerve Giovanni.

"Who in blazes are you? Standing there like a lump of wet clay. Bothering me with all your nosey Parker questions....and me a defenceless respectable woman....." La Muti's abuse continued in a voice which would have curdled a mother's milk and silenced the chirping crickets.

"Giovanni. Bartolomeo Giovanni. My Aunt is...was...Bianchina Bartolomeo."

"Then you should have said so when you came in! You must be the little pest who used to chase stray cats and dogs into the Santa Maria. So, you're Silvio's younger good-for-something son. Bianchina was never done telling me that you were a gentle genius. Unlike your brother who was a thug like your father....*but of the dead, I say nothing but good.* Or, as a smart ass like you would be more likely to say: *Nil nisi bonum.*

16

"The last I heard about you was that you were a student at the University of Glasgovia. You look like your mother, may she rest in peace with Bianchina. The three of us were great friends....until your father jilted me and ran off with your mother."

La Muti made no attempt to apologise for her earlier rudeness. Lips puckered, she offered Giovanni a manly handshake while looking at his face with scepticism. "A genius, according to Bianchina. Well, I suppose looks can be deceiving." So saying, she took Giovanni by the arm and escorted him from the premises.

"Go past the lime tree and back the way you came. Turn left at the crossroads where my cousin Michele dropped you. Michele would have told you how things were with your house had you asked. He probably thought Don Pietro would tell you what you needed to know. Yours is the house standing between the ruins of two other houses Michele and I bought from cousins of ours before they left for America. Man proposes and …......."

Apart from a few pockmarks on its façade and several broken terracotta slates caused by flying shrapnel, the Bartolomeo home had made a miraculous escape from the fate which had destroyed the Verrecchia investments on either side.

Giovanni was sure a cosmetic job by Michele would put things right. While his father used to say that there were no sentiments in business, he believed that Michele's account would take into account the friendship once shared with his father.

The front door was unlocked. Inside the air was fresh and cool. The floors were spotless. Soot and ashes had been removed from the fireplaces. Every area in the house had been stripped of the furnishings and fittings his father had had installed prior to the arrival of Lucrezia and his aunt. It occurred to Giovanni that some of the furniture might have been stored in the cellar where Lucrezia and his aunt had been murdered.

17

Its trapdoor was in the kitchen. On the floor, at a handy distance, sat a wrought iron candlestick with matches on its base plate. Giovanni lit the candle before venturing down the concrete steps to a terrazzo floor speckled with black marble chips. The cellar was empty. No furniture, no fittings and no sign of the fifty-litre demijohns used to store oil and wine. Nothing: other than some debris partly concealed by a makeshift broomstick. However, nestling under the stairway's recess, Giovanni found a camp bed fixed to a steel frame. Morose speculation about sleeping at the scene of two crimes was interrupted by the appearance of a boy on the stairway. He was dressed in a man's suit, overhanging at the shoulders, sleeves rolled back to the elbows and trousers truncated at the knees. Wearing no socks and shoes, his feet were filthy. He had an incongruously clean face showing bruises from a recent beating.

"Don Pietro," he announced, his dark-eyes staring fearlessly at Giovanni, "wants to see you in the chapel house. He says he's sorry he wasn't able to welcome you when Brigante's bus dumped you at the terminus. He was called away to old Mora's and had to wait until he snuffed it. Mamma says Old Mora is a sure thing for Hell because he farmed his wife to the Moroccans in return for French tobacco and cigarettes. Do you smoke?" he asked waving two fingers and an imaginary cigarette in front of his lips.

"One, I don't smoke, two, you're too young to smoke and three, I don't know who you are."

"Fabrizio, Fabrizio of the Fabrizi at your service. I was born in the eighteenth year of the fascist era ....which makes me ten by Don Pietro's reckoning. And I know who you are. You're Lucrezia's brainy brother as she said more than twice. She promised to marry me so she did...and take me to Scotland on a honeymoon.

"She died right here so she did." Fabrizio outlined an X on the floor with his heel. Walking a few paces to his left he made another X. "And here's where old Bianchina and the darky got theirs ...Your aunt had black teeth and bad breath so she had. Don Pietro says I've to help with the cases. Will you be paying me? I'll take Fi-Boyz chocolate bars as payment which is how Lucrezia used to pay me when I carried her shopping.....she called them *messages* so she did."

"Of course she would since she came from Scotland. It's a deal. If you carry the smaller case and I'll give you two bars of Five Boys[1]. But only when we get to the Santa Maria Maggiore."

Every step of the way to the Santa Maria Maggiore was accompanied by Fabrizio's lively and incoherent chatter: about how Don Pietro had ordered his mother to clean the Bartolomeo house...especially the cellar....how he expected his father to return any day, wearing medals won fighting for the Duce on the Russian Front ...where the snow never melts...where Pollacks worked as slaves...and worms farted like Don Pietro ..and only last week he heard that someone from Sesto Campana had got back from the Russian Front, safe and sound, except for having no fingers, toes ....and no tip on his nose.

Unaccountably, as soon as they got near the steps which led up to the Santa Maria Maggiore, Fabrizio lapsed into silence. Ears alert and eyes wide. Like a rabbit sensing the approach of a ferret.

"You must see my collection of war souvenirs whenever you can, so you must." His whispered invitation was shared with furtive glances right, left and over each shoulder.

"Good evening to you my dear Giovanni." A leonine head of white hair roared a greeting from the window above a door to the far left of the Church's façade. It was the head and voice of Don Pietro Verrecchia, Parish Priest of Milignano since Adam flexed his muscles in the Garden of Eden.

When Don Pietro's head disappeared, Giovanni heard him telling someone called Rosaria that Fabrizio had arrived with his expected guest and that she should open the chapel house door to welcome him, rather than leave young Fabrizio to do the

19

honours. Such words were spoken as if opening the door to visitors weren't part of Rosaria's everyday duties as a Housekeeper.

Whereupon, Fabrizio dumped Giovanni's case and took off like a startled hare. This done, the presbytery door flew open and a furious Rosaria, in widow's weeds and headscarf, lunged past Giovanni knocking him off his feet. The ferret had arrived too late to prevent the hare from making good its escape as the crepuscular curtain fell on the dying day.

"He's for a thrashing tonight when he comes home. And I'll be waiting until he falls asleep so he can't run when he gets what's coming to him, as sure as there is a Christ and a Madonna." Don Pietro's housekeeper, breathless with rage, said no more. She yanked Giovanni to his feet, making no apology for having knocked him over.

Effortlessly carrying Giovanni's suitcases, she led the way to the Presbytery. Giovanni followed her up the dark stairwell with a smile on his face. The darkness concealed his amusement not only at Rosaria's behaviour but also at the subtlety of Don Pietro's warning to Fabrizio that his mother was on the warpath.

In the light of several paschal[1] candles, Don Pietro and an army of soldier ants waited to greet him at the top of the narrow stairway. Muttering grim retribution for her son, Rosaria brushed past Don Pietro carrying Giovanni's cases with hands that would inflict considerable damage when Fabrizio's moment of reckoning arrived. That Don Pietro was thinking the same was evident when he spoke after Rosaria was out of earshot.

"One of these days Rosaria will do Fabrizio a mischief. I keep telling her, if punish she must, she should smack him on the backside rather than use his head as a punch-bag. He's a spirited lad, intelligent and streetwise for his age. He adored your sister and was heartbroken when he came back from Frosinone to find her gone.

"Rosaria can't cope with Fabrizio. She's still in mourning for her husband. Despite the fact that he was a good for nothing layabout before he left for the Russian Front five years ago.......as part of what that scoundrel Mussolini called *The Italian Expeditionary Corps* [1].

"Unlike his mother, Fabrizio still thinks his father will come home a hero. As they say, where's there's hope, forlorn as it is......Besides, as a priest what else can I say to the lad? But between you and me, if Fabrizio's living on hope he'll die from malnutrition"

Giovanni said nothing. If he didn't eat soon, he would die from malnutrition. He was hungry and thirsty. His last meal had been on the Rome-Cassino train earlier that day.

"You know, Giovanni, you were about Fabrizio's age when your father brought you here shortly after your mother died. May she rest forever in peace."

Again Giovanni said nothing. His attention was drawn to the opulent furniture which he felt was inappropriate for a parish presbytery.

Sensing his thoughts, Don Pietro explained. "I suppose you're surprised to see some of your father's furniture here?" Giovanni looked at Don Pietro but said nothing. He had other things on his mind besides furniture. He needed food.

"The Goumiers stripped your house like they did here while I was in Frosinone. They carried off what they could and destroyed what they couldn't. My nephew, Michele reclaimed most of your father's furniture from the Goums after making a fuss with French Command for what happened to Lucrezia and Bianchina. I needed furniture. Michele, brought the best of what he had from his storehouse. Since it's your furniture, it will be returned as soon as you are ready to move into your home. I understand Ettore and Maria will be joining you here in Milignano once they've settled family affairs in Scotland." Giovanni nodded. He had no intention of reclaiming the furniture. He'd settle for bread, cheese, salame and a bottle of

San Pellegrino mineral water.

"Meanwhile you'll stay with me for as long as it takes to repair and refurnish your home. Besides, I'll be glad of the company. But tell me, did Fabrizio say anything about Lucrezia and Bianchina?"

"Not a word, apart from showing me where their bodies were found."

"From what the Borelli sisters told me, I understand there were three Moroccans involved. Apparently, they operated in groups of three. According to the sisters, Lucrezia died first. It would appear that when Bianchina went to your sister's assistance, they turned on her. A turban was tied around Lucrezia's neck when her body was discovered near a dead Goumier. He was killed by the other two when they squabbled over your sister. She died defending her honour. Of this, we can be sure. May she rest in peace. As I told you in my letter, three Americans arranged the funerals."

"Were the culprits brought to justice?"

"Apparently, French Officers picked two Goumiers at random, marched them up to the piazza and had them executed by a firing squad. Thereafter, the matter was closed as far as they were concerned."

"But tell me, Don Pietro, how and why did the Americans get involved?"

"It's a long story. At the time, I was with the village's evacuees in Frosinone. I had to leave Milignano because my parishioners wouldn't leave without me. We got there hours before the Allies locked horns with the Germans. Apparently, a group of Yanks took a shine to Lucrezia when they discovered she spoke English. She was young, beautiful and innocent and, according to the Borelli sisters, they took an interest, a paternal interest in your sister. And Bianchina was always there, like her shadow, to make sure that their interest remained paternal."

"Why didn't Lucrezia and my aunt leave with the others for Frosinone?"

"They stayed for personal reasons. Your aunt and I were once very close. In fact, we were engaged to be married. She refused to leave with me and the others because she didn't want tongues wagging. I accepted her decision and that was that. Lucrezia, of course, wouldn't hear of leaving without her aunt. Word of what happened to them reached me in Frosinone and I wrote to you as soon as I returned to Milignano."

"Is there anything more you can tell me about the Americans who befriended Lucrezia?"

"I've got their names and addresses which they left with the Borelli sisters. I suppose you want to write? To thank them for what they did?"

"All in due course, Don Pietro. But I need to rest after four days of travelling and would like something to eat if that's possible at this late hour."

As if on cue, further exchanges were interrupted by Rosaria who burst into the room without warning Her chores in the kitchen were done. She was going home to welcome Fabrizio with open arms and clenched fists.

"Good night, Don Pietro and Good night to you too," she added turning to Giovanni, "I've left bread, cheese and mineral water at your bedside."

"Buona Notte, Rosaria. And may God bless you for providing supper for my guest ….and for forgiving Fabrizio's trespasses, just as He will forgive those who trespass against Him.". Rosaria made no comment other than slamming two doors as she left in high dudgeon. Don Pietro waited until he heard the second door slamming against the lintels at the foot of the stairway before continuing.

"One last word before we retire, Giovanni. Have you made any plans for the future?"

"I have nothing definite in mind, Don Pietro. On the one hand, I would like to pursue postgraduate studies in Latin and Greek at Naples University if they'll have me. My degree from Glasgow University[1] might not be recognised and then....."

"Of course those half-baked scholars in Naples will recognise a degree from one of the most ancient and honourable universities in the western world. But that's not the problem, is it Giovanni?"

"The fact is, Don Pietro, I think...No, I want to be a priest. I believe studying in Naples might be the best way to settle my peace of mind and guide me to where I want to go."

"Young man, listen to your discerning heart[2]. Doing so will help you decide what's right for you. Hiding away in a tuppence-ha'penny university is running away from reality. The place for you is the *Pontificale Seminario Campano*, which as it so happens is in Naples. The teaching language is Latin so you will have no communication problems until your Italian is up to speed. You can stay there or hide there if you prefer, until they ask you to leave."

"And why would they throw me out if I had a mind to stay?"

"Your tutors have all the experience needed to decide if your late vocation is a true one. Staying the course depends on both you and them. But at the end of the day, they, and they alone, will decide on the validity of your vocation and whether you are destined for a life of chastity, celibacy and obedience."

"If I do as you suggest, who'll look after my affairs here? The house has to be repaired and refurbished before my uncle gets here. A chapel has to be built at the Cemetery for Lucrezia and my Aunt...inheritance transfers and taxes have to be negotiated and settled ...."

"Giovanni, Giovanni. Stop looking for excuses. If you are accepted at the Pontificale, then you won't start until October. You will have two months to settle your affairs and Ettore will tie up any loose ends after you leave. Now be off with you to bed. We'll carry on with our discussions during tomorrow's lunch after I've celebrated the midday mass. And I'll dig out the names and addresses you need.

"One last thing you ought to know. Our Bishop has a particular interest in the atrocities committed by the Moroccans in his Diocese. He compiled a report for His Holiness based on details supplied by every parish in his Diocese, which means the Bishop's report contains details of what happened to Lucrezia and Bianchina.

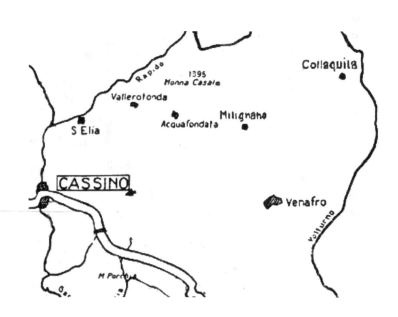

Chapter Three

Sunday 4th August 1946

It was the smoky-tobacco aroma of coffee blended with chicory which woke Giovanni rather than an erotic dream in which he was consummating his marriage to Irma Rossi in La Muti's Post Office. Don Pietro's waspish housekeeper was pouring coffee from a one-cup percolator into what looked like a porcelain thimble.

To hide his embarrassment from Rosario's indifferent scrutiny, he self-consciously pulled a wrinkled bed sheet over his thighs. There was no sign of the supper tray. Rosaria must have removed it while he was asleep. He blushed at the thought that she might have been present at the moment of consummation.

The Church bell began to toll. "And before you ask," Rosaria grouched, "that's the last warning for the mid-day mass. If you want to catch it... you've got ten minutes to move your delicate backside. I won't open the shutters I don't want tongues to start wagging... saying I've got another lover in the bag …as if I'd be interested in an old goat and a little milksop. Talk's cheap. But this Rosaria don't sell matches to fire-bugs…so this Rosaria,"pointing once again to her ample bosom, "looks after her good name."

Don Pietro's comely housekeeper made a hasty sign of the cross to ward off the Evil Eye[1] before adding, "And to think those gossiping piles of fat...stick out their twisted tongues to receive Communion!" So saying, Rosaria marched off with the percolator and empty cup, returning, moments later, with an enamelled basin and matching water-jug, both of which had seen better days.

It took Giovanni no time at all to wash his hands and rub off a five-day growth of fluff on his face with a pumice stone. A serious wash would have to wait until he discovered the extent of the presbytery's facilities. In the meantime, he would have to make do with the basin and water-jug Rosaria had provided.

When Giovanni strolled through the open double doors of the Church, in a wrinkled Hector Powe[1] suit, Mass had already begun. Don Pietro was bending over the centre of the altar: "*Cleanse my heart,*" he intoned in Latin, "*and my lips, O Almighty God.*" The Gospel was about to begin

Giovanni walked down the central aisle and headed for the empty pews nearest the pulpit. As he passed, Giovanni heard obscene whispers attributing his late arrival to services rendered by a shameless Rosaria.

He watched as the altar boy, having moved the missal from the right to the left of the altar, faced the congregation before returning to his place at the foot of the altar steps. It was Fabrizio sporting the bruises and black eyes of his mother's latest retribution.

It didn't take Don Pietro long to race through St. Mathew's parable about the Unforgiving Servant. Giovanni surmised that the essence of Don Pietro's homily would focus on the Spirit of Forgiveness.

Fabrizio handed Don Pietro a battered biretta making the latter's hair stick out over protruding ears when he pushed it firmly on to his head with forefinger, index and thumb. Then, with contrived dignity, Don Pietro moved towards the four columns of granite, porphyry and green marble which supported the pulpit.

Having paused for a moment at the foot of the stairway, Don Pietro could be heard grunting as he lingered on each of its seven steps. A white marble handrail curved its way up and around three quarters of the pulpit's semi-circular platform which adjoined the curved Maremma marble side panels displaying

27

bas-reliefs of Father, Son and Holy Ghost respectively.

Don Pietro leaned on the rail to catch his breath, scanning the congregation below, noting with disapproval the rows of empty pews where Giovanni sat in isolation. Then, before he began his sermon, he gave the traditional blessing which always precedes it. A similar blessing would be repeated at the end of his homily. "*In the Name of Father, Son and Holy Ghost.*" His blessing sounded like a clarion call against the forces of darkness. "And so be it." came the parroted response from a predominately female congregation.

With the exception of Weddings, Funerals, Christenings, Christmas Day and Easter Sunday, the inside of a church was no place for the men of Milignano. Their place, in normal circumstances, would be on the top steps and landing of the Santa Maria, close enough to hear if Don Pietro had something interesting to say, but far enough to encourage comments about this and that as the fancy took them: bemoaning the continuing occupation of Allied Armies; regretting the absence of the good times under the Duce; lamenting the theft of his body from an unmarked grave and differing views as to where Loyalists had hidden it.

When indelicate matters were to be aired, the men would remove themselves to the shade of the piazza's lime tree. There, they would give and receive updates on the alleged promiscuity of the Presbytery's Merry Widow or exchange stories of real or imagined encounters with the Borelli Sisters or the trollops who plied their trade on the Venafro-Cassino highway. But not today.

Today's discussions focused on Giovanni Bartolomeo. The manner and reason of his arrival from Scotland and his disrespectful exchanges with La Muti had spread like wildfire. Within hours, their respective details were common knowledge to every man, woman and child in Milignano. Thanks to Michele and his eight passengers.

Vital questions needed answers. How much money did the boy-genius have in his money belt? How many Dollars? How many Pounds? How many AM lire? Had he really preferred to sit with the pigs and hens? Had he refused to pee into Michele's radiator? Had he cried like a baby when the bus was passing the cemetery? Could someone as unremarkable as Giovanni Bartolomeo have terrorised the Old Dragon in her Post Office lair? Was it true that he had overslept that morning because of the demands made on him by Rosaria Fabrizio?

Giovanni Bartolomeo's arrival was news. The biggest news in Milignano since Don Pietro announced the Armistice on the steps of the Santa Maria Maggiore on the eighth of September seven years ago. It also provided the men with an opportunity to rake up tittle-tattle about his aunt's affair with Don Pietro and how Bianchina, may she rest in peace, had seduced Don Pietro during hours of mutual weakness in the Church's Sacristy[1].

"My dear people, we are an ancient race in an ancient land. Throughout our history, we have suffered at the hands of many invaders. More than 2000 years ago our Samnite ancestors, were attacked by powerful Roman armies who came to plunder, pillage and violate our women in the name of Pax Romana[2]. One thousand years later came the Saracens. After destroying our Sacred Abbey on Monte Cassino, for three long winters, they attacked our villages, pillaging, plundering and violating our women and children.

"And today, history has once again repeated itself." Don Pietro looked at his congregation who were listening with attention. Even the men, assembled under the church's open portals were, for once, giving him similar attention.

"For four years our country was protected from the horrors of the war in Western and Eastern Europe. Little did we know what would become of us when the King dismissed Mussolini and fled like a coward into the arms of the Allies after they had landed in Salerno.

."Little did we know that our former German allies would wreak vengeance on us by setting up their defences on our doorstep in order to block Allied advances on our Capital City; little did we know our American Allies would bomb our towns and bomb our beloved Milignano; little did we know that our Sacred Abbey on Monte Cassino would once again be destroyed and worse still, little did we know that once again our villages would be sacked and our women and children violated and butchered.

"Only this time, my dear people, they were violated and butchered by those the Allies had sent to liberate us from the Germans who occupied our country. Crimes committed by infidels from Africa whose atrocities have been minimised by calling them *Morocannisms* when they should have been described for what they were- crimes against Humanity."

Giovanni could hear sobs coming from the congregation. So far, Don Pietro' sermon had made no connection with Mathew's parable about Forgiveness. Having stirred up raw memories of the atrocities committed by the Moroccan troops, Giovanni felt the Spirit of Forgiveness was the last thing Don Pietro and his parishioners had in mind.

Nevertheless, Giovanni sat back and waited for what he expected would be an appeal for Forgiveness rather than a Cry for Vengeance.

"Every family here present today has had its sorrows to endure, every family its wounds to heal....every family a story to tell.

"Milignano has written the finest page of its history. It is a page shedding light on heroism and on suffering." Sobbing had ceased and in its place, the silence and the stillness of the tomb. After what seemed like an unaccountable age, Don Pietro continued. "It is a page which must be chronicled for future generations so that they might share the experience of their parents, grandparents and great-grandparents, who were participants and spectators in Milignano's theatre of war." Delicately, carefully, Don Pietro stopped for a moment to wipe rivulets of perspiration from a wizened face with the unbuttoned and unfolded cuff of his shirt, "Recently, this morning, in fact, I came across a notebook from my seminary days. In it, I found the words I ought to have spoken when our women and children returned with me last year from Frosinone.

"The words are from Tibullo's Elegy in *Praise of Peace:* Who, asks Tibullo, *was the first to unsheathe the sword of war? How ferocious was such a man.... because his words set in motion the slaughter of our fellow men as nation fought against nation... and opened a shorter path to death.*

"My dear people, these are the words of Tibullo, written over 2000 years ago.

"My dear people, we know who first unsheathed the sword of war in our country... and we know who is to blame for giving birth to a war which was soon to engulf our villages and show our daughters a shorter path to the cruellest death.

"As a priest, I remain shocked by the manner in which our former Prime Minister was mutilated before and after his dead body was hanged in Milan's Piazzale Loreto[1].

"However, as a man, my wrath was appeased by his burial in a an unmarked grave.

"Milignano.... our Milignano.... my Milignano.... has suffered too much for me to feel otherwise. I cannot forget and, as God is my witness, I cannot forgive. As a priest, does this makes me unworthy to serve you? And why do I ask?

"Because, my dear people, forgiveness, for the sins committed by our political masters, can find no place in my heart because they let loose the dogs of war which savaged our people. I will let you be my judges when you can find it in your hearts to forgive the atrocities and depravities endured by our women, our children and our men.

"Nevertheless, my dear People and Brethren in Christ, our Bishop in last week's pastoral letter asked us to forgive our tormentors and aggressors. His Grace asks us not to indulge in

31

selfish ends and selfish feelings." Once again sobbing erupted in the tiny Church. Giovanni felt uneasy listening to comments which were too close to home for comfort.

"My dear people," Don Pietro resumed, almost in a whisper, "we have borne .and are bearing.... our crosses with commendable fortitude. For this, O Lord, we are truly thankful. But which of us can measure suffering to the same degree as the last of Silvio Bartolomeo's family who is with us here today?

"Does the fate of his family not bear the hallmarks of a Greek Tragedy? Father, lost at sea.... in a catastrophe which affected many of our kith and kin .....When an English Prison Ship, with hundreds of Italians on board, was sunk by our then German allies .....His elder brother, Roberto .... himself a survivor of that catastrophe...deported like a galley slave across the oceans to Australia... only to be sent back to England within a year, health and mind broken, to die in tragic circumstances....and then here in our beloved Milignano, the final act of this Greek Tragedy, when his sister and his aunt..... were butchered by the Berber Beasts from the Atlas Mountains of Morocco...degenerates who would pass for men .... When no better than infidel savages and beasts.

"My dear people I would ask you to pray for all of the faithful who have lost their nearest and dearest in the recent theatre of war. And in particular, for the Bartolomeo family, who as Providence would have it, has suffered more than most here present today. *In the name of the Father, Son and Holy Ghost. Amen."*

Chapter Four

The original structure of Rome's railway station was erected in 1867 among the fields and vineyards of the Esquiline Hills to serve the needs of Lazio, the last Papal State remaining in defiance after Italy's Unification six years earlier by Vittorio Emanuele 11, the former King of Sardinia and first King of a United Italy.

As it stands today, Stazione Termine is one of Rome's many surviving monuments to fascist propaganda. Its immensity took Fiachre Fahy's breath away when he arrived on the overnight Genova-Roma express. Having walked along a tediously long platform, Fahy finally reached the cockpit of Rome's principal railway station. Its main access, a neoclassical structure with an imposing portico, loomed ahead of him. Refracted rays of early morning sunshine filtered through the countless narrow windows of its facade.

It was six o'clock and the station was already teeming with an early morning swirl of humanity. A motley collection consisting of sailors, soldiers, nuns, priests, monks, gipsies, prostitutes and peasants. The latter, balancing mountainous bundles of baggage on their heads, followed behind the swaggering menfolk who exploited their labour and fertilised their wombs.

Fiachre Fahy ignored approaches from gipsies, prostitutes and vendors of contraband cigarettes, fake Swiss watches and archaeological artefacts allegedly abandoned by retreating German looters when Rome was declared an Open City eight years earlier.

The vendors' monotonous harangues, supplications and muttered oaths undermining his mother's virtue fell upon deaf ears. Fahy was unmoved and gave them short shrift. He had seen and heard it all before: *The more things change, the more they remain the same.*

With time at his disposal, Father Fahy made for the northern exit and the source of the breeze which was disturbing the careful arrangement of the long strands of hair he had threaded over his bald pate. When he reached its source,, he expected to set foot on Via Porta San Lorenzo. To his surprise, the street had been renamed *Via Marsala* in honour of Garibaldi's eponymous horse... *trust the Romans to name a street after a horse....they lacked the courage to rename it Via Pio Nono knowing that Pio Nono was the abusive name Garibaldi gave his mule.*

Acting on impulse, Fiacre Fahy turned back into the station to check the fate of Via Principessa Margherita at the far end of its western exit. There, he discovered it was now called Via Giovanni Giolitti. He wondered what the former staunchly Royalist Prime Minister might have had to say on hearing his name had replaced the great matriarchal icon of the recently exiled House of Savoy.

Fahy looked at his gold-plated watch, a farewell token of appreciation from fellow army officers when he left Adelaide seven weeks earlier. He found it hard to believe that he had served fifteen years in the Australian Army. But it was true. He had the discharge papers and the ill-health to prove it. *Good, it's only six thirty-two. With any luck, I'll have time for a quick natter with Old Seamus before classes begin.* Fahy's eyes lit up at the prospect of seeing his old friend Seamus.

Seamus O'Fainnaide. A boy-hood friend who never seemed to get enough to eat. Either as a seminarian or as a Member of the teaching staff at the Pontifical Irish College. As far as Seamus was concerned, heaps of delicious pasta, in any of its three hundred and sixty-five varieties, could never be preferred to potatoes, be they boiled, roasted or fried.

Fahy had no doubts that Seamus' first decree as Rector of *The*

Irish College in Rome would have been the abolition of what he referred to as *Unspeakable Continental Breakfasts* which consisted of stale bread dunked in coffee laced with greasy milk. In its place, he would have Donnelly's Irish Sausages and Bacon, served with fried, scrambled and poached eggs, beans, black pudding, white pudding and grated Dubliner cheese.

Sure enough, Seamus had done well for a priest with a modest intellect and a mischievous sense of humour. But Fahy had reason to be pleased with Seamus' promotion. As Rector, he had been able to offer him a part-time teaching post and a roof over his head. *God willing, I'll remain at the Irish College for four years until Seamus retires. After which we'll go back home to Liscannor in Kilfenora County Claire. And every Irishman on the planet knows who was both Bishop of Kilfenora and Parish Priest of Liscannor[1].*

Neither Fiachre nor Seamus had set foot in Kilfenora since the day they left the local primary school as twelve year olds for the Preparatory Seminary at Maynooth on May 16th 1916. The very day Bloody Maxwell[2] executed two injured Sinn Feinners in wheelchairs.

Fahy ran his index finger along the inside of his Roman collar. The starched cotton was already wilting in the heat of the early morning sun. It was chaffing his perspiring neck, as it used to do in the sweltering heat in Adelaide's Internee Camp. He wondered if his Italian had lost any of its fluency since resigning his seconded post as Chaplain to Italian POWs deported from Liverpool by the British Home Office.

Thinking about the internees stuck a chord in Fahy's mind. Tomorrow was the feast of *Santa Maria Maggiore*. It made a connection with one of the internees whose village church bore the same name. The village where the internee's sister had been sent from Scotland shortly before Mussolini's Declaration of War against the Brits and the Frogs.

He wondered whether the moribund internee had survived the

journey by sea from Adelaide to Newcastle. If he had, given the tubercular state of his lungs, the damp Tyneside weather would surely have finished him off. However, the possibility remained that the Red Cross might have sent get him back to die in the warmer climes of his village in Southern Italy.

By the time Fahy got to the National Museum Palace, he decided he had had enough exercise for the day. Given his heart condition, he was wary of over-exerting himself. He would take a horse-cab to Piazza Barberini. It was something he had always wanted to do and couldn't afford when he was a student-priest.

Today, there were only seven horse-cabs in the piazza facing the National Museum. Fifteen years ago, they were lined up on all four sides. He chose the first cab he came to and climbed in without asking the driver how much the ride would cost. He didn't care. His dog collar would, if he were lucky, minimise the over-charging. He sat back. Determined to enjoy what he knew would be the most circuitous of routes to Piazza Barberini.

The carriage trundled along Via Castelfidardo to the Church of Sacro Cuore, and then crawled along a busy Via Venti Settembre into Via Delle Quattro Fontane until it reached Piazza Barberini. Fahy asked the driver to drop him off at the Fontana Del Tritone. From there, it was a short walk to the Via Veneto and the Capuchin Church of Santa Maria della Concezione, where corpses of monks were on display.

Facing the Santa Maria della Concezione were the familiar steps leading to the Pontifical Irish College, which would be home to Fiachre Fahy for the next four years. Or so he thought.

Chapter Five

"Dear Heavens, Tofanelli, take this muck away and bring the Garibaldi biscuits instead. At least, I can dunk them into my coffee without turning it into a greasy mush."

The Bishop's Secretary removed the plateful of offending bagels. "*Greasy mush indeed!*" he muttered as he made his escape to the kitchen. The bagels were made locally by his brother and fried in the finest olive oil. At times, the Bishop behaved like a bagel, *a bagel cooked in water.*

It had been on the tip of Tofanelli's tongue to inform His Grace that a bagel cooked in water was one of the many expressions locals had for describing an idiot. He resisted the temptation because he knew His Grace was too conceited to have a sense of humour. Especially in his present ill-tempered mood.

The Bishop pushed the coffee cup to one side and sat back....*heaven alone knows what's making me irritable these days....venting my frustrations on a numbskull Secretary...over a plate of the baps the locals rave about...people who detest his favourite biscuit because it was associated with Garibaldi's[1] native city. And here I languish...with the responsibility for the care of the Faithful in my diocese...losing my temper over a plate of inedible bagels.*

His Grace, Cataldo Lorenzo Pantaleone, Bishop of the Ancient Diocese of Venafro which dated from the fifth century, was bored. He was bored with the dull routine of Episcopal duties. Bored with the dull provincial people he had to deal with. In his mind, he was a victim of his own success in Venafro and needed the stimulation of a meaningful intellectual challenge.

Six years ago when His Holiness had sent him to tidy up the mess left behind by the French Army, he had done precisely that. His ingenious layout of the French Military Cemetery, where the French Army of Liberation's dead were to be buried, had not only placated the local community but also a sceptical General de Gaulle.

Bishop Pantaleone's reputation was further enhanced with De Gaulle when, thanks to information provided by local Partisans, he was able to prove that leaflets authorising French Moroccan soldiers to terrorise, violate and murder men women and children with impunity, were dropped by German V1 Propaganda Rockets[1]. But that was six long years ago.

Somehow, Bishop Pantaleone had to find a way to get himself transferred from Venafro to Rome where he longed to be be. Once achieved, a Red Hat would be his reward for doing whatever it was that had to be done. The answer was out there somewhere and by the Grace of God, he would find it.

When Papa Pacelli had confirmed his appointment, at the age of thirty six, he was the youngest Bishop in the Province of Caserta. Local gossip put his success down to arse-licking in high places, tyranny in low places and putting politics before his priestly duties. Apart from his mentor, Monsignor Angelo Roncalli, few were able to comprehend the extent and nature of Cataldo Pantaleone's intellect and acknowledge his efficiency as an astute and able administrator. If the Bishop had a future, then it was light years from diocesan routine.

......*Confirmations here, Confirmations there, and Confirmations everywhere*..... Bishop Pantaleone was absent-mindedly thumbing through his diary until his eye rested on *Ordinations*: *Cathedral, October, Saturday,28th.* The first such ceremony since his appointment. The first since 1943, the year his predecessor died. Rumour had it that the late Bishop Tartaglia had died of a heart attack on 25th July when he heard that Mussolini had been arrested by order of the King Vittorio Emanuele 111.

Once again, he rang the bell on his desk to summon his Secretary, Monsignor Salvo Tofanelli. Tofanelli hurried from the kitchen wiping bagel crumbs from his chin with the tip of his index finger.

"Your, Grace, if it concerns the biscuits......"

"Never mind the insufferable biscuits, Tofanelli. I want to know why you've set the Ordinations at the end of October. Why so late in the year?"

"Bishop Tartaglia always held them on the last Saturday of October, Your Grace. But we can bring the date forward if you so wish....."

"No, no, Tofanelli. We'll leave things as they are for this year. Then we'll see. Meantime, bring me the list of Ordinands and today's *Osservatore Romano*[1] if it's arrived. Don't keep me waiting, Tofanelli and bring a fresh pot of coffee."

There were seventeen names on the list of Ordinands. Bishop Pantaleone glanced at the names, Stefano Bandello, Giovanni Bartolomeo, Guido Coia, Mario Franchitti, Celestino Mancini, Manlio Fabrizzi .... he stopped scanning the list. His eyes darted back to the second name: Giovanni Bartolomeo. *Bartolomeo: not a common surname*. It rang a bell. In fact, it rang three bells. The first, Pantaleone couldn't as yet quite place. The second reminded him of Cristofero Bartolomeo the inventor of the pianoforte. The third reminded him of the palace built for Giacomo di Bartolomeo and demolished by Benito Mussolini[2].

Once again Pantaleone rang the little brass bell. Tofanelli reappeared carrying a large silver plated tray containing a Neapolitan coffee pot, Garibaldi biscuits and a newspaper.

"As requested, Your Grace," placing the tray on the Bishop's desk with studied servility, "the list of Ordinands, Your Grace, fresh coffee, Your Grace, and, of course, the Garibaldi biscuits, Your Grace....*may you choke in peace.*"

"For the love of God, Tofanelli, stop fussing. Bring me a copy of my letter to Monsignor Roncalli regarding the Moroccan atrocities. It's in the file containing the names and parishes of the men and women who were violated." While waiting for Tofanelli to bring him the documents, he glanced at the first page of L'Osservatore Romano. Its headline article caught his eye:

MARIA GORETTI: THE SAINT AGNES OF THE 20th CENTURY

Yesterday, His Holiness Pope Pius XII, in an outdoor ceremony in Piazza San Pietro, announced: We order and declare, that the Blessed Maria Goretti can be venerated as a Saint and duly introduce her into the Canon of Saints.

Some 500,000 people, the majority of which were teenage girls, had come from around the world. Pius asked them: Young people, pleasure of the eyes of Jesus, are you determined to resist any attack on your chastity with the help of the Grace of God? A resounding "yes" was the answer.

Eureka. The connection he had been trying to make came to him like a bolt from the blue. He glanced at the newspaper paper again. In an amoral and indifferent world, Santa Maria Goretti was to be the patron saint of chastity, rape victims, teenage girls, poverty and purity. A Saint who would help young women safeguard their innocence.

Bishop Pantaleone didn't believe in coincidences. He was by now fairly sure one of the young women violated and murdered by the Moroccans was called Bartolomeo. Moreover, he was sure his former parishioner would serve as an inspiration to other girls like Santa Maria Goretti.

Once again he rang for Tofanelli. Within seconds, Tofanelli appeared with the requested documentation.

"My dear Toffo, thank you so much for your kind cooperation. And now, if you please, I would like you to pull out the *Santa Maria Maggiore* Parish File and a copy of my *Marocchinate Report* to His Holiness. But do it as soon as you can find a moment, my dear Toffo. However, before you go, have a seat and tell me what you know about Our Holy Mother Church's latest triumph."

Tofanelli looked at Pantaleone in bewilderment until the Bishop waved the *Osservatore Romano* in front of his nose. "Papa Pacelli has seen fit to canonise Blessed Maria Goretti well within the twenty year period as stipulated by Canon Law. Have you any idea why His Holiness brought forward this particular canonisation?"

Tofanelli shrugged off his scepticism, regarding the Bishop's sudden mood change. before replying, "Well, your Grace, I remember reading in the Osservatore that on the evening of the beatification ceremony in 1948, Papa Pacelli approached Maria Goretti's mother, laid his hand on her head and said, if memory serves, *Blessed mother, happy mother, mother of a Blessed One*.

"Apparently, His Holiness was so moved by the presence of the girl's mother that he decided it would be a wonderful experience for her to witness the canonisation of her daughter. She would be the first mother so to do."

"Yes, indeed, Tofanelli.....in point of fact, I was thinking on what must have inspired Papa Pacelli to do what he did after a horrific war when so many atrocities were committed against young girls in the areas of conflict.

"In the person of Maria Goretti, the Faithful now have an icon of chastity to aspire to. The Faithful in my diocese, as you well know my dear Tofanelli, suffered horribly from the outrages perpetrated by the French Colonials. Especially those crimes committed against our young women.

"You will have read my Report on the *Marocchinate*? I was horrified when writing it and still have nightmares about what happened, particularly in the parish of Milignano.

"But, this whole Goretti tragedy, a young girl stabbed fourteen times while protecting her honour, has reminded me of what

41

happened to one particular girl in my diocese. A girl who might well be related to one of the Ordinands whose name is on the list we got from the Pontificale Seminary in Naples."

Chapter Six

"LET HE WHO WISHES TO ENTER THE PRIESTHOOD COME FORWARD". In Latin, the Archdeacon's sing-song voice summoned the Ordinand into the presence of the mitred Bishop sitting in his portable faldstool[1].

A young man stepped forward. He was about to receive the ultimate privilege of the priesthood: the honour of offering the Holy Sacrifice of the Mass, the power to bring souls into the fold of the Most Holy Catholic and Apostolic Church and the right to forgive the sins of his fellow men.

The Ordinand approached the faldstool from the left side of the altar, crowded with the Bishop's entourage of three Monsignors, two Deacons, the Archdeacon and the Parish Priest of the host Church.

The Ordinand was wearing the amice, alb, cingulum, stole and maniple of the Deacon. He held a long white mappula which would soon be used to bind his hands. He bowed reverentially before kneeling in front of the Bishop. As he did so, the Archdeacon introduced him in Latin for the first time.

"Your Grace and most Reverend Father, the Holy Roman Catholic Mother Church asks that you ordain this Deacon, Joannes Bartolomeus, here present before you, to the burden of the priesthood."

The Bishop studied the Ordinand intently: intelligent eyes; the face of docile innocence;....good. "Do you know him to be worthy?" Pantaleone asked in Latin. He did not listen to the Archdeacon's predictable answer. Liturgical prescriptions for ordination ceremonies were enshrined in Canon Law.

The Bishop let his eyes wander over the redecorated church. With the eye of the expert he held himself to be, he put this, the smallest Church in his diocese, into the artistic and architectural category of the nondescript: blue and gold were the predominant colours in its single nave: its lateral walls presenting an expanse of turquoise distemper as a backdrop to two identical baroque statues of the Madonna bedecked in trinket necklaces and bracelets gazing upwards at the domed and garishly gilded ceiling.

The Bishop smiled to himself. He was an El Greco-like figure in his early forties. The over-refined elegance presented by his elaborate purple robes was flawed by rounded shoulders and an elongated neck. A supercilious look of self-assurance was incongruously set in a far from handsome face: lean, with puffy pouches supporting two ebony eyes, set so close to a short squat nose that the overall effect was simian.

For the first time since he left the Sacristy, the Bishop became aware of the individuals staring at him from the body of the Church, wonderment and awe on their faces. Faces which in all probability had never known contentment or had long since given up hope of obtaining it. The drabness of their dress was in marked contrast to the purples, reds and gold brocades of the Bishop's entourage.

As to the faces he saw, they were no better or worse than those he had to endure since His Holiness had seen fit to appoint him to an Episcopal seat in the God-forsaken diocese of Venafro: once a waterhole for wealthy Ancient Roman plutocrats summoned to Capri for reward or elimination by Tiberius, the deranged Emperor who had succeeded Augustus.

Then there were noisy children. As yet innocent of the experiences that would make them mirror images of their elders, their features carved from the same stratum of decay and degeneration that had once driven Bishop Pantaleone from the poverty of his native Apulia.

Milignano had turned out in full for the ordination ceremony. The biggest gathering in Milignano since Don Pietro announced the Armistice from the steps of his Church on the eighth of September 1943.

Everyone in Milignano was proud of its historic Church. Even the men, who rarely darkened its portals, spoke of it with pride. It had been built by *La Duchessa Miranda* as a monument to her dead husband of whom the less said the better. Legend had it that the lime tree in the piazza had been planted by the Duchess to commemorate its first mass, held on All Souls Day. In thanksgiving rather than grief for the death of her detested husband.

"......*AND DECLARES HIMSELF WORTHY OF THIS HONOUR.*........" Recognising his cue, Bishop Cataldo Lorenzo Pantaleone turned his attention once more to the ritual.

"Since, dearest Brethren in Christ Jesus Our Lord," he began, his high octave voice, carrying to the rear of the Church, "both the Captain and the Passengers of his ship have the same grounds for security or common fear, so the opinion of those whose cause is common ought to be equal. Nor has it been established in vain by the Fathers of our Church that the people should be consulted ....."

Bishop Pantaleone's words, delivered in Latin, drifted incomprehensibly over the hypnotized congregation whose concentration was fed by the superstitions of centuries, in which mysticism was stimulated by ignorance.

How were these uneducated peasants to know that the words uttered by their Bishop were a request for their authorisation and not some magical spell which would endow the young Ordinand with unseen supernatural powers? Had they known that they were being invited to question Giovanni Bartolomeo's right to be ordained, some of them might well have been disposed to oblige and answer accordingly.

Many of those present remembered the arrogance, the violence,

45

the self-esteem and imperious manner of the Ordinand's father before the scandal of his future wife's pre-marital pregnancy had forced them to flee from Milignano.

Some remembered the stories of relatives in Glasgow recalling how Silvio Bartolomeo, a Fascist Blackshirt, had terrorised them in Glasgow's Casa D'Italia or in their business premises when found wanting in loyalty to the Duce.

Most knew of his sister's relationship with Don Pietro who was officiating at the ordination of his former lover's nephew. Would the sins of Silvio Bartolomeo be visited on his younger son? Just as they had been on his sister Bianchina, his elder son Roberto and his daughter Lucrezia?

Irma Pacitti's eyes were drawn to the young man who was being ordained. How unlike his father, whose trademark was a pencil slim moustache, bushy black eyebrows, thick salt and pepper hair in a middle parting and long sideburns. Reluctantly, she had to admit that Giovanni's black closely cropped hair, clean shaven and delicate appearance, made him look rather handsome. If anything detracted from his appearance it had to be that silly looking tonsure on the crown of his head, looking like a cat's arse when it raises its tail.

Irma had been Roberto Bartolomeo's fiancée before being handed down, like second-hand clothes to his younger brother....*a kind and gentle soul...extremely intelligent...unlike his brother who was a thug....unpredictable like his father....even more violent... as things turned out when he got back from Australia...Roberto was all hands and tongue and reeked of wine and tobacco...but he excited her... when she was with him it was a struggle being the good girl her mother expected her to be...he got what he wanted from other women...it was his father's decision to break off the engagement ...and replace him with his younger son ...so unlike his brother...non-smoker and non-drinker... a real gentleman.*

Irma watched her former fiancé genuflecting once more before the Bishop and felt no resentment because he had turned her down. Had it been for another woman it would have been a different matter. Giovanni would never have been unfaithful. As Roberto would have been had she been permitted to marry him.

Giovanni had always treated her with respect. Too much respect as it so happened. She had done everything any decent woman could do to induce him to make a pass, short of exposing herself. A complete waste of time and adrenalin rushes. Domenico, her big brother, said that if Giovanni never stood to attention when close to a girl like her then there was something wrong with him.

Irma felt herself blushing. Furtively, she glanced on either side of her to see if Mauro and her mother-in-law had noticed. As usual, they were ignoring her. Of course, Mauro had asked about her relationship with the Bartolomeo brothers. Given she was no oil-painting, she knew he had married her for the cash she had smuggled into the country in her underwear.

" ….......*therefore, what you know of his deeds or morals, what you think concerning his merit you must discuss with a free voice; you must assign the testimony of the priesthood to this man more from merit than from affection.......*"

Mauro's eye fell on Don Pietro's face, asking himself how a man like him had the nerve to appear on the altar with the nephew of the woman he had fucked. A renegade priest who was currently taking advantage of his sex-mad housekeeper. Momentarily, he looked reverently at the statue of the Virgin Mary in the side altar to his right, before venomously shifting his gaze back to Don Pietro.

When the Bishop laid hands upon the Ordinand's head, Mauro switched his attention to his wife's former boyfriend. He was struck by the innocence which radiated from young Bartolomeo's face. The stories circulating about him and Don Pietro's Housekeeper were untenable..The nature of his wife's relationship with Roberto Bartolomeo was another matter.

47

It was all Mussolini's fault for shipping him off to Abyssinia where he lost a leg in the Battle of Enderta[1]. With one leg, none of the local girls would have him. Not that he regretted marrying his mother's import. Irma's dowry was more than enough to pay for the tractor Michele il Brigante had ordered for him in Cassino. It would be delivered as soon as hand controls had been fitted.

The Bishops high pitched voice began to yet another of those prayers which mesmerised the congregation into further immobility. "*Let us pray, Brothers......*" he intoned in Latin when he invited his Con-celebrants to join his prayer. The recitation over, Bishop Pantaleone looked at the Ordinand kneeling before him.

"*Beloved son, to be consecrated to the office of the priesthood, you must be eager to undertake it worthily and when undertaken, to carry it out in a praiseworthy manner.....*"

Don Pietro wriggled uncomfortably on his seat, which was nearest the sacristy door and the furthest from the Bishop's faldstool. He believed that the Bishop's words were directed at him rather than at Giovanni.

Pantaleone always made him feel uncomfortable. He always seemed to be reminding him of his past, which made him feel spineless. Why did he put up with such torture? A man who had stood up to the Germans and had persuaded them, against all the odds, to provide transport to take his flock to the safety of Frosinone before the bombings. Don Pietro knew the answer. Pantaleone had the power to deprive him of his Living.

He had the power to make sure he would never be able to retire in Milignano where he had been born and raised, where his father's freehold of vineyards and olive groves were waiting for his husbandry.

The Bishop's animosity had been evident from the day he was

summoned to Venafro to answer a charge of improper conduct with his childhood sweetheart. How Pantaleone had relished his humiliation when giving him a lecture on the mortification of the flesh, on the dangers of lust and vice, on the integrity of a chaste and holy life and so on and so forth.

Most certainly, Pantaleone had wanted to unfrock him but could not do so because of the requirements of Canon Law. Before dismissal could take place, it needed formal complaints from at least three independent sources. His parishioners had closed ranks. Pantaleone was from Apulia, the land of brigands, adulterers and sheep molesters... no more needed to be said.

Although he could depend on the support of his parishioners, Don Pietro took no chances with Bishop Pantaleone. All Episcopal directives and letters were read obediently and without comment.

When his housekeeper died, he sent details of Rosaria Fabrizio's personal circumstances, sure in the knowledge that the devious Bishop would put temptation his way by rubber-stamping her appointment. On the understanding that she should be replaced as soon as her War Widows' Pension had been approved.

Nor did he question Bishop Pantaleone's surprising decision to hold a singular ordination service for Giovanni Bartolomeo in Milignano. Everyone, including Giovanni, had expected his ordination to take place in Venafro's Cathedral.

Rumour had it that Giovanni's rich uncle had paid for a private ordination service by providing the money for the redecoration of the Santa Maria Maggiore. Don Pietro knew otherwise. The funding had been donated secretly by the Borelli Sisters.

This was the price they had negotiated to receive the sacraments in the Santa Maria Maggiore after a three-year exile in France, to expiate the infamy of cohabitation with the French Officers who commanded the Moroccan Troops who had run amok in Milignano, plundering, raping and butchering at will.

"…. *and so, beloved son, whom the decision of our brethren gathered here today have chosen to be consecrated for our assistance, preserve in your morals the integrity of a chaste and holy life. Recognise that you….*"

Colour drained from Giovanni's face as he listened to his saintly Bishop's holy exhortation.

"*….must mortify your limbs from vices and all carnal desires. Let your teaching be a spiritual medicine to the people of God. Let the odour of your life be a delight to the Church of Christ Jesus our Lord so that by teaching and example, you will build...*"

As Giovanni knelt before the faldstool, the coldness of the marble floor was absorbed by his robes. He was anxious. Not because the alleged burden of chastity would cause him problems. On the contrary, he felt anxious because the burden was non-existent. He had never found it difficult to mortify flesh which needed no mortification.

Even his sub-conscious fantasies were marginally erotic. In the Seminary, his Father Confessor went to unnecessary lengths to point out that there was nothing morally wrong with what he was pleased to call *little nocturnal emissions* because they were inconveniences rather than occasions of sin.

In his humble way, Giovanni believed he was worthy of the honour of being a priest. He knew that it was the loving memory of his sister's sacrifice which had given him the strength to carry on with his studies, particularly during the first year in the Seminary. Without her inspiration, he would never have reached this happy day in the Santa Maria Maggiore.

Ettore Bartolomeo watched his nephew prostrate himself at the Bishop's feet. He had met the Bishop on a number of occasions since he and his wife Maria had arrived from Glasgow three years ago. The Bishop had impressed him, but never more than today. Don Pietro, with typical relish, had told him that the Bishop was from Matera rather than Apulia although nobody was supposed to know. According to Don Pietro, the Bishop was the brother of the notorious Calabrian brigand Mammone[1].

Ettore believed not a word of this nonsense. He never took tittle-tattle seriously. This was why he didn't believe a word regarding the alleged affair his late sister had had with Don Pietro. For a fact, he knew their enduring friendship had started when they all played together as children.

If Don Pietro and Bishop Pantaleone didn't get on, then that was their business. He liked and respected both men. The Bishop, in particular, had proved himself to be considerate in choosing to ordain his nephew in Milignano rather in Venafro with all the other Ordinands.

Ettore watched as the Bishop, still wearing his mitre, rose from the faldstool, genuflected alongside Giovanni and turned towards the Pontificale Romanum held open in front of him by the Archdeacon. Another interminable litany of appeals was about to begin.

As the congregation chorused its *Pray-for-Us* response, Ettore's concentration was interrupted by his wife's sobbing. He moved closer. He watched Maria wipe her tears before they could smudge her impeccable make-up. No mother could have been more proud of a son than she was of her nephew.

He felt happy for her. Giovanni was the son she had longed for and could never have. A careless surgeon had removed more than he should have during an emergency appendicitis operation. An operation which hadn't been done quickly enough to prevent peritoneal dialysis. When Giovanni's mother died, Maria became his surrogate mother. Just as his sister Bianchina had become a surrogate mother to Lucrezia.

Eyes fixed on Giovanni, Maria struggled to control her emotions. Pride lit up her face. Reservations she had kept to herself about Giovanni's vocation had vanished as soon as he appeared on the altar. He looked so happy and all that mattered to Maria was Giovanni's happiness. When her sobbing intensified, Ettore grasped her hand. She wondered how she would react tomorrow when Giovanni offered his first mass and gave her and her husband Communion. Movement on the altar drew her attention to the rituals of her nephew's ordination.

"*Receive ye the yoke of Christ.*" The Bishop was moving the stole from Giovanni's left shoulder to his neck and crossed it over his chest. Then, assisted by the Archdeacon, the Bishop placed the chasuble on Giovanni's shoulders, keeping the rear part folded. "*Receive the priestly vestment by which charity is understood; for God is powerful; that he may increase charity in thee and perfect work.*"

Giovanni's voice was heard for the first time. It was clear and light but loud enough to be heard by all. "*O God, author of all holiness, Bless my vocation as being honest and true.......*"

When his mitre was removed by the Archdeacon, the Bishop turned, genuflected at the foot of the altar and with Giovanni, began to intone the opening words of the Roman Catholic Church's most venerable Gregorian chant: **COME HOLY GHOST CREATOR COME.**

While the Con-celebrants chanted the ancient hymn, Bishop Lorenzo Pantaleone anointed Giovanni's hands with the Oil of the Catechumens[1], making a symbolic cross on the palm of his hands, so consecrated that they may be made worthy to touch and handle the Body and Blood of the Lord Jesus Christ.

"Medieval mumbo-jumbo!" muttered Stefano Ferrara as he watched the Bishop tie the young man's hand with a long strip of white linen. *......might have meant something centuries ago.....rolled up garments... like Masonic Rituals.... what the hell am I doing here? Among this riff-raff,... whose arses have never seen a shirt.... what on earth did his brother have in common with these people.....in this God forsaken dump.... what had brought Artemio running to this hell-hole time and time again when he should have had better things to do.... if I know anything about my brother....the reason must have been a* *woman.... with no track record... beautiful no doubt...and incredibly rich.*

When Ettore Bartolomeo's unexpected invitation landed on his desk in Bolzano, Stefano Ferrara's first reaction was to send a note of regret with a few cases of wine for the celebration festivities. Then curiosity got the better of him. There were questions needing answers. He had to know why his brother had chosen to visit Milignano one last time before moving into the doomed Abbey of Monte Cassino. And days before the Royal Pygmy[1] signed the Duce's arrest warrant tolling the death-knell of Fascism. *......and here I am in the backwoods of Southern Italy....a victim of curiosity..... Bored to distraction..... sitting among country yokels.....watching a ridiculous ceremony held in a language only I and a few others understand.....who are these people kidding?....Receiving the power to offer sacrifice to God.....to celebrate mass for the living and the dead......what absolute bunkum.....*

Despite his cynicism, Ferrara watched with mocking curiosity as the chalice was passed from the Ordinand's bound hands containing what he assumed was wine. If it was wine it was sure to be nothing like any of his vintages. Cynically, his eyes followed the Bishop and the newly ordained as they minced their way to the altar where the latter slavishly echoed the Bishop in a squeaky voice.

Pantaleone glanced at his watch. After two hours it was small wonder the natives were restless. In particular the children, some of whom were playing hide and seek, dodging between the pews and four columns supporting the pulpit. He reminded himself of what St Francis had to say about restless children: *Be still if you can*, which suggested they couldn't. His Grace, Cataldo Lorenzo Pantaleone, Bishop of Venafro, showing patience worthy of St. Francis, ignored the distractions.

"*Receive ye the Holy Ghost,*" declared the Bishop, laying hands on Giovanni's head for the last time. "*Whose sins you shall forgive they are forgiven and whose sins you shall retain they are retained.* Unfolding the anterior part of the chasuble on Giovanni's shoulders with the words, "*May the Lord clothe thee in the mantle of innocence.*"

A cue from the Archdeacon was all it took for the congregation to react. In a time-honoured way and much to the delight of the children, the congregation stood to applaud as Giovanni faced them for the first time as a priest. Modestly, he bowed his head unable to face the gaze of those he loved.

When the applause finally petered out, the Bishop summoned Giovanni from the altar rails for his final warning before finishing the mass.

"*Beloved son, consider diligently the Orders received by you and the burden they place upon your shoulders. Study to live a holy and religious life that you may please Almighty God and acquire His Grace. Do you promise me and my successors' reverence and obedience?*"

"*I do solemnly promise.*"

CHAPTER SEVEN

Sunday 29th October 1950, the Ordination Dinner, Villa Bartolomeo

The legs of the banqueting table were a source of sustenance to wood-worm and local gossips. But it was the largest dinner table available in Milignano to accommodate Ettore and Maria's guests at Giovanni's ordination dinner. For want of better or bigger, it had to be borrowed from the Borelli quadruplets.

The sisters were born prematurely. The Midwife had tagged them Prima, Seconda, Terza and Quarta as and when they first squinted at the light of day. Their parents, emboldened by the fame which followed the birth of two sets of identical twins, refused to change the names given to them by the midwife. They claimed that it would bring bad luck.

Despite pressure from the parish priest, Don Severino Di Meo (Don Pietro Verrecchia's predecessor) who argued in vain that the Liturgical Calendar was full of more acceptable Christian names, the Borelli parents stood their ground. Few expected the tiny quadruplets to survive. There was no time to waste. A reluctant Don Severino baptised them: Prima, Seconda, Terza and Quarta.

Borrowing the table meant adding the Borelli sisters to the guest list. The table had been their passport to countless weddings, christenings and funeral functions in Milignano for over forty years. A period which excluded their three-year exile in France, when storage in the uninhabited Pensione Borelli provided the required conditions for the table's infestation by woodworm.

Few in Milignano wished or cared to separate fact from fiction when it came to gossiping about the use of a table which had laid crockery and men with the regularity of the changing seasons. Many had sworn on their mother's grave that the artisan who carved its legs had used the sisters' sturdy limbs as inspiration. And that he had gifted the table in gratitude for bespoke services rendered in what was to become *Pensione Borelli*.

Yesterday, while Papa Pacelli was proclaiming the virtues of Santa Maria Goretti from the central loggia of St Peter's Basilica, the indispensable table was being lugged, two to each leg, from Pensione Borelli, by sixteen teenage girls, singing, laughing, shouting, arguing, huffing and puffing until it was relocated in Maria Bartolomeo's dining room.

There it made a T-shape with her extendable dining table. A position which made it easy for wood- beetles to cross-fertilise in a superior class of timber. This done, the girls joined Maria and Rosaria Fabrizio in the kitchen to help with the preparation and serving of the celebratory banquet.

There had been some debate between Maria and Ettore as to where the Borelli Sisters were to be seated during the dinner. On one matter they had agreed: Prima, Seconda, Terza and Quarta had to be kept as far as possible from the Bishop. He was still, after all was said and done, a man and as such had to be protected.

They decided to place them at the extreme end of their table, two on each side, as sitting bookends for Stefano Ferrara and the Archdeacon. Ettore reckoned that a man of the world like Ferrara would be able to handle the predatory advances of Prima and Seconda Borelli.

Maria and Ettore believed that the Archdeacon's limited knowledge of the secular world would imbue him with the necessary naivety to withstand the tactile attentions of Terza and Quarta.

To consolidate these quarantine arrangements, the places next to Ferrara and the Archdeacon were taken by guests from the Pacitti and Coia tribes. The remaining places were allocated to the Verrecchia clan headed by La Muti and Michele il Brigante.

As befitted his position, Bishop Pantaleone sat at the centre of the tau's crosspiece, flanked by Ettore and Maria. To his far right, alongside the latter sat Giovanni and to his far left, Monsignor Tofanelli, the Bishop's secretary, and Don Pietro, parish priest of Milignano. The area where the two tables met was left free for the gifts brought by guests as a token of appreciation for having been invited to the Ordination Dinner.

Don Pietro was delighted to have been placed as far away as possible from the man he despised, loathed and detested. He would feel less inhibited about what he ate and drank, but still be close enough to hear and criticise the Bishop's insufferable comments about food, wine and Maria's cooking.

It had taken Stefano Ferrara no time at all to realise that conversation with the Borelli sisters was a matter of logistics. It was like speaking to a many-headed hydra. Since he couldn't tell them apart, he found it easier to follow their syncopated conversation by wearing sunglasses and closing his eyes.

".....You know Dottor Ferrara...."

".....You're as good looking as your brother Artemio....but unlike him you have little to say and gesticulate less."

".....He always stayed in our Pensione when visiting friends....."

".....Like the last time when he told us about the Armistice[1] … before leaving for the Abbey...."

".....No, it was Don Pietro who told us about the Armistice...."

".....No, he didn't.... Artemio gave us the news on September the 5th......"

".....So what! He was his usual charming self that evening....."

"   .But that night he had something on his mind....."

" …He did seem worried come to think of it."

".....We were sorry to see him go the next day,"

".....Stop pretending Artemio was serious about any of us...... despite our friendship...."

"... It's common knowledge Artemio had his mind on a sixteen-year-old ....."

".....Young and beautiful as she was......Lucrezia..... Don Giovanni's sister....."

"..... The envy of every woman in Milignano......" Stefano Ferrara's eyes opened wide as he removed his sunglasses.

Until Lucrezia Bartolomeo's name was mentioned, he had listened to the prattling of the four sisters with detached amusement Smiling and nodding here and there but paying little attention to what was being said. Now, at long last, he knew what had dragged his brother to this God forsaken neck of the woods: Silvio Bartolomeo's daughter and as it so happened, the sister of the tyro priest.

To interest someone like his brother, someone as young as this Bartolomeo woman, she must have been exceptionally beautiful, innocent, healthy, wealthy and educated beyond the limits of basic literacy.

Stefano's attention was momentarily distracted by a woman at the far end of the table. She was holding an apparently strained conversation with a man he assumed was her husband. She was no great beauty. Fairly good looking...small breasts like knots on a thread... pale flawless complexion ....attractively plump.... but spitting sex from every pore..... He would have her if he got half a chance....every dog has his day.... today could be her lucky day.....Small lips meant tight lips. Raised voices from the gruesome foursome rescued him from further lecherous day-dreaming.

"… Love? Love? Of course, it wasn't love!" …

".... It was infatuation, plain and simple! It was infatuation she had for your brother,Artemio."....

".....A schoolgirl's infatuation for a man old enough to be her father....."

".....Far too young to know about the world...."

".....We were younger than Lucrezia ...when the four of us...."

".....Were …. getting acquainted with her father."

The sisters lowered their voices. Nosey Parker Muti was showing too much interest in the exchanges they were having with their handsome dinner companion. La Muti had to be kept at bay. Just as they had kept her at bay in their youth when vying for Silvio Bartolomeo's attention.

".....That's all water under the bridge.....we're not here to offend the Archdeacon's ears...."

".....With tittle-tattle about Don Giovanni's father....."

"......I'm sure he and Dottor Ferrara must be bored with our chatter."

Like the overwhelmed and shell-shocked Archdeacon, Stefano Ferrara said nothing. He hoped his silence would encourage the ghastly foursome to leak further information about a family of infinite surprises. He was sure of one thing. In all the Houses of Tolerance he'd visited, Fivesomes were never on the menu. Threesomes, however, were always available by advance arrangement with the Madam. Evidently, his brother and Silvio Bartolomeo were well acquainted with the Borelli sisters' comprehensive services. The arrival of food put an end to Stefano's conjectures about who did what to whom when the Borelli Sisters played a risqué variation of musical chairs with his brother and Silvio Bartolomeo.

The first course brought waves of oohs and aahs from the guests, silencing all conversation, including the Bishop's and moderating the restlessness of the Coia and Pacitti brats. Guests watched as Rosaria and her team of young helpers emerged with mounds of *Gnocchi di Patate con sugo nero di seppia* and trays of

Canneloni di Ricotta and *Spinaci al sugo di pomodori.*

It was the Bishop's *delizioso* when sampling both varieties of pasta, which broke the spell of silence, bringing expressions of agreement from the other guests and heralding another round of drinking and noisy small talk.

"You're always the same and never happy unless you're making me miserable." Irma was speaking into her plate, anxious that her words with her husband should pass as innocuous small talk to casual observers, like the handsome stranger, sitting with the Borelli sisters.

Call it woman's intuition, but she had the feeling he was trying to attract her attention. She dismissed such a ridiculous notion. A handsome and educated man like Dottor Ferrara could never be interested in a plain Jane like her.

There was frequent sex but no love in her marriage with Mauro Pacitti. Her body readily compliant to his beck and call night and day. Then there was her mother-in-law who treated her like an enemy because she wouldn't bend the knee or give way in the kitchen.

Irma often felt she should have stayed in Scotland. Better there as her brother's skivvy than being treated as her mother-in-law's dogsbody.

However, spinsterhood had not been an option particularly after she was dumped by the Bartolomeo boys. She had agreed to marry a man she had neither seen nor met because, plainly and simply, she needed a man. Mauro, for all his faults, came close to satisfying these needs.

She had known nothing about Mauro before she married him, except that he was ten years older and had lost a leg fighting somewhere in Africa while in his late teens. Her mother-in-law had arranged the marriage with her brother, Domenico, for a hundred Bank of England fivers, payable on arrival in Milignano.

Irma knew that such an amount would have induced any sensible girl in Southern Italy to marry a work-shy, one-legged man who depended on a widowed mother for the food on his plate and a roof over his head.

"Zia Maria used to be the Head Cook in the Bartolomeo restaurant," she mumbled trying to make conversation, despite knowing it would be a waste of time with a stronzo[1] like Mauro.

"I've told you before, I'm not interested in anything about your life in Scotland...I don't like being reminded of your boyfriends and Roberto in particular. When are you going to get this into your thick skull?"

Mauro knew there was no need to hold back when putting his wife in her place. If she left him there would be no repercussions. On the other hand, if he left her, then the dowry would have to be handed back. No matter what, Irma would never leave him. She liked sex too much and he was ready to service her for the sake of keeping the tractor he had bought with her money.

Irma bit her lip until she could taste blood. She knew Mauro hadn't finished with his abuse. There was more to come. There was nothing she could do. She was trapped for better or for worse.

"You enjoy humiliating me at every turn, throwing in my face I'm your third choice.... a cripple married to soiled goods..... I'm too good for the likes of you.....isn't that right Ma?"

The expected agreement was interrupted by the arrival of the main course. It was a Godsend to a relieved Irma: *Stufato di Vitellone al vino rosso, purè di carrote, pepperoni arosto e zucchini ripieni.* While Mauro turned his attention to the food, wine and mother in that order, Irma stole a glance at the handsome stranger.

This time it caught and held his eye and tarried longer than it should have done by an honest woman and long enough to return

61

his smile with a hot flush of embarrassment which was anything but innocent. She had experienced similar feelings of excitement when fighting off Roberto Bartolomeo's half-hearted attempts to seduce her.

When the sun was beginning its descent behind the Pantano Hills, the hyperactive brats of the related Coia and Verrecchia families were let loose in the garden at the rear of the villa. This, and the arrival of the *Stufato di Vitellone*, gave Don Pietro a double dose of pleasure.

Children rampaging in the dining room would have spoiled his appetite. Stufato needed undivided attention. It needed peace when consumers were forking chunks of braised veal into the requisite orifice as the Good God intended.

Adding to the pleasure of eating, drinking and criticising the Bishop, was the company of Monsignor Tofanelli, Pantaleone's Secretary. In Monsignor Tofanelli, Don Pietro had found a ready audience for his anti-Pantaleone comments.

"The *Stufato di Vitello*, Signora Maria," Bishop Pantaleone opined, "matches my mother's. I could pay it no higher compliment. And the due praise of course for the wine Ettore has provided to enjoy it with."

"Just listen to him, Pietro," muttered Tofanelli, "the miserable skinflint would be toasting with mineral water if he were footing the bill."

".... and drinking it from grubby skulls," added Don Pietro, "just as he did back in darkest Apulia like his kinsman, Mammone, decorating the table with heads ....freshly severed..... during each and every meal......"

Monsignor Tofanelli and Don Pietro's laughter brought glances of disapproval from the Bishop and envious ones from Giovanni. Apparently locked in conversation with Maria, Ettore and Giovanni, the Bishop nonetheless eavesdropped into what the old reprobate was saying to his Secretary. On hearing something about Mammone and Apulia, he guessed what had made them laugh and felt more flattered than annoyed.

"I believe, Signora Maria, that your husband was a renowned chef in the family restaurant .*The Torquato Tasso,* I believe it was called. Named after one of our greatest Late Renaissance poets...born in Sorrento and spent some time in our Montecassino Abbey recovering from, let's be charitable and call it depression. As Horace[1] said about madness: *it's good to be mad occasionally..*

"But I digress, or as our Gallic friends would say when getting back to the point, *revenons à nos moutons*. If what we have eaten today is anything to go on, the food served in your restaurant must have complimented the great traditions of Italian Cooking.....unsullied by the extravagance of sauces .so beloved by the French....as the great Rossini used to say. I'm sure you agree, Signora Maria?"

"To be honest, Your Grace," replied Maria, emboldened by the wine she had glugged, "I always thought Rossini was a musician. Someone who wrote operas long before Puccini wrote his wonderful *Madama Butterfly.*

Lorenzo Pantaleone beamed with pleasure, patting his hostess on the back of her hand. "Rossini was not only a famous musician but also an amateur chef of great distinction. He created the *Alla Rossini* dishes you and Ettore probably prepared in your restaurant."…..

"He's got it wrong again Pietro. Those dishes he's referring to, including *Tournedos alla Rossini*, were the creations of Rossini's friend, Master Chef Marie Antoine Carême."

"Well, I never knew that, Your Grace. Rossini sounds like he was more of a Master Chef than a Master Musician." Maria giggled at the boldness of her exchanges with the Bishop.

"It's time he talked about the wine, Toff, which is another area of his self-proclaimed expertise." On cue, the Bishop duly obliged.

"......and to complement your fine food, Signora Maria, let's not forget the superb wine Ettore here has selected for us." Pantaleone held his glass up to the light. "As soon as I tasted it, I knew it was something special... and nothing like the local Trebbiano vintages which plumbers, I do believe, use to unblock municipal drains."

A tipsy Maria laughed at Pantaleone's corny joke even though she enjoyed drinking the local wines but hesitated to share this information with the Bishop.

"We can't really take the credit for this wine, Your Grace," said Ettore coming to his wife's rescue when he noted her hesitation. "The wine was a gift from Dottor Ferrara," pointing him out. "He's the gentleman we must thank for the wine which comes I think from his vineyards in the Alto Adige."

Bishop Pantaleone quick eye made an instant assessment of this Dottor Stefano Ferrara fellow: the elegant cut of his expertly tailored suit; an educated man of discriminating taste; from his blond hair, blue eyes and fair complexion, the Germanic look of a Northerner. He could be a useful man to know. "You must introduce us later, my dear Ettore....."

"And now comes the Overture to Modesty, you can depend on it, Pietro," said Tofanelli with a scarcely concealed sneer.

"..... In all modesty, my dear Ettore, I have to admit to being a lover of good wines.....what experts, like Dottor Ferrara for example, would call an oenophile.....from *oenos* the Greek word for wine."

Giovanni listened with admiration to the conversation his aunt and uncle were having with the affable and erudite Bishop. However, he was happy to remain in the background. On the other hand, he would have given his eye teeth to be a part of the lively exchanges between Don Pietro and Monsignor Tofanelli.

".....and let's make sure, my dear Ettore, that all the glasses are fully charged with this superb wine for my toast to young

Giovanni."

As ever playing to the gallery, Bishop Pantaleone raised his glass to the light, hoping his gesture and comments about its colour and taste might distract Ferrara's attention from the comely sisters.

Maria wasn't really listening to what the good Bishop was saying. All she could say about any wine, be it red, white or rosé, was that if she liked it she drank it irrespective of origin or cost. She had no intention of betraying this confidence to the Bishop. For Giovanni's sake, she wanted to make a good impression.

Friendship with the Bishop had to be cultivated if her nephew were to follow in his footsteps. She believed Giovanni would make a fine Bishop one day... and God willing she would live to see that great day.

October 29th in the Holy Year of 1950 was her nephew's special day. Maria had to keep reasonably sober because it was her job to see that the banquet ran according to plan. It was her responsibility to let Rosaria know when to serve the courses and when to replace empty wine bottles with full ones. It was time to tell Rosaria to bring in the last course, *Pan di Marmo con Crema Pasticciera* and to remind her that the Sweet Course had to be served with coffee and *Mandorle Ricci[1]*.

When the meal was over and the guests had gone, she could look forward to spending what was left of the day with her nephew. Maria intended to spend as much time with Giovanni as possible before the Bishop whisked him away.

She didn't know how many days' leave the good Bishop would permit. However many they were, they would be too few. She hoped His Grace would be true to his promise and not send him to some remote parish in the far-flung reaches of his diocese, which covered, according to Don Pietro, an area of nearly one thousand square kilometres. After the speeches and toasts, she would make a point of reminding the Bishop of his promise.

"Your Grace, honoured guests, my dear wife Maria, Ladies and Gentlemen I welcome you all to our celebration on this the occasion of our nephew Giovanni's ordination to the priesthood." A round of applause interrupted Ettore's opening remarks. It was his first public speech since his wedding reception in the Grand Hotel, Charing Cross Glasgow, twenty-eight years before. The same week in which he had become a Naturalised British Subject, with the full approval and encouragement of his brother.

"On this most happy occasion, I have but one regret which is that my brother, Silvio, my sister, Bianchina, my nephew, Roberto and my niece, Lucrezia, are not with us today to share our joy on this great day. Before asking His Grace to say a few words, I would like to thank all those who have helped make this occasion the success I hope it has been and will be until it is concluded.

"To our Bishop, who has honoured us with his presence and who permitted the ordination ceremony to take place in our Santa Maria Maggiore, to Don Pietro for lending us the services of his housekeeper, Rosaria, to the Borelli Sisters for the use of Milignano's famous table, to the young ladies who brought it here and served our modest fare with such charm and grace and especially, to Dottor Ferrara for his most generous gift of the wine we have enjoyed with our meal and to Michele, for helping us beg, borrow and steal all the additional crockery and cutlery needed to enjoy Maria's wonderful food and above all else, for providing us with the four ceiling air fans, from his sources in Naples, which have kept us comfortable during our celebrations."

There was laughter when Ettore tapped his nose with his index finger, making an I-know-where-you-got-them gesture, which Michele acknowledged with a smile.

"I would ask you all to be upstanding for a toast to all those who have made our dinner the special occasion I hope it will prove to be." When the applause and stamping of feet subsided, Ettore invited Bishop Pantaleone to deliver his keynote address.

66

CHAPTER EIGHT

Bishop Lorenzo Pantaleone rose to his feet, leaning heavily on outstretched fingers and thumbs, more for effect rather than to steady himself. Struck by the general silence and the rapt gaze of the guests, he waited a few moments before breaking the spell of silence.

"*CONTICUERE OMNES!*" The Bishop smiled a smile of circumstance, his words accompanied by a benign gesture of goodwill. "Fear not my good people, I promised Ettore and Maria that my speech would not be in Latin. I think most of you will agree that we had enough Latin this morning, during the ordination ceremony... in your beautiful Church." A round of applause, led by a well-lubricated Don Pietro, interrupted the Bishop.

"But when I stood up to speak, Virgil's[1] immortal words seemed appropriate given your kind reaction.....*CONTICUERE OMNES INTENTIQUE ORA TENEBANT....All were silent and fixed their eyes in close attention.* This was how Virgil described the guests waiting for Aeneas to speak. But what I have to say to you this afternoon is not as dramatic as Aeneas was about to say to his guests." Bishop Pantaleone stopped to take a sip of San Pellegrino before continuing. "No, not as dramatic, but far more important and as such worthy of your attention. This morning on the Church of Santa Maria Maggiore you were all witnesses, Artemio, to a service whose importance is emphasised by a ritual full of symbolism. When you saw me bind Father Giovanni's hands..... his anointed hands....this was to show you that here, in the village in which his father was born and bred.... in the Church which baptised him ....here his surviving son was bound forever in the Service of God and Our Holy Mother Church.....Giovanni Bartolomeo... YOUR Don Giovanni … is now an accredited Ambassador to God Himself."

The last sentence was uttered with such emphasis and feeling that it provoked more applause and cheering. "Viva Giovanni!" shouted one voice. "No. Viva Don Giovanni!" corrected another.

Stefano Ferrari joined in the applause. *This guy's good....got them eating out his hands. He'd make a great salesman...if only he looked less shifty and smarmy.....and given half a chance I would soon have Peg-Leg's wife unbuttoning my flies with her teeth....*

"....to an outsider, perhaps, to a non-Christian certainly, this afternoon's festivities might seem something of an anti-climax after the pomp and majesty of the ordination ceremony....but my dear people, what could be a more fitting sequel?

"Did not Christ Our Lord start his Public Ministry at a marriage feast? And does not our Feast this afternoon ....does it not celebrate Don Giovanni's marriage to the Church?" Giovanni smiled nervously, blushing at the applause the Bishop's words drew from the guests.

"However, my dear people, there is one main difference between our Feast today and the one in Cana. I will not be calling on Don Giovanni to perform a miracle. Instead, I will be calling on you to rise and toast him as our new priest. But first I would ask you to put your hands together for Signora Maria for the miracles she performed in the kitchen." A prolonged ovation followed Bishop Pantaleone's invitation.

"And yet, my dear people," continued the Bishop when the ovation subsided, "while today is a great day of rejoicing for the Church... it does bring both joy and sadness to Don Giovanni, as Ettore indicated earlier in his eloquent address. I refer to the absence of his father, Silvio, his aunt, Bianchina, his brother, Roberto and his sister, Lucrezia......may they rest in peace...all of them snatched from his presence by the hideous contamination and vengeance of War....and united now with his mother, Livia, may she rest in peace, who passed away fifteen years ago."

The Bishop took in the guests with two sweeping looks before fixing his eyes on Giovanni. "My dear people let us remember

Don Giovanni in our prayers, especially in the coming weeks, when he will begin his service to the Lord. Honoured hosts...... Honoured guests, I bid you be upstanding...... to Don Giovanni Bartolomeo, *Let's drink from the joyful cups[1].*

It was a virtuoso performance, delivered with such ease, élan and panache, that it struck a responsive chord in the hearts of the guests who rose to their feet in acclamation.

Once the formalities of the dinner were over, most of the guests gathered in tribal groups to criticise or praise the events and incidents of the day. Each group noisier than the other in order to make themselves heard. In no time at all, the Coia contingent, having drawn the short straw, rounded up the children who had been running riot in the garden, before escorting, dragging or carrying them to their respective homes in the falling darkness.

Stefano spotted Mauro Pacitti limping off to relieve himself in the garden's pit latrine. He sauntered over to where Irma was sitting but Milignano's parish priest got there before him. To hide his dismay and frustration, he sat beside Michele Verrecchia and made a pretence of discussing the possibility of providing haulage services from the Alto Adige to commercial outlets in Cassino and Venafro respectively.

First to leave was the Pacitti clan, led by Irma's mother-in-law. It was followed by the Verrecchia contingent but not before Michele il Brigante had settled on a figure with Ettore for supplying and installing the fans purloined from the US Military Headquarters in Naples.

As he waited to be introduced to Bishop Pantaleone, Stefano Ferrara was still under siege from the Borelli Sisters. He had to wait while the former was exacting apologies from Don Pietro and Monsignor Tofanelli for their lack of attention during his address.

With the excuse of making arrangements for returning their

table, Ettore rescued Stefano from the clutches of the Borelli Sisters and steered him towards Bishop Pantaleone who was instructing the Archdeacon, still in a state of moral confusion after a two-hour mauling from two of the Borelli sisters, to have his limousine ready for departure.

"Your Grace, let me introduce you to Stefano Ferrara. I'll leave you together, if I may, and join Maria who's with Giovanni and Irma in the kitchen. Perhaps the Archdeacon would care to join us?"

With Ettore and the Archdeacon out of the way, Bishop Pantaleone got to the point without the need for further pleasantries.

"My most sincere compliments, Signor Ferrara!"

"It's Dottor Ferrara...but call me Stefano, Your Grace."

"My sincerest compliments on your selection of wine for today's celebrations. Your name rings a bell... I never forget names...I recall a certain Ferrara Artemio. He was an important man in the Foreign Ministry under Galeazzo Ciano[1]. I remember arranging transport for a certain Signor Dottore Ferrara from Venafro to Montecassino...first to Milignano and then to the Abbey of Montecassino....shortly before the end of the Fascist Interval. A most unfortunate decision was made by Signor Dottore Ferrara in going to Montecassino where he was to perish in the bombing."

Bishop Pantaleone raised an eyebrow asking a question to which he knew the answer, "Was he a relative perhaps?"

"Artemio was my elder brother. He was a great friend of Don Giovanni's father. Very close they were. Partners in crime I might add, being honest. Which is what brought me here today." concluded Stefano as Ettore joined them again.

"My wife wants Giovanni and Irma to herself....to discuss old times in Scotland. Not for me. So here I am. The Archdeacon and Monsignor Tofanelli are dutifully waiting in the limousine."

"I'm sure they won't mind if I keep them waiting just a little longer. And it's highly understandable that your charming wife Maria feels nostalgia for Scotland, where she was born and reared....before you joined us, Dottor Ferrara was telling me his brother, Artemio, was a great friend of your brother, Silvio."

"Indeed he was. And it was thanks to him that we were able to keep in touch after the Arandora Star disaster... at least until he entered the Abbey. He kept a paternal eye on my niece, Lucrezia. Silvio would have wished no less. Artemio loved her like a father and she, in turn, adored him like a daughter.

"That's why we were so pleased when Stefano was able to join us for the ordination...not forgetting the pleasure of being able to thank him personally for his generous gift which arrived in good time for today's celebration."

Stefano made a dismissive gesture with his hand. It was wine acquired at knock-down prices from failed and failing competitors.

"No, no, Stefano, Ettore is quite right to speak of your generosity. The wine you gifted was superb. And most appropriate for today's occasion: t*he fruit of the vine and work of human hand* … as we say in the Holy Mass. And what fruit of the vine you brought to us today! But, tell me, my dear Stefano, why have you tantalised us with unlabelled bottles? We know that in them there is no ordinary wine..." Ettore could only nod. Conversations like this were well above his head.

"Ettore tells me you are a lover of wines. This wine has a history. It's ....No, don't tell me Caro Stefano...let me guess. I like nothing better than surrendering my palate to a taste which still lingers and loiters on its memory after today's sampling. Perhaps Ettore you might care to refresh it by opening another bottle?"

"Enough of this talk about Scotland, Irma. You and Aunt Maria should be tired out by walking down long memory lanes and back again," chided Giovanni in mock protest. "Tell me about Mauro. I've been hearing all about him from Michele. I suppose you're the best one to confirm if it's true what he was saying."

Maria suddenly found something to do, muttering excuses about making sure Rosaria had taken the marble cake she had set aside for her son, Fabrizio, before sidling off red-faced with embarrassment, leaving a devastated Irma wondering who on earth had spilt the beans about the state of her marriage. The incongruity of chatting in a broad Glaswegian accent, in the shadow of the Mainarde Mountains of Southern Italy occurring to neither of them.

"Come, come, Irma, it's not my intention to embarrass you. All I want to know is if Mauro did or did not do what I've heard he did. That's all I want to know."

"Did....what?" Irma asked, her expression displaying absolute panic.

"Come on Irma, enough of this bashfulness. Did he or did he not play for Milignano on the day the Armistice was announced?

"You mean," relief clearly showing on her face, "did Mauro keep goal against our local rivals, Mozzilli, on Santa Maria Maggiore's Feast day without wearing his artificial leg?"

"What else would I be referring to? Michele tells that the Mozzilliani to this day can't live down the shame of being beaten by a team playing with a one-legged goalkeeper.... I believe the game was abandoned when Don Pietro's Church Bell summoned everyone to the piazza to hear news of the Armistice ..."

"........if it's not a Barolo......full bodied....like a Gattinara....better obviously than a Spanna." The Bishop was dominating Ettore's impromptu wine tasting, swirling the wine noisily in his mouth before swallowing. "Heavy...violet bouquet with delicious drops of cherries, roses and carnations with just a hint of almonds....strong and decided after-taste....dry...smooth like velvet. Undoubtedly from the Nebbiolo grape. The last time I tasted a wine like this was in Rome...to honour the appointment of Baron von Weisaeker as the Reich's Ambassador to the Holy See. The wine was much favoured in Fascist Circles at the time. Now what was it called? No, don't tell me, Stefano.......Santa Margherita... the name has religious connotations....no, not Santa Margherita.... it was Santa Maddalena. Yes, that's it. Santa Maddalena. A wine patronised by the abstemious Mussolini."

Until the wine was identified, Bishop Pantaleone had been gazing at one of Michele's black-market air fans, but as soon as he named the wine he transferred his gaze to Stefano's face which such intensity that it made him start.

Ettore had no idea what was going on between Stefano and the Bishop. He was completely out of his depth and he knew it.

The momentary blinking of Stefano's cold blue eyes and the slight twitching at the corner of the mouth convinced the Bishop that he had discovered, not only the reason for the unlabelled bottles of the now proscribed Santa Maddalena, but also the cheapskate nature of the gift. The Bishop smiled to himself wondering how Stefano could possibly save face with Ettore.

"You do have a fine palate, Your Grace." Stefano agreed, angry with himself for having underestimated the Bishop. To save face, he would have to quibble as he had never quibbled before. "This wine is similar to St Magdalener, the name we give to the Santa Maddalena. When I was arranging to send a shipment to Von Ribbentrop's estates in Wiesbaden ….in exchange for a commensurate number of vintage Henkell[1] we had already received. ...and when we jumped ship I was unable to honour our agreement....it's a long story. For another time perhaps.

"However, the wine in question is a Kaltarese. One of the Alto Adige's most popular red wines......made like the St Magdalener...or the Santa Maddalena if you prefer....from the schiava grape....and not from the Nebbiolo grape as you seem to think." Stefano looked at the Bishop defiantly, wondering if his sophistry had fooled the Bishop.

"Forgive the vanity of this fond and foolish man, my dear Stefano. As my mother used to say, *Pride leaves on Horseback and returns on Foot.* I just wonder whatever became of all the Santa Maddalena... or St Magdalener...when the name became unfashionable ....given its association with Mussolini .... all those poor wine merchants left with a great deal of it stocked in their cellars ....on the expectation of plenty... and we've all heard of the farmer who hanged himself on the expectation of plenty[1].

"Besides, I take my hat off to those Wine merchants who bought up all the Santa Maddalena they could from bankrupted competitors and put it back on the market under a different name. Perhaps as a Kaltarese."

"Sounds like good business sense to me, Your Grace. I'm sure Ettore would agree?" Ettore smiled but said nothing. What he was sure about that a cat and mouse game was being played between Bishop Pantaleone and Stefano Ferrara and that His Grace was the cat.

"Many Congratulations, Your Grace. I congratulate you on your formidable knowledge of wines."

"I'm flattered you think so, my dear Stefano. I've always been interested in the subject of wine. I find it fascinating....its history...its different vintages... the different grapes ....where they are grown. Things like that. I was wondering, Stefano, if you would be interested in arranging a wine tasting for me in Venafro? We have an Archaeological Society there. Now and again we arrange ...a social evening .... A change from our usual lectures ....last month's we had someone telling us all about the Ancient Roman Colonies in Porto Torres on the island of Sardinia."

"From what Michele Verrecchia was telling me, I'm sure it would be more appropriate to bring in somebody to lecture on Venafro's Olive Oil Industry[2]... but this Society of yours....has it got any members connected with the catering industry...like hoteliers,

74

restaurateurs, bars...."

"You mean would it be worth your while holding a wine-tasting in Venafro?" The Bishop smiled. He had the measure of this city slicker.

"Put it that way if you like, Your Grace, but business is business and there's no business like more business."

"Rest assured you will find it worthwhile. I'd be surprised if you didn't shift at least two hundred cases. If you can lay hands on some Santa Maddalena, with or without labels, you can put me down for thirty cases. I'm sure my friend, Cardinal Roccaravindola, will order the same if I can persuade him to come along."

"Very well, Your Grace. Sometime in October or November would be fine. There's a chance it might coincide with Don Pietro's annual pilgrimage to Montecassino. As you know my brother is buried there. I'll leave my card so you can get in touch once you have decided on a definite date."

"Will you be staying overnight in Pensione Borelli? I understand your brother stayed there when visiting Giovanni's aunt. If not, I can offer you a lift to Venafro or, if need be, to Cassino."

"Unlike Artemio, I have my own car. Must be off... have to be in Caserta tonight. We used to sell a lot of wine there before the ..."

"The end of the what we diplomatically refer to as '*The Fascist Interval*'?"

"No Your Grace....before the abolition of the monarchy,"

Bishop Pantaleone shook hands with Stefano. They had reached an understanding. But it wasn't an understanding between equals. It was an understanding between master and pupil, like the understanding between Jesus and John the Baptist.

When Stefano took his leave for Caserta with his tail between his legs, Ettore led the Bishop into the kitchen where Maria and Giovanni had been waiting for them. Both were surprised to hear that Stefano Ferrara had left without saying goodbye.

The Bishop embraced Maria and gently brushed her cheeks with his thin dry lips. Then he shook hands and embraced Ettore. After which he turned to Giovanni, embracing him warmly. As he did so, he looked at Maria with reassurance before nodding a silent agreement to a question she didn't need to ask. "Report to me on Friday morning, Giovanni, Venafro, 9 o'clock sharp. When I will inform you to which parish I have decided to send you."

Chapter Nine

Bishop Pantaleone was true to his word. He had promised Maria Bartolomeo that her nephew would not be sent far from Milignano. Collaquila, the hill of eagles, was where Giovanni was heading in Michele's pre-war Fiat Ardita.

Collaquila, to the north side of the Pantano Hills, was, as the crow flies, thirteen kilometres distant from Milignano. However, Giovanni knew that while Michele was no Juan Fangio[1], he would nonetheless tackle the road distance of thirty-four kilometres at breakneck speed.

Today, all going well, would bring an end to a perfect week which began with his ordination and would end, Michele's driving permitting, when he was installed as a curate in the parish of San Sebastiano. The catalyst which was to wreck his happiness was the National Flag of France flying high above a row of fledgeling cypress trees.

"That's the French Military Cemetery," Michele proclaimed when he noticed Giovanni's interest. Giovanni smiled at Michele's tendency to state the obvious.

"The French visit it, usually in November....last year De Gaulle came with a few Big-shots. The General complained that the trees weren't growing fast enough....said so in the comments column of the visitors' book. There's a photograph of his Big Bourbon Nose in the Chapel. At least there used to be." When Giovanni asked him to pull over, Michele made no attempt to conceal his disapproval.

"You don't want to be going in there. There's nothing of interest for decent folk like us. Besides, I've been hired to take you to Collaquila. The deal didn't include making a detour to a French

Military Cemetery, which is the last place a Bartolomeo should want to visit. You're as pig-headed as ever your father was...and that's saying something," adding sincerely, "with all due respect."

Leaving a perturbed Michele in the car, Giovanni headed for the entrance of the Campo Santo at the centre of an imposing semi-circular parapet. Giant Double wrought-iron gates were chained and padlocked. Of the two smaller gates on either side, the one on the right was unpadlocked.

A Y-shaped pathway, paved in the same granite as the parapet, cut through an impeccable sward. Where the pathway narrowed into a single track it extended as far as the doorway of a Memorial Chapel. On each side of the pathway, three rows of six marble crosses, with names inscribed in black, reached out at right-angles.

The front apex of the little Chapel was crowned with a metal cross. Facing the cypress trees, at the far end of its roof, covered in clay roof tiles, the National flag of France hung from a white wooden flagpole.

In contrast with the appearance of the ornate wooden entrance doors and the whitewashed façade of the chapel, its interior was unexpectedly bleak, dingy and smelled of decomposing rodents. Austerity had waylaid simplicity in what had been a successful attempt at cutting costs: four pews built from recycled railway-sleepers, languishing on nondescript grainy tiles; a token plaster-of- paris altar, its bare surface covered by a layer of dust and mouse droppings; two small candlesticks encrusted with verdigris and wax stood like sentinels in each of the two niches on either side of the altar; at its centre, an open tabernacle, shorn of its silk lining and empty save for the carcasses of two mice and the Visitors' Book.

Giovanni's first thoughts were to offer a *De Profundis* prayer in commemoration of the dead but he dismissed the idea because of the altar's desecration and absence of the all-important sanctuary lamp. Disillusioned with the poor state of the Chapel, he hurried into the shade provided by the trees. Michele was standing by the gates, pointing at his watch and beckoning him to the car.

Acting on impulse, Giovanni opted to have a look at the area behind the trees. To his surprise, he discovered a free-standing minaret, encircled by a projecting balcony. Perched on the top of its onion-shaped crown was a gilded crescent moon. The minaret's side door was unlocked and opened easily.

The tiny mosque was empty, spotless and smelled of lavender. There was no stairway for access to its balcony. The floor and walls were dressed in glazed blue ceramic tiles while the domed ceiling was decorated with a lapis lazuli mosaic speckled with white stars. Set low on the wall facing the entrance was a long narrow ogee window, glazed with translucent brown alabaster marked with swirling streaks of yellow and black. Below, a plaque, written in French:

OSER SOMMEILLER À L'OMBRE D'UNE SECURITÉ BIENHEUREUSE,

DANS UNE VIE COMME LES FLORAISONS D'UNE VERGER.

(Abu I-Muzaffer al-Abiwardi)

The shock of reading sentiments inviting rapists and murderers to rest among the blossoms of an orchard grove hit Giovanni with such intensity that it expelled notions of forgiveness. Instead, a savage thirst for retribution and vengeance momentarily possessed him. Overcome with conflicting emotions, he sank to his knees, forehead on the floor, tapping it with his forehead to assuage his turmoil, in an inadvertent parody of a Muslim at prayer.

His mind was dominated by the opening words of a prayer. The same prayer he had refused to offer in the memorial chapel moments before: *Lord hear my prayer. Let Thine ears be*

79

attentive to the voice of my supplication.....

The fervour expressed in his prayer brought Giovanni a measure of serenity. He knew that a desire for justice and vengeance was at odds with his Church's teaching on Forgiveness. Forgiveness, not only for what the Moroccans had done to his sister and aunt but also for those who saw fit to encourage them.

Unlike Don Pietro, Giovanni knew there could be no place in his heart for retribution and that the Spirit of Forgiveness must always prevail. To this indispensable end, the Scriptures were uncompromising: *Vengeance is Mine, I will repay, said the Lord.*

Still in turmoil, he emerged from the mosque. Instead of turning towards the gates where Michele was waiting, he stumbled into the clearing behind the mosque. There, he saw countless rows of ogee slabs each bearing Arabic names: Ben Loudi, Halilou, Djillali, El Achebe, Ben Mustapha, El Nahiri, Ben Hakimi......

Shaken to the core, Giovanni was scarcely aware of walking back to the car.

Michele's I-told-you-so speech was lost in the ether until his reckless driving brought Giovanni back to reality as the Military Cemetery disappeared behind in a cloud of dust. It was only when they were in the final stages of their ascent to Collaquila that Michele resumed his well-intentioned reproof.

"You know now why I didn't want you to go in there. The Officers who permitted those savages to do what they did in Milignano and Collaquila are buried in the front show-piece section.....the animals under their command are buried behind the trees. One of the many compromises negotiated by Bishop Pantaleone and General Juin, De Gaulle's mouthpiece."

"But why in Venafro .... here, on our doorstep? ...Why not in Cassino where the British Colonial Troops are buried?"

"The English wouldn't hear of it. The Indian Rajputs are Hindus and couldn't be buried anywhere near Muslims. Doing so, would have caused a riot in British India."

"But hundreds and hundreds of Moroccans are buried in Venafro. I had no idea there were so many of them fighting in this area."

"They include those who fell in Acquafondata and Vallerotondo....all of them carted down to Venafro like cholera victims. Tunisians and Algerians are in there too."

"Aren't soldiers supposed to be buried where they fall?"

"The Allies bent the rules when it suited them and the Bishop agreed to bury all those who fell within terracotta his diocese. With the proviso that they were kept out of sight. At least the Russians kept to the rules."

"Santo Cielo Michele, what on earth have Russians got to do with....?"

"What I'm saying Don Giovanni, is that my brother was in the 63rd Tagliamento Blackshirt Division in Russia. He's buried near Stalingrad where he and his comrades fell. No fuss. No bother. And no, I'm not a Communist...being one would be bad for business in these parts." The sighting of Collaquila's terracotta rooftops interrupted Michele's history lesson.

"That's Collaquila up there!" announced Michele, again stating the obvious when they passed the word Collaquila written large on a road sign. "We'll stop on the first clearing we come to ...I need to do something."

"Radiator trouble?" asked Giovanni with a semblance of a smile.

"Nothing wrong with the radiator. I need a pee."

"Look, Michele," said Giovanni when Michele returned, "before we get to Collaquila, let me say I appreciate why you wanted me to steer clear of the cemetery. I should have realised that such an elaborate Campo Santo would never have been built for a handful of French Officers...seeing all those people, probably among whom are those who murdered my sister and aunt, tore me apart. I should have listened to you."

Having made his peace with Michele, Giovanni gave Collaquila his attention. From where the car was parked, he had a good view of faded terracotta roof tiles on houses clinging to volcanic rock like shrivelled grapes on a withering vine.

A stratus cloud shrouded Collaquila. The euphony of its name could not mollify the disillusionment Giovanni felt on realising that Collaquila - the hill of eagles - wore its poverty with ostentation. Collaquila, built on the convulsions of a prehistoric earthquake, would, in a perverse way, be a paradoxical reminder of the world he had left behind in Scotland. Giovanni shook his head in disappointment. A reaction which Michele picked up immediately.

 "Hardly panoramic, is it? And the smell! This place is known for growing vegetables. Good strong manure is the key. You can smell the quality.....and the quantity. It will get into your hair and clothes.... you'll get used to it ......" The sight of Michele screwing up his nose brought a grudging smile from Giovanni. A reaction which merely encouraged Michele to continue with his characteristic parochialism.

".....I could tell you stories about these people that would push the tonsure down the back of your neck. But since they're not for the delicate ears of a priest..... I'll keep them to myself. Besides....." Giovanni felt he had to stop the flow and show some loyalty.

"That's enough Michele, it's time to stop criticising my parishioners."

Not that Michele had said or could say anything he hadn't heard before. His father used to say the Collaquilani were a strange tribal group descended from renegade Samnites. He called them Spartans because, like them, they never rose above the heights of mediocrity.

When his father was examining Defoe's 'Robinson Crusoe', a school prize awarded for knowledge and understanding of English Literature, he had burst into laughter. "Here's a poor soul dressed like a Collaquilano shepherd....living in the middle of nowhere wearing goatskins." Even his aunt Maria had got in on the act. When Giovanni informed her where the Bishop was sending him, she told him that Collaquila was where the natives bred cats and dogs for *Stufato alla Collaquilana*."

".....mind you Don Giovannino, the Americans should have made a better job of this mule track they call a road. When this country gets back on its feet, we'll build a real road from Milignano to Collaquila and bring them civilisation...... like introducing the natives to scented soap and cutlery and selling them wine fit for human consumption.

"Besides, my belly's telling me that lunchtime has been and gone. The sooner I get back to Venafro, the sooner the Bishop will pay me and the sooner I can have a working dinner with somebody's wife, with all due respect, Don Giovannino."

Giovanni didn't give much credence to Michele's impending adultery. His thoughts were focussed on the old parish priest he was about to meet. He was unsure of the reception which awaited him.

Bishop Pantaleone hinted that diplomacy would be required if he were to establish a working relationship. After nearly fifty years of dedicated service in the Diocese's poorest parish, the Bishop said that Don Agostino deserved assistance to see him comfortably through the twilight years of his ministry.

According to Bishop Pantaleone, Don Agostino thought he was as fit as ever and that, until now, he had refused to break in a new curate. He had warned Giovanni not to discuss the *Marocchinate* unless Don Agostino himself brought the matter up.

When saying their farewells earlier that morning, Don Pietro had given him a different slant on his colleague in Collaquila. "Trust Pantaleone to give you a baptism of fire. Sending you to help Don Agostino in his hour of need? Poppycock! He's up to something. However, whatever you do, don't ever bring up the subject of the atrocities committed by the Goumiers. Unless Don

Agostino does so. The Goumiers ran amok in Collaquila for two days before French officers brought them under control. Other than that, all you need to know about Don Agostino is that he is a erudite authority on Horace and a penny pincher as tight as a toad's backside."

Michele's car was moving at walking pace, testing Gianni Agnelli's[1] patented suspension system to the limit as it bumped in, out and over the potholes of the track leading into Collaquila. Giovanni could hear him muttering about the damage flying gravel was doing to his precious paintwork. Then the car came to a sudden stop. The way ahead was blocked by a flock of tintinnabulating goats. Black ones and brown ones seemed to be materialising from nowhere. The air was thick with their stench.

The goats were being encouraged to scrape between the car and the houses on either side of the track by two goatherds dressed like Defoe's Robinson Crusoe. They were flogging the goats with merciless impartiality causing them to have bowel movements whose stench made Giovanni's stomach turn. He lowered the window and retched over the goats as they inched past Michele's car.

"Don't worry about the mess, the goats will eat the evidence," Giovanni said nothing, using a handkerchief to wipe dribbles of vomit, first from his mouth and then from his sleeve. After which he leaned forward until his head lay on the dashboard, muttering repeatedly,"foedissimum...foedissimum.....animalium...foedissim um..."

"What's this about animals??"

"It means the foulest of animals. That's how the Ancient Romans referred to goats. Just pull over for a minute, Michele. … I don't want my new parishioners to see me in this condition. First impressions....you know what I mean........"

Like Giovanni, Michele had never before been in Collaquila. Nobody went there unless they had to. The fact that there was no sign of life didn't fool Michele. He knew enough about peasant life to know that the emergency stop and subsequent occurrences would have been witnessed from behind every shuttered window on the way to the village. He kept this knowledge to himself and held his peace as requested by his pale-faced passenger.

Still, at walking pace, Michele followed the track knowing that it would lead him to the inevitable village piazza and the eponymous Church of San Sebastiano. He felt sorry for the young priest and wondered how he would cope with the hill-billies of Collaquila. For sure, he would have his work cut out for him. But if the lad was anything like his father, he would survive. Time would tell, in a place where it had stood still for nine hundred years.

Winged rumour was alive and flourishing in the backwoods and pastures of Collaquila. The news of Don Giovanni Bartolomeo's arrival in a flood of vomit was channelled through the village's human relay network: from Maria Mangiabambini, dispenser of love potions and herbal abortifacients and *Devoured Babies* on demand, to Simonetta *Semprepronta*, the *Ever-Ready* friendly village strumpet, offering around the clock service, then on to Don Agostino's housekeeper, Erminia *La Iatale*, whose *hiatal hernia* produced an acid reflux as sharp as her tongue and finally to Carmelina *La Cappriciosa*, the capricious midwife and arch enemy of *Maria the Baby-Eater.*

It was *Carmelina La Cappriciosa* who regurgitated the news about the condition of Don Giovanni's terminal stomach disorder to her husband Pasqualino *Chiaccherone*, the village *Blether* and self- appointed Mercury. He carried news of the new curate's diverticulitis to the resident hangers-on who loitered in Paladino's American Bar after the Angelus Bell had summoned them from the morning's toil of supervising their women while they laboured in the fields and lowland pastures.

The end result from the grapevine gossip and rumour was seen when Michele's car finally inched its way into Piazza San

Sebastiano: half the village population had turned out to welcome the invalid priest. When Giovanni stepped out of the car a combination of embarrassment and pleasure quickly brought the colour back to his pallid cheeks.

He hardly had time to say goodbye to Michele before being engulfed by the reception committee. Giovanni felt himself being manoeuvred towards the Church steps. An unseen hand was tugging at his suitcase. Rather than lose balance, Giovanni let it go.

Standing at the top of the Church steps was the venerable figure of Don Sebastiano Porrini.

The Apulian breezes from the Adriatic Coast raised the bottom of Don Agostino's soutane where three of its lower buttons were missing. A biretta impregnated with dust and candle grease was perched on a disproportionately small head. A deep scar ran across his cheek as far as his chin on a craggy face, which was a network of deep intersecting wrinkles. Behind him, partially concealed, an elderly lady who Giovanni assumed was Don Agostino's housekeeper.

As soon as Don Agostino began to moved down the stairs, arms behind his back like a disgruntled schoolmaster, the crowd retreated and dispersed, leaving Giovanni and his suitcase to face the music. His first test in the art of diplomacy was about to begin.

Giovanni controlled the desire to comment on the horrific scar which ran across Don Agostino's face and upper lip. Neither would he joke about the layers of dandruff which decorated the threadbare shoulders of his soutane.

Chapter Ten

"I don't need or want an assistant," declared Don Agostino wasting no time on pleasantries when introducing himself. "And leave that blessed suitcase to my Housekeeper. There's no need to shame her in public by drawing attention to her condition. Let's get this straight, now that you've been foisted on me."

If pushed, Don Agostino's admirers would be happy to admit that he was a cantankerous and loveable pain in the arsc. The Bishop had warned Giovanni, more or less, what to expect. He decided to take Don Agostino seriously, opting for an innate silence.

Diffidence was a virtue Giovanni's father encouraged in his children. He was forever saying that children should be seen and not heard. "*Speak when the hen pees*" was the way he actually put it. Giovanni never dared ask how his father knew a hen didn't or couldn't pee, but he would shut up nevertheless.

Outwith the family, Giovanni's father held that there was a proper time and place for children to have an opinion. However, with regard to his own children, a hectoring and ruthless Silvio Bartolomeo would be the one to decide the time, the where and the what of that opinion.

".... but if Pantaleone thinks I need a Scotch assistant then Don Agostino needs a Scotch assistant. The reason he sent you here is a mystery. Another one of his Machiavellian brainwaves, I suppose. Blessed is he who gives orders. And blessed is he who ignores them .....*and damn'd be he who cries, 'Hold, enough*!*"

Strutting ahead, Don Agostino addressed the latter quotation from Shakespeare to the heavens. He made no attempt to sidestep the goat and mule droppings which lay in the track leading to the dingy presbytery at the rear of the San Sebastiano. He was too busy regretting his half-hearted efforts to block Giovanni's appointment.

"Don't bother scraping your shoes. Leave that to Emilia when you take them off. And don't bother sitting down. You'll want to go straight to your room, no doubt, to rest the idle limbs of youth. You'll be wanting time to prepare your sermon for tomorrow? You don't say much, do you? You'll take tomorrow's mass at seven. Give me a chance for a long lie. The first in forty odd years. You don't say much, do you? Not that I need a rest. I deserve one. You won't be expecting something to eat, will you? We expected you for lunch. What kept you?" Remembering the Bishop's advice, Giovanni said nothing about the unscheduled stop at the French Military Cemetery in Venafro.

"I hear you were sick. Delicate stomach, eh? What a Pity. Emilia's preparing my evening meal. She's got three speeds: slow, dead slow and stop. Don't worry. I'll manage the lot if you're too weak to join me. It'll be a struggle but I'll make the sacrifice. So put your mind at rest. We don't believe in waste in these days of scarcity. As my mother used to say, may God Bless her and keep her: *he who saves, gains.*

Giovanni stood beside his suitcase, concentrating hard to conceal his amusement in the face of Don Agostino's self-assurances.

"Pantaleone thinks I'm too old to manage on my own, does he? Well, we'll see about that. I just get a little tired these days. Which doesn't mean that I'm ready for the knackers' yard or that dilapidated monastery in Gallo Matese for worn-out priests. You don't say much, do you? That's the stuff. Listen and learn, that's my motto....curates should be seen and not heard and speak when the hen pees. And one more matter, remember Emilia's my housekeeper..As such, she's at my beck and call. She's not fit enough to run after both of us. She pretends to be deaf when it suits her. ....And don't touch my books. I've got them classified in a certain order according to my preferences.

88

"Pantaleone tells me you are a man of means...your expensive new cassock and made-to-measure shoes say it all. I suppose. You can obviously afford to buy your own books. I suppose you've brought some books with you? It's probably why Emilia did all that grunting and wheezing when you forced her to carry your heavy suitcase."

"Pantaleone tells me you're a clever soul. That you have a degree from a second-rate Scottish University. The star student of your year, no less, at the Pontificale. The best of a bad lot more like. Born for greater things he says. Clever enough to be a Jesuit, he says, and good enough to have his very own ordination ceremony in Milignano. Something here doesn't add up but who am I to question a future Prince of the Church? But it cuts no ice with me.

"You don't say much, do you? You can tell a man from the books he reads. Brought up, I hear, the land of Macbeth, Castles and Whisky...where they eat sheep-guts and oats we feed to our cattle, get drunk every Saturday on horses' piss and wear skirts instead of trousers."

Giovanni expected a mention of the Scotsman's legendary parsimony. None came. Probably because it was the only Scottish trait Don Agostino could bring himself to admire.

"I hope you've brought your own towels? Don't want you using mine. The more Emilia rubs them and slaps them against the rocks or beats them with a stick, the thinner they get and the more time she wastes patching them when they fray. My towels are made from home-spun linen...they belonged to my mother, God rest her precious soul. You don't say much, do you?

"I might borrow your soap. From the smell you trail, I'm sure you've brought a good supply. It'll make a change from the stuff the locals make from goat's tallow and wood ashes. I'm fed up smelling like an old goat...it's the least you can do seeing you'll be using the water Emilia lugs from the basement well.

"You don't say much, do you? But you don't fool me for a minute

89

because I know the deepest rivers make the least sound."

Emilia limped in carrying two coffee cups on a tarnished tray. No saucers, no sugar, no spoons.

"You shouldn't have brought Don Giovanni coffee. Remember he's got a delicate stomach and vomited over Staffieri's goats. But leave the coffee. They say too much caffeine is bad for you. Rubbish! I'm been ingesting it five or six times a day for years. Did me no harm." Don Agostino quaffed both cups in two loud gulps followed by an exaggerated smacking of lips.

"And another thing, my parishioners will leave gifts at the altar rails after your first mass in my San Sebastiano. And this whether or not your sermon impresses. Just don't speak down to them. They enjoy sermons most when they don't understand a word. With any luck, we'll get eggs, chickens, fruit and vegetables. The downside will be if they offer wine...undrinkable.... but it'll do for dressing salads and pickling gherkins.

"The gifts are produced in my parish, so you hand everything over to Emilia. We'll keep what we need and redistribute what's left to those in need. Just remember: charity begins at home.

"And one last thing before you rush off to your room. We eat here when it suits me. If you're on call when it's time to eat then too bad. In this heat, food won't keep once its cooked. If I have to eat for two, then I will eat for two. Don't believe in waste. One last thing, you will need a horse and saddle to get around the parish. I see from the look on your face that Pantaleone didn't tell you how far-flung this parish is. Don't worry, I'll sell you my spare saddle and throw in the parish horse for good measure. Not much point in keeping two horses is there? It's bad enough having to feed two priests."

"I was thinking of buying one of Michele's cars. It would be a great help getting around the parish and less tiring for you, Don Agostino."

"This isn't a rich parish. you know. We can't have ostentatious displays of wealth. It would affect the collections made on Sundays. Parishioners won't cough up if they get the idea into their heads we don't need the money. So, you buy my saddle and make use of my carriage. I'll use your money to replace the altar carpet.

"E-M-I-L-I-A! Come and show Don Giovanni to his room. He won't be joining me for dinner. He doesn't feel up to it after dining with the goats. Santa polenta! I hope Pantaleone hasn't sent me an invalid suffering from tapeworms. That's all I need at my age. It's a great responsibility having to prevent a smart-arsed curate from joining the nearest Trappist Monastery where silence is de rigueur. I hope your diffidence is a sign of strength rather than weakness."

Don Agostino was still muttering about Giovanni's propensity for silence when Emilia ushered Giovanni away before he could hear further admonishment. She held a gnarled finger against her lips and beckoned him to follow. Giovanni felt a number of black hexagonal tiles loose under his feet as he followed Emilia's shuffling figure along a dank and narrow corridor.

"His bark's worse than his bite, Don Giovannino ….he needs help and he's glad to see you. When he heard you were coming, he dusted and rearranged his books and asked me to make up your bed with brand new sheets. He needs somebody to talk to. He's a scholar and he's lonely.

"I can't read...can't write....you'll see for yourself how clever he is...from his books...he went to a great deal of bother hiding them during the war. First from the Germans and then from the Marocchini...not that they were much interested in books when they ran amok........"

Giovanni wasn't listening when she mentioned the unmentionable. His attention was taken by the chaos in Emilia's kitchen in which filth and grease battled for supremacy.

Bundles of twigs and saplings were strewn on the floor at

random in the two corners of the wall which contained an open hearth. Hanging from its interior, a bulbous cauldron was partially buried in a mountain of glowing white ashes dotted here and there with red hot-embers.

The remaining corners of the kitchen were cluttered with open casks of sand, water and unwashed crockery. From the indentations, serrations and debris on the undulating surface of the table, Giovanni guessed that it was used to chop meat, fowl, vegetables and firewood.

Flies and bluebottles buzzed over a heap of rotting vegetables and scraps of meat littering the floor around the table. A cluster of ants in circular formation was closing in on the remains of a dead mouse under the table.

Giovanni watched Emily fishing out a steaming coffee percolator from the hot ashes with uncanny dexterity. Having noted how she used sand and water to clean and rinse a cup, Giovanni decided to forego the pleasure of Emilia's unauthorised hospitality.

"I'll pass on the coffee Emilia. I'm sure Don Agostino will drink it. I'll be glad if you could show me to room."

The bedroom was no more than a glorified storeroom. From the light of a tiny bulb hanging from a cobwebbed ceiling, Giovanni saw enough to reinforce his initial impression that Emilia was a conscientious objector in the war against filth and cleanliness. With the striking exception of the area around the window ledges displaying Don Agostino's priceless first editions and the bed sporting brand new sheets and pillowcases.

It was obvious to Giovanni that there was nothing haphazard in how Don Agostino had arranged his books. On one ledge, standard Greek and Latin Classics, on the other Latin Theologians, Greek Philosophers and the Giants of Italian Literature.

The thought of delivering his first sermon brought him down to earth from the intoxicating ether of Theology, Philosophy and Literature. He was glad his Uncle and Aunt wouldn't be in Church next morning when he delivered his maiden sermon. He had a dread of drying up in the pulpit. If this happened he could expect no mercy from Don Agostino, no matter what Emilia said.

Tomorrow was the Feast of Saint Sylvia the patron saint of mothers-to-be. And, logically, the Gospel of the day contained the *Magnificat*. There was enough inspiration in its words for a dozen sermons. From one of the suitcases, Giovanni retrieved his Roman Breviary containing St Luke's moving words.

Thumbing through its pages, his father's memorial card fell out. Ten years, four months and two days since the *Arandora Star* had been sunk without trace in the Irish Sea. A maritime disaster in which his father had drowned and from which his brother had been one of its survivors.

Giovanni stared at the memorial card and thought of his uncle's speech at the ordination dinner. The recent war had indeed cost his family dearly. His labours as a priest would be dedicated to the memory of his family and in particular the memory of his sister. Giovanni knelt at the bedside and prayed beneath a fading portrait of The Madonna of Pompeii.

Later that evening when Emilia called to ask if Giovanni wished to join Don Agostino for supper, she found him asleep. In the gloom, she discerned serenity on his angelic face. She smiled. "Welcome, Don Giovanni," she murmured, "God has sent you to Don Agostino who needs you more than words can say. May the Good Lord look down on you with favour tomorrow." Emilia bent over Giovanni and gently kissed his forehead.

At that same moment, within a stone's throw of the San Sebastiano's neo-classic facade, a Collaquilano was plotting Giovanni Bartolomeo's downfall.

Chapter Eleven

Casa D'Italia, Park Circus, Glasgow, 24th May, 1940.

"According to information received from our Embassy in London, the Duce yesterday assured the Führer that he would realise the legitimate aspirations of Italy by sticking to the obligations of the Secret Supplementary Protocol, as agreed when the Pact of Steel was signed last May in Berlin. We don't know the exact day and time war will be declared. No, don't interrupt me Ettore...... but declared it will be. Just listen and follow Roberto's example."

Ettore held out his hands in resignation. The thought of gainsaying his elder brother, let alone interrupting him when he was laying down the law, never ever entered his head. He had been in thrall to both his brother and sister since their parents died in the cholera epidemic which broke after the earthquake of 1908.

The thought of following any example set by his brother's bull-headed son was another matter. However, Ettore thought it best to keep this particular reservation to himself. From experience, he knew that criticism of the seventeen-year-old Roberto, however mild, would irritate a doting Silvio.

"It's impossible to say," said Silvio with assurance, "when we will declare war. Rest assured, it will be within the next few weeks. Churchill will live to regret his refusal to accept the Führer's proposals for peace after the conquest of Poland.

"The coming war," continued Silvio boastfully, "will enable us to break the chains which suffocate us in the Mare Nostrum[1] and in so doing eliminate, once and for all, tyrannical Anglo-French domination of the Mediterranean."

"Just tell us what's to be done, Dad and we'll do it. You've made up your mind, haven't you? Otherwise, you wouldn't have ordered Zio Ettore to come here in the first place."

"Watch your tongue, Roberto, watch your tongue. Both of you know that when it comes to the welfare of the family, I never have or will ever be found wanting. As sure as night follows day, the success of my activities here in Scotland....on behalf of the Party.... will ensure my arrest in the event of war. I understand, from what Ambassador Grandi tells me, that the British Home Office, acting on direct orders from Churchill, has drawn up contingency plans to arrest all Italian citizens over the age of sixteen and send them to the Isle of Man. Ambassador Grandi, I'm proud to say, also tells me that prominent members of the Fascist Party like me will be shipped overseas, probably to Canada or Australia." Pausing for effect, a self-satisfied Silvio poured himself a glass of San Pellegrino mineral water.

"What makes you think the British Home Office has the resources to send any of us overseas, Dad?"

"Porca Putana, Roberto! Put two and two together and show some savvy. You know damn well our informant in the Clyde-side Shipyards has reported that passenger ships from the Blue Star Line has been requisitioned by the Military and put out to tender for refurbishment as prison ships."

"You mean the two liners sitting on the dry dock in the Cammell Laird Naval Shipyard? The ones waiting to be painted battleship grey?"

"Exactly, Roberto. They are being prepared for VIPs like me. Unless they are redirected to Dunkirk for the evacuation of what's left of the British Expeditionary Forces ....before Rommel's 7th Panzer Division arrives to annihilate them."

"Ironic isn't it Silvio," Ettore ventured to say, "That we should be praising Rommel when he's the little stronzo who won his spurs leading the Stormtroopers who chased us across the Piave from Caporetto."

95

"Yes! Yes! Yes! "retorted Silvio dismissively. "That all happened because General Capello was bedridden with malaria..... so we were left to the mercies of that bungling imbecile Cadorna[1].

"But that's all in the past and we should never look back. History will never repeat itself. We have nothing to fear from the Germans. It's the future which counts. And it's only a matter of time before Goering's Luftwaffe wipes out the Cammell Laird Docks and heads north to Clydeside for more target practice. For my liking, once the bombing starts, the Meadowside Shipyard is too close to home for comfort.

"Which means that we will have to think of Lucrezia and Bianchina's safety. With this in mind, I've decided to send Bianchina back to Milignano with Lucrezia. Once in Italy, they will be out of harm's way and want for nothing.

"We'll join them when the war is won. I've opened a Post Office Account in Bianchina's name with one million lire transferred from my account in Rome, with instructions to transfer more as and when required."

"Do I take it you plan to leave Giovanni with us?"

"Of course, Ettore. Maria has been like a mother to him since Livia died. You'll be looking after the brains of the family."

"And I suppose I'm the brawn, Dad?"

"We spoiled you, Roberto. Both of us did. And even more so after the Jesuits expelled you in your first year."

"The little stronzo deserved all he got for saying Harry Lauder was a better singer than Gigli. And it's hardly my fault his pals made the mistake of trying to save his skin. What was I supposed to do? Run? The three of them deserved what they got."

"Be that as it may be," said Silvio proudly, "but we still made a mistake in keeping you at home for two years until you reached leaving age. We should have trusted the Marists to finish your education.

"Who knows what you might have achieved. You were clever enough. This was the reason your mother made me promise, on her deathbed, that Giovanni would be the one to redeem the family name by living up to the academic expectations of the Jesuits. Speak up, Ettore, say something for God's sake and stop standing there as if impaled to the bloody floor."

"Rest assured, Silvio, I'll make sure Giovanni gets to the University, bursary or no bursary. Maria will carry on treating Giovanni like the son we never had. Besides, he's been living with us in Kelvinside since Livia died. There will be no great upheaval involved for all concerned. But, if you and Roberto are to be arrested and sent to God knows where for the duration, what do we do with our Kelvingrove and Mount Vernon properties?"

"You and Maria will move from Kelvinside to Mount Vernon with Giovanni. As far from the Shipyards as possible. The properties we own are held in your name. Sell both houses, grab what you can and get back to Italy after Giovanni graduates. Even if our properties survive the bombing, they won't be worth a cent after we've brought this country to its knees.

"I've taken the precaution of closing my account with the British Linen Bank and have transferred the money to Giovanni's savings account. I've done the same with Roberto's account. For practical reasons, we'll close the Casa D'Italia for the duration. Most of the staff will be rounded up for internment. Same goes for the Torquato. But keep paying wages while the conflict lasts. They deserve nothing less for loyalty to us as a family. Dependents will need money when the breadwinners are locked up."

"How soon do we close the Torquato, Silvio?"

"Honour all dinner and function reservations until next week then close it down. Say it's for refurbishment. Roberto will help you mothball the interior before our lads brick up the front entrance and windows. This will protect the place from attacks by patriotic arsonists and looters running amok during their Glaswegian Kristallnacht[1]. The same goes for the back entrance. As a red herring, have the doorway boarded to conceal the brickwork. Leave a pile of bricks, sand and cement handy. This will create the impression that work is on-going. When they're stolen, as they surely will be, report the theft to the Police. Just for the record. Roberto and I will continue to live in the *Casa* until we are arrested. Unless Roberto wants to leave with Lucrezia?"

"Never! If you stay, I stay. No matter where they send us. We'll be back within the year. Mark my words! We'll get back to revel in the glory of victory. I'm looking forward to our first victory parade from Park Circus to George Square. To be welcomed by the Podestà of Glasgow, looking swell in his black shirt and fez emblazoned with our double-headed eagle."

"There's one more thing you have to do Roberto before we take a holiday at King George's expense. You must persuade Irma Rossi to break off your engagement and leave Giovanni free to take your place. She's a good all-home-and-chapel-girl and I'm very fond of her. I've discussed this matter with her mother and she's more than happy to welcome Giovanni into the family.

"We both agree that a Casanova, like you, could never make her happy. At all costs, we must protect the girl's reputation. Besides, none of us, least of all Maria, would approve of Giovanni being foisted with shop-soiled goods. So do what you have to do for your brother's sake

"Once we've attended to these matters, we sit back and wait for the Duce to make his announcement from Palazzo Venezia. Which he can't do until loudspeakers are in place in public squares and bars throughout the peninsula and on our two major islands," adding with cynical satisfaction, "which is good news for me and Artemio since we have a controlling interest in the Sarzana factory which produces loudspeakers and rigging kits.

"Together with our Ordinance Factory in Porto Torres, we will do well from this war. In Scotland, our assets will be safe in the hands of Ettore and Giovanni since both are British Subjects. Together with our assets in Italy, our future welfare is assured.

"After the war, we will enjoy our wealth on both sides of the Channel. And when Giovanni graduates, we can look forward to his wedding with Irma. Just bear in mind," Silvio added with irrational self-assurance, "that while Patriotism, unlike Socialism, cannot be seduced by wealth, it can find a home wherever and however it is accumulated. Meanwhile, the delay will give Roberto ample time to arrange a short wave radio link-up with Artemio from OVRA[1] Headquarters in Rome, so that we can hear the Declaration of War in the Casa D'Italia."

"I suppose Churchill will be doing his eleventh-hour best to keep us out of the war, Silvio?"

"If he does, Ettore, he's sure to be wasting his time. We can't be seen to be negotiating like a Neville Chamberlain [2]. This would be seen as a sign of weakness and would not, I repeat, would not be in accordance with the spirit of Proletarian Fascism. The Duce will ignore any attempt to prevent him from fulfilling his destiny with the Führer."

"And tell me, Silvio, will this broadcast be made be in the morning or the afternoon?"

"Probably in the afternoon if it is to take effect at midnight. According to protocol, the Duce's Declaration of War will be delivered in the first instance to the respective Ambassadors of Great Britain and France.

"Meantime we have to turn our attention to arrangements for Bianchina and Lucrezia's departure. Ettore, contact our man in Thomas Cook's and have him deal with the travel agenda. First Class all the way to Rome. Roberto, get Artemio to arrange transport from Rome to Milignano for Bianchina and Lucrezia. It's more than likely Artemio will get my old friend Michele Verrecchia to pick them up at the Stazione Termine.

"Ettore, use the back entrance when you leave today and take our cache of gold sovereigns with you. I've emptied all but a few into two Gladstone Bags. Keep them stashed until I get back. Take the Building Fund Cash Book with you and burn it as soon as you get back to Kelvinside.

"Roberto, deal with the Irma situation. Take Maria with you. She's a friend of Irma's mother. Make Irma feel that she's the one to have broken the engagement. She won't find it hard to swallow that you're not the marrying kind and that Giovanni will be a better bet in the marriage stakes after he graduates. This will leave you free to continue sowing wild oats in the gardens of the local tarts before you are arrested. So make hay while the sun shines.

"This done, gentlemen, we can look forward to the Duce's broadcast. I'll have what's left of my nest-egg sown into the hem of my overcoat, pack my valise and wait for the arrival of His Majesty's Black Maria."

CHAPTER TWELVE

Collaquila, Church of San Sebastiano, Sunday 5th November 1950

Emilia had spread the news that Don Giovanni Bartolomeo would be celebrating the first rather than the second Sunday Mass. As a result, the Church of San Sebastiano was packed to capacity for the former. The chance of avoiding one of Don Agostino's sermons was an opportunity to be savoured.

The excitement of the congregation was reflected in a hum of anticipation. Like an expectant theatre audience,it waited for the curtain to rise on the matinee performance of Don Agostino's understudy. The delay was by no means unwelcome. It gave the congregation an opportunity for a free and frank exchange of tittle-tattle with friends, relatives and adversaries, about Don Agostino's first-ever curate.

........HE'S A FOREIGNER....... SPEAKS TEN LANGUAGES...... A SCHOLAR JUST LIKE DON AGOSTINO....... HIS FATHER WAS A FASCIST BIG-SHOT......HIS MOTHER WAS THE BELLE OF THE DREADED VILLAGE.......WHERE HIS FATHER HAD BEEN COCK OF THE WALK... HIS BROTHER WAS A CONVICTED THUG....... HIS MOTHER PREGNANT WHEN SHE ELOPED......... HE WAS SICK OVER STAFFIERI'S GOATS....... HIS MOTHER RAN OFF TO SARZANA WHERE HIS FATHER WAS STATIONED.DURING THE GREAT WAR...... HIS SISTER WAS RAPED AND MURDERED BY THE MAROCCHINI....... HE'S THE BISHOP'S LOVE CHILD...... DON AGOSTINO WANTS HIM TO LEAVE.....

To the villagers of Collaquila, the Church of San Sebastiano reflected the limitations of their religious beliefs. They knew no more than the garish frescoes illustrating the two macabre deaths of San Sebastiano[1] and a giant statue of *Our Lady of Sorrows*,

101

face glowing with tinted red cheeks and three gem-encrusted swords piercing her heart.

To most, if not all, of its congregation, attendance at the San Sebastiano provided a passport to that desirable Garden of Eden where every day, like Sundays, was a day of rest from the labours of the fields and pastures.

To the left of the High Altar, a bell near the sacristy door tinkled above the din and loud enough to hush voices and cause necks to crane. The persistent clattering of children's feet was stilled. Two altar boys, bedecked in red soutanes and white surplices trimmed with lace on sleeves and hems, marched out with hands joined. A few paces behind, came a composed and radiant Giovanni wearing a gold satin chasuble and stole. He carried a chalice covered by a veil and burse in the coordinating colour of his vestments and held in place by the palm of his right hand.

Having removed the white linen corporal from the burse and placed it over the altar, Giovanni carefully positioned the chalice at its centre, covered it once more with the veil and replaced the burse over the veil. This done, he genuflected and then turned to walk down the three steps to the foot of the altar. Before he reached the last step, the congregation broke into loud and sustained applause

Giovanni stood on the carpeted platform, head bowed in embarrassment, wondering how the congregation would react when he made a hash of his sermon. Giovanni looked up and smiled nervously until the applause ended.

When he faced the altar to begin Mass, the servers were kneeling on the first of the three altar steps, eager to parrot their responses, in a centuries-old language they did not understand. With Don Giovanni, they began a Latin litany dating back to the sixteenth century: *I will go unto the Altar of God; unto God who gives joy to my youth.*

When the Gospel reading of St. Luke's Chapter on the Visitation was over, Giovanni felt inspired and ready to deliver his first sermon. Taking one glance at the precarious condition of the pulpit which looked like a giant matchbox on crumbling concrete stilts, he decided to speak from behind the open gates of the communion rails.

Giovanni's decision caused a murmuring among the good people of Collaquila. Weaned on Don Agostino's obstinate and predictable conservatism, the Curate's unorthodoxy had to be savoured while it lasted before he was brought to heel.

"In the name of the Father, Son and Holy Ghost." "Amen." came the response from all save one of the congregation.

"My Brothers in Christ Our Lord." Giovanni's initial nervousness vanished as soon as he began to speak. The adrenaline of confidence pulsed through his body adding strength and purpose to his otherwise gentle voice. "...the Gospel of this day marks the Feast Day of the Visitation when two mothers meet for the first time after learning that each was with child. Elizabeth and Mary, cousins exchanging ordinary everyday words about their happy condition and looking forward to …....."

*Antipatico, a pain in the arse just like his father. Looks like him... except for the spiv hairstyle and the gangster moustache... but the same arrogant expression of superiority....I'll get a better look at his ugly face when I take Communion.....*Standing alone at the back of the Church, Raffaele Staffieri, the village Undertaker and Itinerant Pig Slaughterer, listened to the new priest's words with loathing in his blasphemous soul. He hated this priest more than life itself because he was the son of the man who had beaten, humiliated and robbed him when he and his mother lived in Scotland.

And now, after sixteen years of agonising, the day of reckoning had come. Like a bolt from the blue and manna from heaven, the Bishop of Venafro had sent Giovanni Bartolomeo to serve as a Curate in Collaquila.

".......it is St. Luke himself who raises the meeting between the

103

two women above the normalities of everyday life. He puts into the mouth of the Virgin Mary the words of that wonderful prayer we call the Magnificat:

"MY SOUL DOTH MAGNIFY THE LORD, AND MY SPIRIT HATH REJOICED IN GOD MY SAVIOUR.

"What, my dear people is Our Lady saying to us? She is telling us that God has chosen her.....for her humility. She is telling us that her very lowliness has been the cause of her elevation. "FOR HE THAT IS MIGHTY HAS ELEVATED ME.

"You see, my dear people this is how the Lord Our God works.... he works through the humble and lowly....not through the rich and the powerful. HE HATH PUT DOWN THE MIGHTY FROM THEIR SEAT AND HATH EXALTED THE HUMBLE AND THE WEAK.

"And yes, Mary's exaltation was unique. And something that was never more to be repeated. But this does not mean that He has stopped working with and through the lowly and the humble.

"God works through mothers struggling to raise their children, and through husbands labouring in the fields and pastures to feed them and clothe them.

"My dear people, God works with and through the victims of the world we live in...the victims of poverty and hunger ...the victims of disease.... the victims of injustice and yes, my dear people, the victims of war." Giovanni paused, head bowed and hands tightly locked for a few moments, giving him time to dismiss the temptation of raising the taboo subject of the *Marocchinate*. There were a few coughs here and there echoing through the Church. In a quiet yet still audible voice, Giovanni continued, eyes firmly fixed on the central aisle. "And finally, my dear people, I would like you to know that I am dedicating this mass not only to you, my new parishioners but also to my parents. My mother died on this day fifteen years ago in Scotland, the land where I was born and ten years ago, on the second of July, my father perished in the *Arandora Star* sea

104

disaster. I would ask you to keep them in your prayers during this mass."

While he was speaking Giovanni had a vague impression of somebody leaving the rear of the Church in great haste, but he did not dwell on it.

"I would also ask you to pray for my late brother, sister and aunt, who like my father were victims of the recent war which touched all of us, in one way or another. Humbly, I would also ask you to pray for me, that I may be worthy to serve as your priest and in so doing honour the memory of my family. I would now ask you to kneel for my blessing."

During the Offertory, while Giovanni and the altar-boys sat on the right facing the altar steps, the absence of the traditional collection of alms was taken as a signal to the congregation to come forward with gifts for the new priest, placing them on the side-altar dedicated to *La Madonna Addolorata*, with tinted cheeks and three gem-encrusted sword handles embedded in her bosom.

During the distribution of Communion Wafers, the congregation kneeling at the communion rail were able to have a closer look at their new curate. Such were their numbers that the mass lasted nearly two hours. Almost double the time it took Don Agostino to plough through his regular Sunday Mass and a laboriously long homily.

When his inaugural mass was over, Giovanni retired to the sacristy to disrobe. There he found the stern figure of Don Agostino ready to deflate him with constructive criticism not only about his sermon but also from where it had been delivered.

Chapter Thirteen

"Why so glum face, Giovanni?" asked Don Agostino when Giovanni entered the Sacristy to disrobe. "If anyone has a right to be glum then it's me. Not much point in wasting good candles for the second mass when nobody will be there. Your sermon took the words out of my mouth.

"Not much point in giving the same sermon, is there? People would think it's me you've been copying. That's the way it should be. I can't have my parishioners thinking that in you I'm met my match. And that, my boy, would never do. So let me start with some criticism of your sermon, in case you get ideas above your station.

"Let me begin by saying that you should have included the relevance of St Silvia in your homily on the Visitation. Just as I did last year and every year before that."

"If this was a test, Don Agostino, then I've failed it. I should have made this connection."

"Listen and learn, young man. Given your comments on Mary and Elizabeth, need I say more?"

"No, Don Agostino, that won't be necessary. Unless you were going to add that St Sylvia was Gregory the Great's mother?"

"I would have done that during my homily if you hadn't been responsible for the cancellation of today's noonday mass. Which would have been reason enough not to cancel the noonday mass if I had known you didn't intend to mention St Silvia, Don Smarty Pants. But I'm more than pleased to have saved parish money by not burning candles needlessly. But I've said that already, I think, before you went off at a tangent.

"Emilia's spreading the good news about the candles as we speak. You'll serve my mass on the side altar once I've disposed of your gifts. You don't say much, do you? Except when it matters. Like your sermon this morning? Like promoting your family? I suppose you're pleased with yourself?" Giovanni said nothing. "Well, I suppose as first sermons go, I've heard a lot worse. I'm here to give you advice which you will take of course, unless you plan to irritate me with irrelevant minutiae about Gregory the Great's family."

Giovanni held his silence and continued to disrobe. Slowly and carefully, he untied the cincture around his waist before he removed the chasuble, folding it twice and pushing it to the rear of the dresser, where the Sacristan had earlier laid it out. He thought he detected a hint of humour, even a suggestion of praise in the old man's comments.

"…...and don't speak to these people with such familiarity. If you do that they might start thinking they're your equal. We simply can't have that. We must always speak above their heads. That's why we've got a pulpit. Not good enough for you was it? These people respect what they don't understand....ignorance gives strength to their faith...makes it survive...makes it thrive. Take away the ignorance, you take away the magic.

"Remove the magic and you remove their need to come to Church. And it's their duty, their exemplary duty, to contribute to the support of their pastors. Which they can't do if they don't come to church. I suppose, no, I know there's little likelihood that contributions will double now that the Bishop has foisted you on me. So, remove the magic and we'll starve.

"You don't say much, do you? Which suits me down to the ground. I've had years of practice keeping my mouth shut. I've sent Emilia to find out why the village Undertaker left mass during your sermon.

"Get out and about. Meet your parishioners. Don't get yourself too involved... if you do, you might miss lunch, given that abstinence is good for the soul..." Giovanni had no intention of missing the entertainment of a lunchtime monologue from the irrepressible Don Agostino.

The San Sebastian Presbytery

The"Emilia! E-M-I-Li-A!" bellowed Don Agostino sitting centre stage with Giovanni in the dining room. "Emilia! Are you waiting for those carrots to grow fingernails or for our mule to have a foal?

"Get a move on woman! Don Giovanni here is getting more impatient by the minute. In fact, so impatient that he's beginning to hum while we're waiting here for you to show your face." Don Agostino looked at Giovanni to see if he was paying attention. Satisfied that he was, he continued. "What does it take to boil a few carrots I ask you? Now, tell me, Giovanni, while we're waiting for poor Emilia to produce a meal from that hell-hole she calls a kitchen, did you meet any of our local worthies during your tour of duty? No need to beat around the bush. Emilia will tell me who you met and who said what and to whom.....later, after she's done her rounds. Shouting, you should know, keeps Emilia on her toes.

"She's well-off with me here, believe me. Better than most of her cronies who would swap places with her in an instant, if ever they got the chance. But what's all this humming? Am I boring you? One of your Scottish pibrochs?"

"It's not a bagpipe variation, Don Agostino. It's from a cello concerto by Dvorak, inspired by Horace's Ode, 'O Fons Bandusiae'. It's a great favourite of mine. I was reading it in one of your......sorry Don Agostino...I know you told me not to touch your books but ...." Giovanni's face reddened. Don Agostino had told him to steer clear of his precious books. He had defied him. Like a wayward schoolboy, caught red-handed in a misdemeanour, Giovanni waited for the expected rebuke.

But Don Agostino wasn't listening to Giovanni's sheepish apologies. That it could be a misdemeanour never crossed his mind. For the first time since the young priest's arrival, Don

Agostino's wistfulness vanished as his lips curved into a smile.

"Horace? Your favourite Latin poet you say? ....*the fleeting years are slipping fast away ......and piety will bring no respite from pressing old age.* These are my favourite lines.....not that they refer to me in particular. I've always liked them. Even when I was a young whipper-snapper like you and when old age was the last thing I had on my mind. Horace sums up how I have strived to live my life here in Collaquila: *A LIFE BLAMELESS AND FREE FROM SIN.* Which, if you will forgive my shameless presumption, is what I would I would like on my tombstone: *INTEGER VITAE SCELERISQUE PURUS.*

Don Agostino seemed lost in his thoughts. Giovanni said nothing. He had a feeling the old man was going to bring up the subject Bishop Pantaleone had warned him not to mention.

"Not that I've got death on my agenda for the moment. I don't suppose Pantaleone told you what happened when the Goumiers raided Collaquila? I suppose he told you that the Germans manned a look-out post here on the Liri Valley? They were here for nearly two weeks. Until they got wiped out one night in a commando raid by Goumiers stationed in Milignano.

"In the morning we welcomed them as liberators. The rest is history," he added pointing to the scar on his face. "There are those who know what happened here and those who don't know. Of those who know, many of them have remaincd silent and kept what they know to themselves."

Don Agostino nodded his head from side to side and exhaled a long and weary breath, which seemed to come from the depths of his soul, before continuing. "I went to Pantaleone to report what they did to me and my housekeeper. He invited me to say what I had to say but only in the Confessional.

"And so Bishop Machiavelli's lips were sealed with regard to our unspeakable personal experiences here in my presbytery. Our ordeals didn't figure in the *Marocchinate Report* he sent to Papa Pacelli. And believe me, I'm thankful for this exclusion, for

Emilia's sake rather than for mine.

"What I didn't know then was that he had been appointed by His Holiness to whitewash the behaviour of the Goumiers and allow their dead to be buried with full military honours in land owned by the Church. But the less said about Pantaleone the better. I can say no more without impugning his reputation ...... I've said too much already. The devil is in the details and speaking of the devil, out jumps its tail."

The tail on this occasion was Emilia. For once her interruption was welcomed with relief rather than sarcasm. A chance to stem further revelations about how he and his housekeeper had been violated by the Goumiers.

"This young man thought you had trekked over to Scapoli for the water, gone down to Milignano for the matches, before hauling firewood from Capriati." As usual, Emilia ignored Don Agostino's ironic comments.

"Serve the lad first. And don't ladle too much soup into his plate. I don't want him leaving any. Don't believe in waste. It's always better to have less than more. Let him get used to the richness of your greasy soup before we trust him with bigger amounts. Leave the bowl here beside my plate. I'll serve myself while you incinerate the capon."

With relish, Don Agostino slurped his way through the contents of the giant tureen: yellowish greasy chicken stock with globules of overcooked pasta. The noise he made reminded Giovanni of how his father and brother used to slurp at the table, much to his and sister amusement.

"You don't want some of this awful wine, do you, Giovanni?" The question was asked in a way which invited refusal. "Collaquila's best vintage. Goats' shit does nothing for grapes cultivated on volcanic rock. I hear from Emilia that Mussolini's Santa Maddalena was served at your ordination dinner. A gift from some big-shot operator from the Alto Adige.

"Emilia tells me this Nordista tried to flirt with the wife of Milignano's one-legged goalkeeper. A delightfully plump young lady from what I hear and one of your admirers.

"Never trust these Northerners. I suppose you think it's ironic that Mussolini promoted wines when he was a teetotaller? Nothing of the sort! He took back-handers just like the rest of his thieving band of scoundrels. Rogues, degenerates and cut-throats the lot of them. And I'd bet my pension on Pantaleone snaffling a few cases.

"I'm sure my Uncle will let you have a bottle or two. I'll send word."

"Just you do that. When you write to him....do it tonight. Strike when the iron is hot is my motto before it becomes water under the bridge. But I don't want charity. Ask your uncle if he would like a few trusses of garlic. Cloves as big as orange segments. Goat shit works wonders on frost free hill soil.

"Tell your uncle I'll send him one truss per two bottles of wine. No, let's be sensible and prudent here. Make that two trusses for every six bottles. We could maybe throw in a few rounds of goats' cheese. No, better to make that one round to seal the deal."

Further discussion on hypothetical bartering was interrupted when Emilia appeared with a mummified capon, shrivelled and black. Complete with shrunken head, neck and claws.

"And here she comes with the speed of a rampant tortoise. Alleluia! Alleluia!" There was a hint of amusement on Emilia's face when she approached Giovanni with her burnt offering.

"Snap off one of the legs from the pyre, Giovanni. I'll have the breasts and I'm happy to polish off the other leg. Bring it here Emilia. Giovanni will understand why I am pulling rank. One of the privileges of ruling the rooster, or the capon as it so happens. What are you saying, woman? Speak up!" Emilia was leaning over Don Agostino's ear, close enough to see the wax behind its sprouting hairs.

111

"Now? Here? While we're eating?" Don Agostino muttered, showing considerable irritation.

"The Mayor and the Brigadier," said Emilia raising her voice in exasperation, "they insist it's urgent official business. Something that can't wait. They've brought a *Salame* and an enormous *Caccio di Cavallo*. The cheese was brought by the Brigadier."

"A salame and a cheese? An enormous Caccio di Cavallo? From those two skinflints? Then their business must be serious. Give them coffee....in those small cups without handles... while we finish off your sacrificial offering." Emilia stifled what could have been a yawn or a sigh as she limped off.

Giovanni watched the old priest bending over his plate tearing at the capon with vigour. Despite its appearance, Don Pietro's smacking lips indicated that the bird was succulent and tasty. At regular intervals, Don Agostino wiped his fingers on a chunk of bread, from which he broke off a sizeable morsel, used it to mop up the grease on his chin, before sliding it into his mouth.

A loud belch and a sonorous breaking of wind followed the emptying of yet another glass of the undrinkable' wine. Only when the capon's bones had been gnawed and sucked dry, did Giovanni venture to say what he had in mind.

"Do you want me to leave you alone with the visitors, Don Agostino? It might be that what they have to say is for your ears only."

"Not at all, my boy. If it's parish business, then it's your business. And parish business it must be since those two dolts have seen fit to come at this sacrosanct hour of the day.

"Besides, it's time you met the Mayor and our local Bobby. I can't wait to hear what those two imbeciles have to say that's worth a salame and a giant cheese, let alone interrupting my lunch. The Brigadier has been with us...now let me think.... must be about five years. He's still to make an arrest.

"As for the Sindaco, he got the job by appointment because

nobody else wants it. We tolerate him because of what the Germans did to his wife Miriam, the daughter of a Polish Jew. It was a reprisal for refusing to organise Labour Gangs to extend Kesselring's Gustav Line fortifications. The Germans sent the Sindaco's wife to a holding camp for Jews in Rome from where she was sent to the gas chambers of Auschwitz. Requiescat in pace.

"As it so happens, our Sindaco is also the village Doctor but as such he's rarely called. Women here don't trust him. I get to hear both sides of the coin in the Confessional, so my lips are sealed.....if you know what I mean.

"Besides, I'm sure a lad like you isn't interested in what the Doctor apparently gets up to in Collaquila. However, if you want to know chapter and verse, have a word with Emilia."

Chapter Fourteen

Friday 7th September 1951, Pontifical Irish College, Rome

Fiachre Fahy sat back studying the massive physique of his friend seated opposite him at the far end of the table in the Rector's dining room. Since he last saw him fifteen years ago, Seamus O'Fainnaide had moved from middleweight into super heavyweight class with a vengeance.

"Well now, me old friend Father Fiachre Fahy from Kilfenora County Claire, you'll be feelin' like a new man after your spell of dooty with the kangaroos. You've lost weight an' most of your hair. We'll soon get you back on your feet with the blessed trinity of Pasta, Vino and Potatoes...... an' I'll see to gettin' you an undetectable toupee.

"You have the lean and hungry look like that Julius Caesar was complain'n about while expressing his preference for jolly fatties like me[1]. Four square meals a day and a runnin' all day buffet will soon rid you o' that washed-out look I saw this mornin' when I clapped eyes on you ..... when you interrupted me breakfast, the most important meal of the day."

"It's fine long-winded welcome so it is for a weary soul like me, after a four week two-ocean jaunt from the back o' beyond and an overnight bone-shaking Genova-Roma express. But you're right there Seamus," shaking his head with exaggerated gravity, "I was feelin' depressed after seein' the Capuchin Church across the road. Just thinkin' o' the place would take the smile from any mother's face. I need no remindin' of death in this condition of mine. *The Fear of death perturbs me[2].*"

"Sweet star of the Sea... you'll not be thinkin' and talkin' about that old bone-yard in the Santa Maria would you now? An old bone-yard, that's what Padraig O'Gallachair, God rest his blatherin' soul, used to call it. You shouldn't be tinkin' maudlin'

114

thoughts. Remember we used to go there before our shavin' days for a good laugh? What was it Padraig called the place?"

"A dog's idea of paradise." Fahy replied without hesitation. "Which got him into trouble with the Rector for blasphemy. Remember?"

"Come now, Fiachre Fahy, Padraig O'Galachair got us into bother every time he opened his mouth. Remember the blanket ban on San Isidora students from sitting on the Spanish Steps?"

"How could I forget, when it was me own question which brought the answer causin' the ban."

"Hardly your fault for being so naive, Fiachre Fahy, now was it to be sure?"

"All I asked the Rector was how we, as trainee priests, could tell a good girl from a bad one. How was I to know that Padraig would pipe up to sayin' all we had to do was have a look at how they sat on the Spanish Steps?"

"You and Padraig should have known better given how touchy the Rector was about female underwear. And didn't Padraig make matters worse when the old dodder overheard him saying he would deprive the dogs of their supper by shovelling all the bones in the Santa Maria into a grinder and ship the lot back to Ireland to fertilise the spuds.

"Listen to me Fiachre Fahy and don't be puttin' your mite's worth in before I'm finished. I'll make a deal with you. Here and now. Don't be makin' any remarks about the fact that I've put on a little weight," patting his rotundity with pride, "I'm a fatty. And so what? I've eaten lots o' healthy food to get like this. In return, I won't mention the fact that you've gone thin on top with two hairs doing the work o' forty. Now, what was I sayin' Fiachre Fahy from Kilfenora County Clare?"

Fiachre smiled. Still the same old Seamus and his puckish way of shocking anyone daft enough to take him seriously. "You were remindin' me about me hair loss."

115

"And so I was, so I was. And I say it's the Good Lord's punishment for all the combin' you used to do when you thought me and Padraig weren't lookin'. Divine Retribution I call it for yer vanity. It's a pity so it is that Padraig isn't here to see a baldy Fiachre Fahy. So, is it a deal, Baldy? You won't be mouthin' off about me weight and I won't mention those few hairs straddlin' that big intellectual skull of yours."

"It's a deal, Fatso. I'll forget about your bloated body, which could feed the cannibals in Darkest Africa and leave room for seconds and you won't mention my vanity in tryin' to conceal me loss o' follicles."

The two friends laughed after their ritual exchange of insults. Honour on both sides had been satisfied and Seamus had succeeded in his intent of reviving Fahy's spirits. It was just like old times. Calling him Fiachre Fahy to distinguish him from a fellow student called Ruairi Fahy. If Padraig O'Gallachair hadn't succumbed to muscular dystrophy, their reunion that day would have been perfect.

"What do you think of all the changes in Rome, Fiachre Fahy?" Seamus asked, dipping his fingers into a jar of soft pecorino cheese crawling with plump white maggots. He looked with delight at the maggots squirming on his fingers before sticking them into the mouth of his moon-shaped face.

"The topography might be different but the Romans are still the same as usual. Still livin' up to their SPQR[1] motto." Fiachre shrugged, waving away an invitation to taste the maggot-ridden muck Padraig used to call Quagmire Cheese.

"*Sono Porci Questi Romani! These Romans are a filthy lot!* The wit who coined this paraphrase was immersed in a River of Light. They are indeed an arrogant bunch of sullen penniless skinflints because they think the whole world owes them somethin' in recognition fer the glories of Ancient Rome. You can measure their respect for strangers and foreigners as the shortest distance between two contiguous points."

116

"Couldn't agree more Seamus. They think people like us owe them something for havin' civilised the world."

"Are you sure you don't want to try this pecorino, Fiachre Fahy? Or have your taste buds been ruined by eatin' too many kangaroos and koala bears?"

"No thanks. I like me pecorino dead on the plate and not lookin' like albino tadpoles trapped in cheese curds."

"You know somethin', Fiachre Fahy," said Seamus changing the subject, "Italians don't rightly know how much they owe the Irish for rescuing them from the territorial waters of ignorance."

"That the why I'm never done tellin' them what Dante owed to Irish scholars in our monasteries during the Dark Ages. Ireland wasn't called *The Light of Europe* for nothin'....are you listenin' to me, Seamus? Or are you too busy fishin' for maggots?"

"I could be telling you, Fiachre Fahy, to keep your hair on but for our pact." But Seamus knew there was no way of interrupting Fiachre Fahy when he was on his hobby horse.

"Ireland owes the world nothin'! That's what I'm declarin', Seamus. Eireann holds pawn tickets from all the countries who've been blessed by the labours of our countrymen. Would the word of God have lit up Australia without the convict priests the Poms sent to Botany Bay?

"You should be writing this down for the memoirs we plan to write. But let me change the subject for a change. Tell me about last year, Seamus. Tell me all about Holy Year. Was it the success the Vatican is claiming it was?"

"It was the Canonisation that did the trick. Attracted millions of pilgrims so it did."

"The canonisation of the twelve-year-old? Murdered for standin' up against a would-be rapist?"

"Blessed Maria Goretti or Saint Maria Goretti as she is now. Her story really got the World's Press goin'. Went on for months.

Makin' up for the fact that it had ignored her story for nigh on forty years. Suddenly, it discovers her story is full of human interest. Made a dog's dinner of the fact that the lass forgave the criminal who stabbed her God knows how many times before the poor soul died. Her mother and her killer were both at the ceremony in St Peter's Square. Side by side. Holding hands. Very poignant. Sold lots of medals and souvenirs. Kiosks and stalls are still full of them. If it's true what my good friend Cardinal Roccaravindola is sayin', they're searchin' the whole peninsula for another Maria Goretti."

"And who would you be meaning by 'they', Seamus?"

"The Press and the Church of course. Who else?"

"And how's the search going?"

"According to Roccaravindola the Church has sniffed a possibility. Whispers about a girl down South... in that part of Italy which produces weepin' statues, monks wi' bleedin' hands and apparitions and miracles wit' the regularity of me bowel movements. We'll just have to wait and see if anythin' comes of it. But tell me, Fiachre Fahy, how's the old ticker? Will it see us through for another few years? Or will I be havin' to go back to Kilfenora County Clare on me own leaving you buried here with Old Luke Waddin?"

"I'll be fine. No strenuous work.... like diggin' for maggots in pecorino cheese. If I can avoid worry and agitation from the likes of you, Seamus, I'll live long enough to see you buried in Kilfenora County Clare. It was enervatin' heat that jiggered me in Australia. Caused a thrombosis in me leg. And that was that as far as the Army was concerned. More or less told me, as Padraig used to spell it out without the vowels, V-F-N C-L-[1]. So I cashed in me service chips, took the severance parachute before the Diggers booted me out the door.

"I saw no reason to snuff me candle among the wild colonial boys of Botany Bay. And thanks to you, Seamus, here I am. I didn't want to get back to Kilfenora County Clare without you.

And that's the God's honest truth, Seamus O'Fainnaide, Rector of the San Isidoro Irish College in the Eternal City of Rome."

"Sweet star of the Sea, Fiachre Fahy, it was nothing at all. You'll be doing me a favour teachin' Italian to my students. And besides, I'm sharin' your talents wi' Father Cassidy, me opposite number in the Scots College.

"Apart from your keep, you won't cost me a farthing. Cassidy will be paying your salary wit'out knowing it. Now isn't that something? Gettin' a tight-arsed Scotchman to fork out for your salary wit'out him knowin' it?"

"Now I know why they made you Rector of the College. Seamus O'Fainnaide. It's a rogue you are. And I love you for it. May God forgive me part in cheatin' a fellow priest."

"God is forever merciful, Fiachre Fahy. And speaking of transgressions, I won't be joining you for breakfast tomorrow. Donnelly's Sausages are bein' flown in from Dublin. I'll be at Ciampino to make sure they don't sprout legs and disappear like the last lot.

"I don't take chances when it comes to me Sausages. After that I've got a meetin' wit' Father Cassidy to draw up your timetable. Salvatore will serve you breakfast. He'll hear you walkin' over the loose tiles when you rise and shine. So I'll say goodnight and see you at lunchtime. Good night and God Bless us both."

Fahy heard the loose tiles clanking under his feet when he entered his assigned bedroom. His, God willing for the next four years. It smelled of lavender and was adequately furnished. Modest and suitable for the purpose. In comparison to the army barracks in the POW camp, it was luxurious.

The pleasure of having his own room, wardrobe, wash basin and pisspot was to be savoured. His bed was soft and formed a comfortable hammock shape at its centre. The sheets and pillow cases were clean even if transparently thin. Once he had stripped to his khaki underwear, he would feel comfortable enough in the stifling heat of the night.

He wouldn't miss the oppressive heat of Adelaide or the kami kazi mosquitoes which the wind sucked from the swamps of the Patawalonga. A pencil-slim wooden crucifix above the bed reminded him of a makeshift cross he had made for one of his POWs.

He would have all the time needed to research the book he planned to write with Seamus on the Irish missionaries. And where better to start than in an Irish Seminary deep in the panting heart of Rome, founded in the 17th century by an Irish Franciscan? Had it not been for Luke Wadding, Fahy would never have been where he was at this precise moment in time. Tiles clanked when he pulled the curtains.

Fahy found it impossible to sleep. The price he had to pay for a *Seamus-Lunch* followed by a long siesta. He got out of bed. Restless. Pacing. Backwards and forwards over the clanking tiles. Reading his Breviary. Yawning. Scratching. Breaking Wind.

When he went back to bed an hour or so later he still couldn't sleep. From experience, he knew that sometimes the answer to insomnia was reading the soporific tomes of Canon Law, but he had no intention of making a nocturnal visit to the College Library.

He got out of bed again, this time heading for some old copies of the Osservatore Romano, La Stampa and An Phoblachts he had noticed on the window ledge when pulling the curtains. Selecting one from each pile he went back to bed.

By the time he finished reading the well-thumbed An Phoblacht[1], he was wide awake. Reading about the IRA's rising star Ruairi Ó Bradaigh and his cryptic plans for military campaigns against the Royal Ulster Constabulary had stirred the cockles of Fahy's Republican heart.

Nor could he find sleep in the turgid pages of the *Osservatore Romano*. Most of which covered the intimate details of Santa Maria Goretti's life, from her birth in 1890, her illiteracy, malnutrition and malaria, to the attempted rape and fatal stabbings in 1902.

Drowsiness was creeping up on Fahy when he picked up a four-month-old copy of La Stampa. As soon as his eye fell on the banner headline Seamus' comments were recalled and the encircling shades of sleep were banished.

DIES DEFENDING HER HONOUR

Another Moroccan atrocity surfaces in the Mezzogiorno. This time near the Ancient Roman town of Venafrum, whose Bishop, Cataldo Lorenzo Pantaleone, has gone to great lengths to play down his rumoured interest in this particular atrocity.

According to enquiries carried out by this correspondent, investigations into the brutal murder of the girl by Moroccan Volunteers in the French Expeditionary Forces have been underway since Papa Pacelli admitted Blessed Maria Goretti into the Congregation of Saints.

Bishop Pantaleone is anxious to prevent the development of cult which per se would impair the progress of the girl's case under the aegis of His Eminence, Ippolito Baldassare Roccaravindola, Cardinal Ponens of The Congregation of Rights, which investigates cases for possible Beatification and Canonisation.

Fahy felt the newspaper slipping from his grasp as his senses succumbed to the enchantment of sleep which soon ensnared him into a labyrinth of distorted images.

He was in the middle of a great piazza paved like a gigantic chessboard. Transparent gauze figures materialised, gradually becoming more and more defined until they assumed human form.

Mud-caked, naked, male and female Aborigines. Faces smeared with translucent paint. Maggots crawling and falling from their nine orifices. Closing in on him, crowding, jostling and jeering. Closer and closer they came. Priapic. Pouting. Gyrating hips. Flaccid dugs. A bloated Buddha flashed through the throng like a bolt of lightning. It was Seamus in the robes of a Cardinal ringing a handbell, beckoning him to the safety of Padraig's boneyard. Louder and louder it rang. Closer and closer came the painted Jezebels. *Jesus, Mary and Joseph protect and save me.*

He was awake. Rescued by the campanologists of the Eternal City.

Through Fahy's bedroom window, came a cacophony of clanging bells echoing from the Vatican and the nearest of the Twenty Two Districts of Rome. Having come to terms with the unfamiliar surroundings, Fahy asked himself why bells were ringing with such persistence. It wasn't Sunday. Today was Saturday. Then he remembered: today was the feast day of *Santa Maria* Maggiore.

Fahy clanked over the tiles and pulled the curtains. The strong morning sunlight filtered through the insect screen. When his eyes adjusted to the glare, he was able to pinpoint the extensive Villa Borghese Park where he, Seamus and Padraig had spent many a carefree morning zigzagging in and out of its nine entrances. He walked over the loose tiles once again to make sure Salvatore got the message.

On cue, there was a knock on the door. Salvatore duly entered carrying the offerings of coffee and mineral water which began the typical Italian day. There was an appealing quality about the deference Salvatore showed when carrying out his duties. It was never obsequious and akin to the humility shown by monks when carrying out their secular duties.

"Are you free to serve my mass this morning, Salvatore?"

"A pleasure, Reverente, it will be my pleasure to serve your Mass." As quietly as he had arrived, Salvatore stepped over the loose tiles and retreated to his kitchen to plan the gourmet menu of the day, leaving Fahy to drink at his leisure a substantial cup of coffee. Characteristically, Seamus had banned the use of thimble cups.

"Sweet star of the Sea! It's a great thing Fiachre Fahy what a modest man like me does for a friend in putting up with that skinflint Cassidy. A thimble of coffee was all I got. Not even a cup of tea although I could smell a pot brewin' in the kitchen. The shame of it, serving coffee in cups made for midgets. He deserves to be diddled. And fer spite, I left him none of me sausages. Salvatore tells me that having served our Masses he now ready to serve us lunch." With self-evident satisfaction, Seamus rattled off the lunch menu of the day: *Calzoni di Mozzarella di Bufula e Salame di Culatello, Linguini alla Marinara, Bistecca di Carne Equina, Contorni di Patate al forno* and *Insalata Mista.*

"This will be followed, you'll be glad to hear Fiachre Fahy, by a few slivers of maggot free pecorino sardo, which knocks spots off the local pecorino romano I can tell you, served with Salvatore's home-made bread and washed down with a white vintage from his home town of Acquafondata.

"You know, that rascally friend o' mine, Roccaravindola, keeps tryin' to lure Salvatore into his household. No chance. He's been with me since 1946...not long after the poor soul got back with what was left of the Eighth Army Musso sent to Russia. Salvatore was an army chef. Holed up he was in the Russian Steppes for nearly two years. Doesn't like talkin' about it....memories are too painful. But I'm sure you don't want to be swappin' tales of war experiences with the likes of me, whose only active service was throwin' flowers at General Clark when he and his men marched into Rome in the summer of '44. So tell me, Fiachre Fahy, what have you been up to besides rearrangin' the unmentionables across your skull?"

"Nothin' much. After visitin' Luke Wadding's tomb, I started readin' *Memories of the Easter Uprising.* Interesting it was to

123

read what Macdermida has to say about Éamon de Valera's[1] parentage. Apparently, there's no record of his mother's marriage to Juan de Valera. Which means, I'm very glad to say, that the Brits have been dealin' with a real bastard in every sense of the word. By the way, Seamus, have you any idea where Venafrum is?"

"Venafro, you mean? Now why on earth should Fiachre Fahy be askin' me such a queer question?"

"Durin' the small hours of this mornin', I was readin' something you mentioned from an old copy of *La Stampa.* It was regardin' what you were sayin' about the Church searchin' for another Maria Goretti. Seems you were right in saying the Press is on to something. Venafro was mentioned in the article and it connected me with one of the internees in the POW Camp who, if I remember correctly, is from that neck of the woods. The internee was called Roberto Bartolomeo. He was never done tellin' me about the celebrations which took place in his village on the feast day of *Santa Maria Maggiore*. Today, a it so happens. I often wonder what happened to the poor lad. If memory serves, the village is called Milignano."

"Never heard of the place....Milimigniano...or whatever. But I sure knows where Venafro is. As a matter of fact, I stopped there overnight as a guest of Venafro's Bishop before we travelled to Monte Cassino for the commemorative funeral service of the late Abbot Diamare when his body was brought from Sant'Elia Fiumerapido...where he died a month or so after the Germans surrendered. Now here's another fine job the Anglo-Saxons did on that ancient monastery. Razing a venerated shrine to the ground for no good reason other than because it was there. God forgive the WASPS [2]. But I digress. You were sayin'?"

"I was thinking you might refer my interest in Roberto Bartolomeo to Cardinal Roccaravindola. He'll be acquainted with the Bishop of Venafro and maybe he could shed some light on whether the lad ever got back to Milignano."

"The Bardilini...Bartolini boy?"

"The name's Bartolomeo, Seamus. Roberto Bartolomeo. That's B-A-R-T-O-L-O-M-E-O."

"Sweet Star of the Sea Fiachre Fahy, keep what's left of the unmentionables on your head. How could I be forgettin' that your man could be related to the Cristofero Bartolomeo who invented the pianoforte? Life's full of coincidences. And this could be the greatest coincidence since Moses arrived at a desiccated Red Sea just as it was about to be irrigated by Noah's Great Flood." Fahy laughed at another of Seamus' absurdities.

"Why not contact Roccaravindola now, Seamus, and satisfy your curiosity about Cristofero Bartolomeo. You never know, he could be one of Roberto's ancestors. Strike while the chords on the piano are vibratin'. And while you're at it, you might ask him how we can go about importing a few kegs o' Guinness."

"I'll be back before you can say Black and Tans." Despite his size, Seamus took himself off with remarkable speed.

Fahy was still enjoying the silence of Seamus' absence when he reappeared with a banana-sized grin on his chubby face.

"Roccaravindola, to be sure, is most interested in this Bartolomeo fellow. Really interested. In fact, he wants to meet you. Tomorrow! The Cardinal has invited himself for lunch. And what's more, Fiachre Fahy, when I mentioncd your weakness for a jar or two of Guinness, he says he'll be more than happy to contact Dennis Devlin, the Irish Ambassador, on your behalf.

"The Cardinal's self-invitation for lunch might well be motivated by his love of Salvatore's cooking, but I know there's more to this than meets me suspicious eye. Nevertheless, Fiachre Fahy of Kilfenora County Claire, when Cardinal Ippolito Baldassare Roccaravindola, to give him his Sunday name, gets here tomorrow we'll find out soon enough."

Chapter Fifteen

Collaquila, 5th November 1951, San Sebastiano Presbytery

Emilia ushered the Brigadier and the Sindaco into the dining room. Snubbing the latter, she grunted the Brigadier's name and withdrew, her nose wrinkled with disapproval. Don Agostino ignored the social pleasantries and got to the point, making no attempt to hide his irritation.

"I hope for your sakes this intrusion during lunch is for something important. So speak up, then get out and leave us to finish lunch in peace."

"Don Agostino, the Brigadier and I would like a private word with you, if possible." The Mayor nodded in Giovanni's direction as he spoke. Taking the hint, Giovanni made to leave.

"Sit where you are, young man. Anything you two have to say can be said to both of us, or not at all. Get a move on. Spit it out."

"Suits me, Don Agostino. But I can't speak for the Sindaco." The Brigadier made no effort to hide his dislike for Milignano's Mayor.

"Just get on with it and stop wasting time and keeping me from indulging in one of the few pleasures permitted to a priest. Emilia has dressed the salad and unlike wine - and my patience - it doesn't improve with age. So spit out what you have to say and then be off with you both."

Giovanni sat back in his chair. Before the Sindaco and the Brigadier retreated to safety, he guessed the curtain was about to rise on what was sure to be an enjoyable farce starring Don Agostino with a supporting cast of two.

"Thank you, Reverente." said the Brigadier, unperturbed by Don

Agostino's characteristic rudeness, "We've come about..."

"Simonetta Semprepronta, Don Agostino," interrupted the Sindaco, "It's hardly my brother's fault there was no second mass today, now, is it? As a result of the cancellation, Simonetta didn't see the pebble signal my brother left on her gatepost this morning, prior to leaving for the mass that never was."

"With all due respect, Signor Sindaco, stop interrupting me. As I was trying to say, Reverend Fathers, my investigations show that Pasqualino, the Sindaco's brother, waited in vain for almost an hour for the said Simonetta Fusarelli or Eveready to show up for an assignation in the Campo Sportivo's pavilion for which he has a key.

"On his way home, Pasqualino bumped into the said Signorina Simonetta Fusarelli or Eveready. Whereupon the said Pasqualino did first remonstrate with and then assault the said Simonetta Fusarelli or Eveready on the face causing grievous bodily harm to her nose which was still bleeding profusely when I did chance to find her lying in the gutter during my morning patrol...."

"There were no witnesses, Don Pietro," interrupted the Sindaco, "I hasten to add, to my brother's alleged assault."

"No witnesses? Here in Collaquila?" Don Agostino laughed scornfully looking at each of his visitors with feigned incredulity.

"Reverente," said the Brigadier correcting the Sindaco's erroneous interruption, "there were no witnesses prepared to make a statement. In such circumstances in my capacity as...."

"For Heaven's sake, Brigadier, that's enough of your Officer-of-the-Law gobbledegook. Let me tell the Reverend Fathers what happened next or we will be here all day. At least I won't be twisting things to suit myself.... and show my brother and me in the worst possible light.

"In the circumstances of the alleged condition in which he found her, the Brigadier took it upon himself to bring Simonetta to my Surgery for examination after the alleged assault by my brother."

127

"An examination, Don Agostino, which took him over an hour for what was no more than a nosebleed."

"I attended to her in my professional capacity, as any Doctor would who has taken the Hippocratic Oath....."

"Hypocritical Oath more like," muttered the Brigadier.

".......after all," continued the Sindaco ignoring the Brigadier's sarcasm, "there are many causes of nosebleeds besides a trauma to the exterior nasal passages. Signorina Fusarelli had to be cleaned up before I could examine her properly. And this was to ascertain if there were any bruises on her ribs, pectorals and thighs...... which might have been caused when she fell into the ditch at the side of the road."

"I see." said Don Agostino, nodding his head with theatrical gravitas, "And so, gentlemen, what happened to Simonetta Fusarelli was clearly my fault? The rendezvous pebble on the gatepost wasn't spotted by Simonetta Fusarelli because I cancelled the midday mass. And you, Signor Sindaco decided to uphold the family honour by acting as a proxy for your hapless brother's missed appointment with a traumatised woman, who can't tell the difference between abuse and affection."

"And, Reverent fathers," intervened the Brigadier. ignoring Don Agostino's sarcasm, "you should also know that our Sindaco paid Simonetta Fusarelli or Eveready, two fifty AM lira notes for his administrations."

"Don Agostino," protested the Sindaco lamely, "I gave her the money as a goodwill gesture for the damage done to her clothing before and after the alleged assault."

"Pitipaft!" exclaimed Don Agostino, "I cancel the midday mass. Pitipaft! Simonetta Fusarelli takes a beating for missing an alleged rendezvous. And Pitipaft! She gets a 100 lira pittance from the Sindaco in compensation for the alleged damage done after the alleged assault. So why come here to interrupt my lunch, our lunch," winking at Giovanni, "to inform me of all this nonsense ...... news of which would have got to me later today, when Emilia takes her habitual early evening promenade and has words with all the non-existent witnesses you couldn't find when she does so."

"Reverend.....Reverend Fathers," protested the Brigadier, "an assault has taken place in broad daylight. The law cannot be ignored. Something must be done. And something must be seen to be done."

"And I say, Don Agostino, that the Brigadier... this meddler in other people's business .... should keep his interfering Sorrentine nose out of our domestic affairs."

"Enough! Enough of this nonsense! You, Brigadier, want me to help you do your duty ...like Pontius Pilate?" demanded Don Agostino arching his eyebrows in disbelief. "Yes, there has been an assault on the character and person of that poor deluded and defenceless woman," looking at Giovanni affirmatively, "who, to this day, has never recovered from what the Goums did to her. But, let me be precise. Let me tell you Brigadier, what you ought to do. After which I'll tell you what you will do.

"Pasqualino should be arrested for having assaulted a defenceless and disturbed woman going about her misguided business in the streets of Collaquila. This same woman, Simonetta Fusarelli, should be arrested for prostitution, having apparently offered herself to the here present Sindaco for the reprehensible sum of 100 AM lire.

"Finally, you should have the here present Sindaco arraigned before the Medical Ethics Authorities in Rome demanding that they investigate alleged misconduct for alleged improprieties past and present with his female patients." Don Agostino looked at his demoralised visitors squarely in the eye, making them squirm in the silence which followed his devastating declarations. An enthralled Giovanni waited for of Don Agostino's coup de grace.

"And now Brigadier, this is what you will do. You will go back

129

to your wife and forget the whole incident of Pasqualino's premeditated attack on Simonetta Fusarelli and I'll forget that it was you who took her to the Sindaco's surgery, despite being aware of their respective weaknesses, weaknesses which most certainly would not have escaped the ears of your good wife, who, in all probability, has tut-tutted sanctimoniously about the Sindaco and Simonetta's perennial weaknesses in the privacy of your rent-free home.

"You have been here five years as Collaquila's Police Sergeant and, to date, you have never made a single arrest. Why, we must surely ask ourselves, after all these years have you finally decided to do your duty? No. Let me finish. I'll tell you why. Shut up and listen. And this goes for you too Dottor Sindaco." Giovanni could see that Don Agostino was enjoying himself.

"It's because you know there are witnesses to an assault which took place in broad daylight, rather than behind closed doors. You were worried the Magistrates in Cassino would get to hear a sensationalized account of this vulgar and sordid little melodrama which happened on your watch.... you wanted to save your backside.... and save your snivelling face.

"So, you thought it would be a good idea to barge into my presbytery, with everyone from here to Venafro knowing why, and have me persuade you to arrest Pasqualino and have Simonetta confined to a prison hospital for the psychiatric care we know the poor soul needs," Don Agostino paused for a moment and gave Giovanni a look betraying the empathy he felt for Simonetta Fusarelli's disturbing wartime ordeal.

"Then," Don Agostino continued, "when all hell is let loose, I'll get the blame for the repercussions. And the Sindaco knows this. So he comes along too, in case I needed to be reminded of what the scandal would do to Pasqualino's family.... and of the great debt we owe him personally for what, as Podestà, he did for us during the war.... for the loss of his wife when the Germans came.... so that we'll continue to overlook his alleged ethical aberrations. Aberrations which, alleged or otherwise will

130

henceforth never occur again in my parish. I hope I have made myself clear?

"Now get out of my sight. Both of you. And I'll forget this conversation ever took place. My advice to you both is to say nothing about what's been said here today. Leave everything to Emilia. She'll spread the authorised version of today's meeting and the rest will be history. I doubt if she's missed a single word eavesdropping at the keyhole. Emilia! Come and show these two cretins the door!"

Don Agostino sat in silence for a few moments after the two mortified intruders had left. Giovanni could see that his visitors had tired him out.

Don Agostino revived however as soon as Emilia reappeared with two cups of coffee on her tarnished tray. Giovanni wondered what had happened to the prematurely dressed salad.

"And before you ask, Don Agostino," she said with a hint of mischief, "We all know you don't like waste, but I had to throw the salad out. It had turned mushy and soft. Had I known beforehand how long your visitors were going to be here, I would have added honey to the vinegar. So don't be blaming me for the waste."

"In that case, just bring me a few slices- make them thick ones- of the Brigadier's cheese and a few slices of the Sindaco's Salame- thick ones if it's my favourite *Soppressata*," adding as an afterthought, "and bring some for Giovanni too. I'm sure his delicate stomach has never had to ingest and digest this particular variety of dried wild boar sausage.

"The Brigadier's cheese is a rare act of sacrifice from our thrifty Bobby. I'll have you know he is and will ever be the Three Wise Monkeys in person. In return for seeing, hearing and saying nothing, my parishioners supply him and his God-Makes-Them-and-Pairs-Them-Wife with all they need to live off the fat of the land. They never spend a cent. Accommodation, heating, lighting and telephone go with the job as does free coffee in Palladino's every day and twice on Sundays. It's a sinecure he doesn't want to lose. Hence the reason for today's farce."

"Solomon, Don Agostino, Solomon himself could not have handled your two visitors with greater sagacity. *Wisdom is found on the lips of him who has understanding......*"

"*... but a stick on the back of him who is void of understanding.*" added Don Agostino, completing the quotation, "as those two idiots found out today.....

*Solomon. Solomon, eh? Maybe the Bishop was right after all.... the lad is bright.... A good listener.... vir sapit qui pauca loquitur....it's a wise man who speaks little..... what was it that Solomon said....he who pampers his servant from childhood...**will, in the end, find his heir.**... and who am I to argue with such prophetic biblical wisdom.....*

Although Giovanni had no real understanding as yet of the petty intricacies, frivolities and complications of village life, he had genuine admiration for the way Don Agostino had handled the exchanges with his two visitors. From the expression on Don Agostino's face, he could see that the old man was pleased for having been compared to Solomon. Wisdom is indeed found on the lips of him who has understanding.

Chapter Sixteen

"Your Eminence, permit me to introduce my old and dear friend Fiachre Fahy. By now his CV will be familiar to you, to be sure, to be sure. Father Fahy...His Eminence, Ippolito Baldassare Roccaravindola...Cardinal Ponens of The Sacred Congregation of Rites, which as you know, is the Vatican Committee which processes the Beatification and Canonisation of Saints. So don't be thinking for a moment that your sinful life is under investigation."

"Ahh! Blessed is he who cometh in the name of the Lord." The Cardinal's words had the two Irishmen looking at each other in puzzlement. Neither could tell whether the Cardinal was calling for a blessing on his own head or on Fahy's arrival. What they knew for sure was that, since the wily old fox had invited himself for lunch, there was something in the air besides his love of Salvatore's cooking.

Of the two Irishmen, Fahy alone found the situation intriguing. For his part, Seamus was too preoccupied that the pre-prandial pleasantries might impinge upon his designated lunchtime and spoil Salvatore's *Gnocchi Acquapendente*, made from flour and soft over-boiled potatoes with nothing else added, neither water alla Napoletana nor egg alla Romana.

An endless interchange of handshakes ensued. Despite an apprehension about a probable delay in savouring Salvatore's Special Sunday Menu, Seamus was delighted with his handiwork in bringing the Cardinal and his friend together.

The Cardinal's nasalized intonation gave a rich resonance to his Venetian accent. His voice, together with his dwarfish stature, his mongoloid features and his sallow complexion, gave him a youthful aspect belying his eighty-one years. In Vatican circles, he was known as Farinata [1].

The Cardinal Ponens of the Congregation of Sacred Rites was nicknamed *Farinata* not because he once had platinum blond hair like his illustrious namesake, but because of his passion for fried farinaceous dishes.

Despite his lack of inches, the Cardinal's long flowing scarlet robes contrived to lend him a quiet aura of dignity and authority, rather than encourage ridicule. He was born on the First of July in Pieve di Cadore, the birthplace of Titian, on the day when Rome became the official Capital of Italy. With characteristic confidence, the Cardinal looked forward to reaching his century in 1971.

The Cardinal had been a brilliant scholar at the Pontificio Seminario Romano Maggiore, graduating as Doctor *Utriusque Leges* at the age of twenty-three and joined the Vatican Secretariat at the invitation of Pope Leo X111. There he has remained to serve each of the latter's four successors.

His Doctorate in both *Civil and Canon Law* had been of inestimable value to Pius X1 when the Lateran Concordat was drawn up for Benito Mussolini's signature in 1929. Monsignor Roccaravindola was subsequently rewarded with a Red Hat and appointed *sine die* as Cardinal Ponens of the Sacred Congregation of Rites.

"And so, Fadder FA-I...we meet at last. Your friend Se-Amus, has been biographic in his account of your career in A-U-stralia." The strong pronunciation of the initial vowels in the word Australia further emphasised the Italianità of the Cardinal's English accent. "Tell us how things were, Fadder FA-I, in fly-infested A-U-stralia." Before Fahy could reply, Cardinal Roccaravindola continued irrepressibly, "We are led to believe that the Antipodean Aboriginal is even more backward than the poor Abyssinian. Porca Polenta! To think that the English Imperialists couldn't wait to drive Italian Civilisation from

Abyssinia after the war. Bringing the hapless Emperor Haile Selassie back to Addis Ababa was a spiteful mistake. A restoration which meant a return to a despotism which thrives on a triad of ignorance, superstition and poverty.

"Mark my words on this the ninth day of September in the year of Our Lord 1951 on the feast day of the venerable Boethius, the Emperor Haile Selassie's days are numbered [1]. But Se-Amus, can you as our host be expected to entertain a humble Prince of the Church in the corridors of the Irish College? Porca Polenta! We have much to discuss before sampling the delights of Salvatore's culinary genius." So saying, the ebullient Cardinal headed for Seamus' drawing room with all the familiarity of a host and reached it despite Seamus' efforts to steer him into the dining room.

Fiachre and Seamus had no option but to follow the Cardinal. "It's your entire fault Fiachre Fahy," grumbled Seamus sotto voce. "Yours and your friend's piano playing great uncle! And now we're in for one of Farinata's long-winded aperitifs....Sweet Star of the Sea don't make it too long and spoil me lunch."

Cardinal Roccaravindola removed his scarlet cape before claiming Seamus' favourite armchair. A magnificent pectoral cross studded with a succession of blue Kashmir sapphires rested over his clasped hands which were a network of wrinkles and pigmented liver spots.

Salvatore edged in sideways like a docile crab, carrying a silver salver with three Waterford Crystal glasses and a bottle of San Pellegrino. Without a word, he served the Cardinal and Fahy with the savoir-faire of an experienced sommelier. While pouring for Seamus, he whispered reassuringly that he had not yet consigned the Gnocchi to boiling water. Superfluous information which nevertheless lifted Seamus' spirits. Besides overcooked pasta, Seamus could think of nothing more repugnant than overcooked Gnocchi.

"*Salvatore!* Living up to his name as the Saviour of Italian

135

cooking. The appetising smells from the glowing Olympian Fires in your kitchen promise much for our palate. Pour what's left of the San Pellegrino.....how apt a name...for the secular pilgrimage we will shortly be making to your Master's dining room. So, off you go my dear Salvatore. Put the finishing touches to a meal we will soon have great pleasure in describing to Cardinal Battandier, whose chef knows absolutely nothing because he trained in France, where he mastered the art of cooking sauces to camouflages his frightful food."

Salvatore bowed bashfully at the Cardinal's complimentary comments, delivered in tandem with his heartfelt disparagement of French cuisine. However sincere his comments were, Salvatore had heard them all before. As soon as he made for his kitchen, the Cardinal resumed his eloquent tour de force.

"Porca Polenta, we don't know what spoils our appetite more. Cardinal Battandier absurd claims regarding the superiority of French Cuisine or Bishop Cataldo Lorenzo Pantaleone's ambition." The Cardinal made a chopping motion with the side of his hand, fingers outstretched and apart. It was a gesture the Cardinal often made when emphasising what he considered to be important.

"Porca Polenta! Nothing but nothing should be allowed at our age to give us indigestion. When we have come this far, what else is there to look forward to other than the sampling of good Italian food- another chopping gesture- Porca Polenta!" sniffing the air, "What appetising aromas we sense wafting through the air!" Cardinal closed his eyes, silently meditating on the words which reflected the pleasures to be enjoyed with Salvatore's cooking. Moments later, he opened his eyes and addressed the issue which had motivated his improvised visit to the Pontifical Irish College.

"Fadder FA-I, when Se-Amus phoned us yesterday we were, to say the least, elated. After speaking to Cataldo in Venafro, we were ecstatic. Your enquiry about this Bartolomeo fellow was simply Providential. May the Lord be praised."

Fahy glanced at Seamus. From the shrugs they exchanged it was clear that neither of them had any idea why the Cardinal was so animated.

"At long last our investigations regarding the Servant of God, Lucrezia Bartolomeo, will be able to move from its present diet of spiritual milk to a substantial diet of spiritual meat." A chopping movement accompanied the Cardinal's remarks. But the two Irishmen were still in the dark. Neither of them could grasp the motivation behind the Cardinal's litany of metaphors.

"Let us explain. This Bartolomeo fellow you were enquiring about, and we say this in strictest confidence, is the brother of the servant of God at present under investigation by our Congregation of Sacred Rites."

Fahy looked at O'Fainnaide. Their faces betraying the amazement shared by this astonishing coincidence. The wonders of God performing in mysterious ways. A simple enquiry about Roberto Bartolomeo had led to Fiachre Fahy stumbling onto the stage as an extra in a developing spiritual drama in which the former's sister had a leading role. Fahy waited for enlightenment.

"Fadder FA-I , the servant of God under investigation, Lucrezia Bartolomeo, can you tell us what you know of her?"

"Not very much, your Eminence. I know she was sent to Milignano from Scotland by her father days before Mussolini declared war on Britain and France. What I wanted to know was whether or not a chronic consumptive like Roberto Bartolomeo had survived the journey back to England and whether or not The Red Cross had managed to get him back to Milignano."

"Which makes your arrival here in Rome all the more Providential, my dear Fadder FA-I. So much for the milk of the matter. Let us give you a few more sips before we get to the meat of what we have in mind for you.

"Lucrezia Bartolomeo was violated and murdered by Moroccan

137

soldiers fighting under the flag of France. Now, according to the teachings of the Church and we have the authority of Doctor Angelicus, St Thomas Aquinas no less, to substantiate this teaching on martyrdom to the effect that, when it is known to have occurred, there is sufficient cause to begin a process which could lead to beatification."

"I understand, your Eminence, but how do I figure in all of this?"

"Patience, patience, my dear Fadder FA-I." Roccaravindola was making his familiar hand gesture as he spoke. All in good time the gesture seemed to say. It was a gesture which did nothing to placate the noisy grumbling of Seamus' stomach.

"Our problem Fadder FA-I, lies, not with the servant of God, Lucrezia Bartolomeo, but with her family and to a certain extent with the personality of Bishop Pantaleone himself. If Se-Amus could delay Salvatore's lunch for a few more minutes?" It was a rhetorical question. The Cardinal pausing long enough for Seamus to realise that what his Eminence was about to say was for Fahy's ears only.

"I'll slip into the kitchen and explain the delay to Salvatore. He can be so temperamental when it comes to the unexpected." Fahy noticed Seamus' dejection as he left and wondered if his body language was the result of yet another imposition on his stomach or the mortification of the Cardinal's diplomatic request for privacy.

"Let us begin, Fadder, with your man Roberto Bartolomeo. He is, so to speak our common denominator. His is another tragic case just like his father and his sister's.

"We are all well aware of the scandal of the Dunera crossing to A-U-stralia in 1940. What you don't know is that the Holy Father received hundreds of complaints, from victims and relatives, regarding the indignities endured by those unfortunate Italians who were forced to make that infamous voyage.

"Roberto Bartolomeo, one of the sixty-eight survivors from the

138

Arandora Star sea disaster, in which his father perished, was shamefully included in the Dunera's passenger list. We say this, not in mitigation, but in explanation of what Roberto Bartolomeo did when he was returned, moribund, to England by the British Home Office for subsequent deportation to Italy.

"According to confidential information our Nuncio in London received from the Commissioner of the Metropolitan Police, Bartolomeo discovered, thanks to information received from fellow Italians in the local community, the whereabouts of the soldier responsible for his miseries on the Dunera. The where was *Nu Cassell*. Given the precarious state of Bartolomeo's health, God alone knows how he managed to make contact with the said local network. But contact was made.

"The ex-serviceman in question, an Anglo-Irishman by name Michael O'Carney, was subsequently found in a disused warehouse near the Ferry. Beaten to death beyond recognition, by a group of unknown assailants.... who, having called for an ambulance.... disappeared without trace.

"When the ambulance and police arrived, they found Roberto Bartolomeo, skeletal and emaciated, propped up against the wall. eyes wide open and stone dead, clutching the name and address of his tormentor who was lying at his feet and here I quote from the Police Commissioner's report "mashed to a pulp in a pool of blood, skin, bone, mucous and bodily fluids etc. etc. etc.".

"Jesus, Mary and Joseph," muttered Fahy. After ten years of wondering what had become of Roberto Bartolomeo, he now had the answer. He now knew why Roberto had no inclination to unburden himself, either face-to-face or in Confessional and why he never attended any of the Camp's masses. With a desire for vendetta eroding his mind and body, Roberto Bartolomeo had no inclination to divulge his homicidal revenge mission.

Had he done so, Fiachre Fahy knew he would have had a problem keeping such information from his Commanding Officer and in so doing further delay or cancel Roberto's

139

repatriation. Fahy kept these thoughts to himself and changed the subject.

"You said, Eminenza, that the Bishop of Venafro was another problem," said Fahy as Seamus reappeared from his sojourn in the kitchen. There were traces of tomato sauce on the corners of his mouth and a few grains of grated parmigiano trapped in the dimple of his chin. From the look of satisfaction splashed across his face, Fahy guessed Seamus had been dipping bread, liberally powdered with parmigiano, into Salvatore's tomato sauce.

"I trust all is well chez Salvatore, Se-Amus? Your friend here is about to learn what he needs to know about Bishop Lorenzo Cataldo Pantaleone. As you know, Se-Amus, the Bishop does everything according to Canon Law. He is an intellectual. Intellectuals are dangerous. Dangerous when they abuse such intellect to further...to hasten their elevation to the Church's Curia of Cardinals.

"Cataldo is capable of writing the finest and most elegant Latin in Italy. Does he offer this God-given talent to the Vatican Secretariat? He does not. But how does he bring this talent to the attention of the Holy Father? Encouraged by his influential mentor, Monsignor Roncalli, he writes articles for the exclusive monthly *Periodica de Re Morali*, which he knows is read by the Holy Father.

"The Holy Father sends for him. To congratulate him on the quality of his writing. Porca Polenta! What does Cataldo do? Knowing the canonisation of Santa Maria Goretti was close to the Pontiff's heart, he suggests that there was an unnecessary delay by the Cardinal Ponens regarding the investigations of a Postulant in the mould of Santa Maria Goretti. Porca Polenta! Beware the sophistry of a flattering tongue.

"We know all this because the Holy Father told us and as Se-Amus here knows, we retain Papa Pacelli's confidence. Cataldo has never been the same since Salotti, his former tutor in the Pontificale, got a Red Hat. It was Cardinal Salotti who charted

140

and promoted the cause of the then Postulant and Servant of God, Maria Goretti, from the time of her death to her beatification and canonisation. A saintly man, who will surely die with a square nimbus over his head [1].

"An honour, Fadders we are unlikely to ascribe to our good friend Cataldo. Not that we are saying he will never take his place with us in the College of Cardinals. Of course he will. His mentor, Monsignor Roncalli, will have his way sooner than later. But all in good time.

"You see, Fadders, the truth of the matter is that there is indeed a *probabilis causa* regarding Lucrezia Bartolomeo. According to the Code for Postulants, we can proceed with her case in the ordinary way of non-cult. This explains why Cataldo is keeping things close to his chest in his dealings with the Press.

"However, we remain suspicious that Pantaleone's might have been less than thorough- unlike Salotti- in his investigations so far and that he might have left several stones unturned in his race for a Red Hat.

Cardinal removed his scarlet skullcap. With great deliberation and with evident satisfaction, he scratched and rubbed his tonsure and the nearest surrounding area. Itch eliminated, Cardinal Ippolito Baldassare Roccaravindola replaced his skullcap and took up from where he had left off: the vexing matter of Cataldo Lorenzo Pantaleone, Bishop of Venafro.

"The problem with Cataldo is that he believes he can be the architect of his destiny. But did I tell you Fadder, there is a surviving Bartolomeo brother?"

"I know Roberto had a younger brother. Born in Scotland like his sister. A genius according to Roberto. His name's Giacomo...if memory serves me."

"Giovanni!" corrected the Cardinal, "Besides Lucrezia, he's another plus in the Bartolomeo family. He was ordained last October by Pantaleone in a special ordination ceremony in

141

Milignano. Why? Probably part of Cataldo's Master Plan with regard to the promotion of Lucrezia Bartolomeo's cas e. We last heard that Cataldo had sent young Giovanni to serve in an obscure village in the Mainarde Mountains, to keep him out of the Press' way."

Egged on by Seamus, Fahy asked the question foremost in their minds. "If, as you say, your Eminence, Giovanni is one of the pluses, does this mean there could be skeletons in the Bartolomeo cupboard?"

"Yes, yes. Of course there are. But before giving you details, we must tell you Fadder FA-I, we must tell you how you can be of great assistance to the Church. To help set our minds at rest regarding Lucrezia Bartolomeo's case, we require a replacement Postulator. Monsignor Schmalzgruber has retired to his native land in Pforzheim now that Marshall Plan [1] funds have helped rebuild the family home.

"According to Canon Law 2004, a Postulator must have a fixed address in Rome. So you see Fadder FA-I, why your arrival here is Providential? Will you accept our nomination?"

"And it's to be sure that he will, Eminenza. Let me be the first to congratulate me ol' friend Fiachre Fahy.

"It seems, your Eminence, that Seamus has accepted the honour on my behalf." Fahy rose from his seat and kissed the Cardinal's sapphire ring which had been held out in a gesture of fraternity.

"You will also have to obtain written or oral statements from the American Soldiers who befriended both the girl and her guardian. This might mean travelling to the United States. You will also have to interview the women who prepared Lucrezia and her guardian for burial. We need corroboration on the statements they submitted to Monsignor Schmalkzgruber through the Parish Priest. We understand that Schmalzgruber never visited Milignano in the course of his enquiries."

"In effect, your Eminence, you want me to go over the ground my predecessor covered and more besides? Like verifying, for example, that the women who prepared the bodies for burial were known for their piety and honesty?"

For Fahy's benefit, Seamus was rolling his eyes and looking at his watch. Blowing silent exasperation from the corner of his mouth. Fahy ignored his friend's frustration.

"You mention the United States, your Eminence, does this mean that you are not satisfied with the statements the soldiers have submitted to the Bishop of Venafro?"

"That's the problem, we have had to date received no statements from any of the soldiers involved. So far they have refused to cooperate. In fact, we don't know for sure if all or any of them got back to the United States.

"But now that we have you on board, we'll get our Nuncio in Washington to check if they are still alive. Something which Pantaleone should have requested through our offices. But it is not within our remit to tell a Postulator what do.

"We know that Cataldo bullied Schmalzgruber. All we are saying is that, unlike Cataldo, we consider the testimony of the Americans to be crucial and indispensable. We look forward to reading reports of your dealings with Cataldo."

The Cardinal had been speaking for half an hour. It seemed a lot longer to Seamus, who was hoping Fiachre Fahy had no questions to ask about   Congregation of Sacred Rites' procedures.

Lunch had been delayed far too long for his liking. Enough was enough. His mind was concentrating on Salvatore's *Fritto Misto di Mare* which would take only took one minute to fry if Salvatore had the oil simmering, Then the *Risotto con Gamberi,* followed by *Fegato Fritto alla Rossini* served with *Bisi* and *Risi alla Veneziana.*

It would be a meal worthy of Farinata's nickname. Seamus' mouth watered at the thought of washing down Salvatore's courses with several bottles of the *Prosecco Tranquillo* cooling beneath the running water of the garden well.

Fahy was paying little attention to the exchanges which followed between Seamus and Cardinal Roccaravindola on what Salvatore had prepared for lunch. His mind was dwelling on the violence which had shepherded Roberto into the presence of his Maker. *....Surely illness had addled his mind? If only I could have been able to reach out to Roberto ..... to make him unburden himself..... to bring him back to the fold......*

"Many congratulations, Monsignor Fiachre Fahy." It was Seamus again. *What on earth is he up to now?*

"It is customary for Postulators," declared a beaming Cardinal Ponens, " to be so honoured. It's an honour within our gift."

The Cardinal held out his ring for Fahy to give it the traditional kiss of thanks in recognition for the honour bestowed. Monsignor Fahy did so with a humility which reflected his modesty.

"We'll be able to return to Kilfenora County Claire as a couple of Church Toffs, Eminenza, to be sure to be sure...seeing that the Rectors of the Irish Seminary here in Rome always retire as a Monsignore. An honour which in my case", winking mischievously at Fiachre Fahy, "will be conferred by the Holy Father himself. Sweet Star of the Sea and Goodness Gracious Me, isn't the Good Lord looking after His own very special people as sure as night follows day?"

"You'll enjoy meeting Cataldo Pantaleone, Monsignore. You will find him insufferably charming, living as he does like a Florentine Grandee. At least until he works out, as he will, what's behind your appointment. But enough is enough. We have kept Salvatore waiting too long."

Cardinal Roccaravindola was on his feet with a nimbleness belying his age. He took Fahy's arm and nodded to Seamus to show the way to the dining room where Salvatore would be waiting. with his legendary patience, to serve them.

"Salvatore! Salvatore!" Cardinal Roccaravindola exclaimed, cupping a hand behind his ear, "Do I hear you saying: *Eat all courses, all ye who enter.*

Salvatore smiled at the Cardinal's amusing parody of the words Dante placed above the gates of Hell which invited lost souls to abandon all hope of salvation as they entered[1] For Salvatore it was a welcome change from what the Cardinal usually uttered after Grace had been said: *Bring forth the Ambrosia and Nectar of your Immortal Culinary Gods.*

Chapter Seventeen

After Work Social Club, 22 Park Circus, Glasgow, 15th August 1933

Basement Office of Silvio Bartolomeo, Italian Fascist Party Official

"Did I not make it clear that *Fuck Music* is banned from this Club? In particular the work of that good for nothing homosexual Jewish plagiarist, Cole Porter?"

"Even if his song *You're the Top* has a verse dedicated to the Duce [1]?"

"Don't you believe it! Porter is mocking the Duce by associating his name with Houdini the son of an Irish Rabbi called Sweeney So do as you're told, Roberto, Fascismo is a virile regime. Our music must be strong and masculine. There can no encouragement for decadent Jewish homosexuals like Porter in our Fascist Ideology.

"Coded messages of homosexuality in music must be vigorously suppressed. Stick to Verdi and Puccini and play Giovinezza[2] on the hour and every hour from dawn to midnight until you hear otherwise. Is that clear, Roberto?"

"If you say so, Dad."

"I do say so. Now, let's get down to today's business which concerns the little turd from Collaquila. Just give me fifteen minutes with Staffieri. That's all the time I need to settle our little misunderstanding. It seems like your last visit to his Gallowgate love-nest failed to knock some sense into his skull. This time he won't fail to get the message.

"Have our transport van ready to cart him back to Mount Vernon

146

when you and the others have finished with him. Show him down as soon as he gets here. Meantime brief our men in the Coffee Bar and prepare for your initiation. Get the lads to bandage your knuckles adequately for the purpose. Just in case, get one of your squad to collect a frog from Glasgow Green."

Silvio Bartolomeo leaned back in his armchair. A handsome man in his forties, he had been an important figure in the Blackshirt stronghold of Sarzana in Liguria where he had settled after the Great War.

In Sarzana, his forte had been the organisation of workers' protests- often violent- against conditions in the factories owned by Jewish anti-fascist industrialists. Such had been his success in promoting Fascist idealism that his talents were eagerly sought by Party activists from Trento to Trapani.

On June 10th 1924 the Italian Socialist leader Giacomo Matteotti[1], an outspoken opponent of the Duce and Fascist policies, was kidnapped in Rome. Two days later, Silvio Bartolomeo and family were escorted all the way by Blackshirts on a first class train journey from Rome to Glasgow via Milan, Paris, Dover and London.

There were unconfirmed reports that Silvio Bartolomeo had been the driver of the Lancia used in the abduction of Matteotti. However, by the time Matteotti's mutilated body was found two months later by a scavenging dog, in a shallow grave on the outskirts of the Capital, Silvio Bartolomeo was living comfortably with his family in Glasgow's wealthy Kelvingrove district.

Silvio Bartolomeo was an important figure within Glasgow's Italian community, holding the position of Gerarca or Fascist Hierarch by order of Rome's Grand Council of Fascism. His compatriots respected and feared him.

His prime function was to organise the collection of prescribed donations for the *Partito Fascista Italian* from the 2000 or so prosperous Italians who lived and worked in Coffee, Ice-Cream

147

and Fish and Chip Shops respectively throughout the Central Belts of Scotland.

His success in this activity and his outspoken support of Fascism brought him to the attention of MI5, the British Intelligence Agency.

The dossier kept on Silvio Bartolomeo recorded, inter alia, details of his and his family's activities in the West of Scotland. Since his arrival, a second son, Giovanni, was born in Glasgow in 1925 followed by the birth of a daughter, Lucrezia, three years later on the day and month Mussolini's Secret Police, OVRA (The Organisation for Vigilance and Repression of Anti-Fascism) was created.

Also noted was Silvio Bartolomeo's close association with Artemio Ferrara, Deputy Commander of OVRA with whom he had purchased a majority shareholding in a Sardinian Ordinance Factory and that he was paid £200 per month by the Italian Foreign Office into an account with the Charing Cross Branch of the British Linen Bank, from which, to date, no withdrawals have been made.

Nevertheless, £100 cash deposits were paid each month into a Bank of Scotland Savings Account (Glasgow Cross Branch) to his brother, Mr Ettore Bartolomeo (naturalised 1922), from which to date no withdrawals have been made.

Furthermore, £20 cash was paid monthly into three savings accounts held for sons Roberto and Giovanni and daughter Lucrezia Bartolomeo respectively in The Airdrie Savings Bank (Tollcross Branch), from which to date no withdrawals have been made.

With the help of leading members of the Italian War Veterans Association, Silvio Bartolomeo organised a ruthless collection of voluntary donations from Italians throughout Scotland for the purchase of prestigious apartments at 22, Park Circus, in the high-end residential area of Glasgow's West End, for the sum of £1,500 which was paid in one single cash transaction.

In 1933, after extensive refurbishment, it opened its doors as an *After Work Social Club* for Italians living and working in Scotland and in the following year, it was officially inaugurated as the *Casa D'Italia.*

It was here, in the basement of this elegant edifice that Gerarca Silvio Bartolomeo was intimidating Raffaele Staffieri.

"....your mother's visa application for the United States will be rejected. As will yours, Staffieri."

"What has this to do with my application for full membership, Comrade Bartolomeo?" Staffieri asked in a hesitant voice.

Without answering, Bartolomeo slowly removed his tasselled fez and placed it on the desk as he rose to his feet. On the dark oak-panelled wall behind him were two large framed daguerreotypes of the Duce and King Vittorio Emmanuelle III. Strutting to where Raffaele Staffieri was seated, Silvio Bartolomeo bludgeoned Staffieri's right eyebrow, making sure the spurting blood did not catch his shirt or fall on his jackboots. This done, he wiped the truncheon on Staffieri's shoulder and returned to his desk where he replaced the fez on his closely cropped head.

Gerarca Bartolomeo's knuckles on both hands turned white as he clasped the jutting axes of the wooden fasces carved on each armrest, revealing a struggle to defuse the adrenaline generated by his savagery. Then, with amusement, he watched Staffieri's attempts to stem the flow of blood with his fingers and the cuffs of his Saville Row silk shirt.

Silvio Bartolomeo waited patiently until the effusion of blood from Staffieri's eyebrow dwindled to a trickle before resuming his verbal onslaught, just as a shaken Staffieri moved to speak.

"Comrade Barto......" muttered a befuddled Staffieri.

"You lost the privilege of addressing any of us as Comrade when you were disciplined in our London Fascio..... punishment for bringing the Fascist Party into disrepute following the shame of your arrest and conviction for criminal activities. The British

Home Office demanded confiscation of your assets and immediate deportation. Ambassador Grandi intervened with Scotland Yard on our behalf and had you released into our custody here in Glasgow," Bartolomeo paused before adding without irony, "in the knowledge that you would be rehabilitated with our unique brand of totalitarian pampering.

"In our Park Circus Fascio, we have a merited reputation for persuading wealthy dissidents and renegades to mend the errors of their ways, return them to the fold wherein they will show all due appreciation for our efforts by contributing generously to our Building Fund."

Silvio Bartolomeo once again rose from his seat. Staffieri cowered as his tormentor moved in the direction of his left eyebrow. A faint smell of excrement came from Staffieri as Gerarca Bartolomeo brushed past him aggressively and headed for the two standing cupboards on either side of the doorway. From each of which he removed a bottle.

With feigned resignation, Silvio Bartolomeo placed a bottle of *Johnnie Walker Red Label Whisky* and a half bottle of *William Hodgson Castor Oil* on his desk before facing a demoralised Staffieri.

"Let me be brief. After we've loaded you into our transport van and shipped you back to Mammina in Mount Vernon, we want you and your mother back in Italy before our Grand Opening next year when our *After Work Club* will be renamed the *Casa D'Italia.*

"Repatriation with assets such as yours is very much welcomed by the Duce and will be brought to the attention of Ambassador Grandi, who technically speaking is your sponsor. Come what may, I want you out of the country before I travel to Hyde Park for the Grand Fascist Rally on 14th September. This gives you two weeks to pack up and get out of my sight."

"But ….. I...we...don't want to go back to Collaquila. If we can't go to America ...we want to stay here..." Staffieri's fear of further violence from Silvio Bartolomeo and memories of punishments inflicted by Blackshirts in the London Fascio silenced further protest and lamentation.

"Your mother's visa was denied because she declared in her application that she was a widow. When we all know her estranged husband is alive and thriving as Collaquila's Undertaker and Itinerant Livestock Butcher, as befits a loyal member of the Party. So much, therefore, for Mammina's application.

"Yours will be denied when our Consul-General informs his American counterpart that you failed to mention your criminal record. We understand you specialised in housebreaking and resetting goods to criminal elements known to Scotland Yard.

"On a tip-off from our informant in the Metropolitan Police Force, you were brought to the attention of comrades in the London Fascio. Speaking of which, you will know what's in store for you from the bottle of castor oil you see on my desk."

Staffieri's knew, from personal experience, how an overdose of castor oil produced a spontaneous mobility disorder of the intestines, causing acute and infectious diarrhoea.

"If you don't leave quietly, we will increase the dosage to a full litre. However, this time we will add petroleum spirit which will make your bowel movements even more productive.....and painful.

"After which we will make you swallow a live frog to alleviate your intestinal discomfort. After all, as I've said before, we are not Communists or Socialists. A frog will help your recovery and forward your departure for the warmer climes of our beloved country.

"Our therapy will encourage political regeneration while confining you to your swanky new bathroom in Mount Vernon for at least a week .... all going well if the frog does its job. We won't lay a finger on your mother. After all, we are not

Communists or Socialists. We are Humanitarians, which is why we will leave your mother unharmed to look after you when you leave us this morning.

"Unless of course, you prefer to recuperate in your whore's squalid Gallowgate tenement for which, we understand, you pay the rent. We have seen for ourselves where she lives with her three little father-unknown bastards one of which is as black as coal.

"Yes, I can see from the expression on your snivelling face that you remember my son and his friends' recent visit to your Gallowgate love nest. And of course, your Mammina is still in the dark about your association with someone who - praise be to God - is not one of us.

"We can easily arrange for Signora Staffieri to visit your Gallowgate whore, so she can get acquainted with the three little bastards. It will certainly come as a shock to your Mammina when she discovers that all the folklore festivals and costume exhibitions you lied about attending here in the Fascio, were lame excuses for betraying your bloodline by associating with a drunken whore you picked up in an Argyle Street tavern."

Reference to his woman's weakness switched Staffieri's attention to the bottle of whisky on his tormentor's desk.

"You're wondering about the Johnnie Walker? Let me explain in simple terms: should you still refuse to go back to Collaquila after taking our laxative and enjoying the unavoidable period of convalescence, we move to elimination. It's as simple as that. The decision is yours.

"How do we eliminate the type of problem we have with someone like you? Let me inform you of our tried and tested method of operation: first, we strip you and swap your clothes with tone of the grateful down-and-out in Glasgow Green who supplies us with frogs, then we pour whisky down your gangarozzo. This done, in the small hours of the night, we drop you over the Suspension Bridge in Clyde Street.

152

"If all goes to plan, you'll be fished out when the Police Barge sweeps the river for its regular Sunday morning haul of nameless vagrants. Then, after an overnight in the Saltmarket Police Mortuary, comes burial in a numbered grave in the London Road Cemetery. Just imagine how your Mammina would feel if you were to disappear from the face of the Earth. And that will be that."

"I can't ... I can't go .... at least not as soon as you say. My house in Mount Vernon? My restaurant in Mitchell Street?"

"No problem regarding the house. We will buy your house and its furnishings in Mount Vernon at the going rate. Clean fresh air in the outskirts of suburban Glasgow will do my Livia's poor health a power of good.

"She's suffering from what our bowler-hatted hunchback Doctor now says is a form of *bacterial meningitis*. Another of his that'll be *Five-Guineas-Please* remedies. He's nothing more than a money-grabbing good-for-nothing Quack.

"In my opinion, lots of fresh air is what my Livia needs to clear her headaches and revive her appetite. There's absolutely no need to waste money on expensive antibiotics. Mount Vernon's fresh air is the best cure my money can buy.

"Now, as for the restaurant, that's another kettle of stinking fish as your whore from the Gallowgate might say. I know what you paid for it because Signora Gilda told me when we met to tie up the deal we thought we had made with her until you butted in."

"In that case, I'll accept what I paid for it: three hundred pounds plus conveyancing fees."

"Nothing doing, Staffieri! Here we, no, you, have a problem. Signora Gilda had agreed to sell *The Torquato Tasso* for two hundred and twenty-five pounds. A fair offer which she accepted. Then you come along, days later, to upset the Bartolomeo applecart with an offer of £300. What's more, you told Signora Gilda you would better any further Bartolomeo offers by fifty pounds. You should know that Signora Gilda has graciously agreed to donate the difference of £75 to the Party's Building Fund.

"So you see, in principle, the Bartolomeo family can't offer you more than our first and only offer of £225. You will also be expected to settle last year's associate members' fees for you and your mother. We will, of course, expect you to pay this year's full membership fees before you leave- over and above a voluntary donation to our Building Fund.

"Such loyalty will stand you in good stead when you get back to Collaquila and present your papers to the Mayor or *Podestà* as we now call our Chief Municipal Magistrates.

"I repeat, we are not Communists, Socialists or Gypsies. If you cooperate with us this morning, we will send you back to your mother and encourage her to pack for your return to Collaquila. In the meantime, my son Roberto is anxious to make acquaintance with your miserable hide. To establish his bona fides …. or as our comrades across the Atlantic would put it ..... to make his bones, by breaking yours when we punish you- as punish you we must- for all the inconveniences you've caused the Party and the Bartolomeo family.

"Just bear this in mind: you must never feel ashamed of admitting the error of your ways .... this will help to justify the punishment you are about to receive." Gerarca Bartolomeo rose to his feet to give emphasis to his well-rehearsed words of Party Propaganda.

"Our measures will help to remould your future behaviour as befits our Duce's plans for political reclamation according to the Duce's regeneration diktats for wayward citizens ..... in Italy or wherever they may have chosen to fly our flag ......"

Gerarca Bartolomeo paused for a moment, as if turning the pages of his well-thumbed script of illogicalities, "And remember this," he continued pompously, "It is our sacred duty to cure symptoms of deviant and decadent impulses. Any action taken will help us

154

to escape from the shackles of inferiority and help us take our rightful place in the front row of the World's Political Theatre.

"This said, Staffieri," continued Gerarca Bartolomeo, nodding his head with self-satisfaction, "after Comrade Roberto has vindicated the family honour with your purification, our Blackshirts will escort you to the wash room.

"There, your soiled clothes and underwear will be incinerated while you are having your miserable carcass cleaned with a high-pressure hose, Roberto will take your wallet to RW Forsyth's and buy quality ready-made replacements and provide you with relevant receipts. After all is said and done, we can't have you leaving here looking like a Communist, a Socialist or heaven forbid, a Gypsy.

"What could be fairer than that, I ask you? Nevertheless, when all is said and done, we most certainly want you out of here as soon as possible before our paid-up Members arrive to enjoy the amenities of our After-Work Club.

"What's even more important, we want you and your mother well and truly repatriated by the time Comrades Ambassador Dino Grandi and Consul-General Ferruccio Luppis come here next year for the official opening of our Casa D'Italia.

"By which time a son will have been reunited with his father and a wife will have been reunited with her husband. And we will live happily ever after. And before you leave the country, pay off your whore in the Gallowgate with a year's rent. That should keep her mouth and legs closed long enough before she finds another sucker to feed her habits and her bastards."

Chapter Eighteen

Collaquila, Saturday 12th August 1952

"Now look here, young man ...." Giovanni braced himself for what was likely to be another of Don Agostino's paternal admonishments, to be delivered in his inimitable curt style. Hardly surprising after his Housekeeper had brought him news about how Staffieri had once again slandered his father in Palladino's Bar.

Giovanni knew that whatever Don Agostino had to say was justified. Something had to be done to shut Staffieri up. Something should have been done to stop the rot months ago. Nine months ago to be exact. Perhaps, from the day of his first mass in Collaquila, when he learned that Staffieri had stormed out of the San Sebastiano during his sermon. Since then, Staffieri had never missed an opportunity to slander his father's memory and reputation.

Giovanni's apparent indifference to what Staffieri was saying had merely encouraged him. But now, after the previous evening's outburst in Palladino's, Giovanni's restraint had reached breaking point. Tittle-tattle about his father and brother was one thing, but insinuations that his sister had flirted and more with American soldiers stationed in Milignano was another matter.

Innuendo regarding his sister was something he couldn't tolerate. Lucrezia would never have compromised herself. Her death was a testament to that.

".... you must do something about that idiot Staffieri. You will have to strike now, figuratively speaking of course, rather than tomorrow and tomorrow and tomorrow before the damage becomes irreparable. *Seize the day, trusting as little as possible in tomorrow.*"

Don Agostino's concern was written on his face. "Raffaele Staffieri has always been a malcontent. He has few real friends even among the riff-raff who get drunk every night at his expense. His over-protective mother, a dreadful woman, saw to that. Father was always too busy butchering pigs or burying people to be bothered with his son and heir.

"Believe me there were few in the parish sorry when she left Collaquila to join him in London. Least of all the father who was glad to see the back of both of them."

"I remember my uncle saying something about Staffieri leaving London in a hurry and that he had been sent to Glasgow for his own good. A wealthy man apparently. He brought his mother with him. Aunt Maria said she was a pain in the backside and upset lots of people including my mother."

"We were all surprised when mother and son came back to Collaquila. I knew nothing about his criminal activities in London until you informed me about them. When he learned your father was in Milignano in '35 he said and did nothing. It would have taken guts he hasn't got to air a grievance against a prominent PNF official like your father.

"According to the Brigadier, Raffaele Staffieri was classed as an undesirable by the United States and refused a visa. This is probably the reason he and his mother came back here long before the outbreak of war. Not many were glad to see them, including Raffaele senior. Why not ask Ettore to deal with Staffieri?"

"I'd rather not, Don Agostino. I don't want to worry Ettore and Maria any more than I have done."

"Come what may, you will have to deal with Staffieri. As a priest, you must be respected. I could get Emilia to spread the word that you know why he had to leave London and why he was refused a visa to the United States. At the very least, it will let him know you are somebody to be reckoned with.

157

"Besides, if your father bought him out, he must have done well in the deal because Staffieri didn't come back to Collaquila empty-handed. He paid over the odds for land he bought from the Marchesa, not to mention a herd of goats. The goats you fed on the day you arrived belong to Staffieri.

"Last year, when his father died, he took over as Itinerant Pig Slaughterer and Undertaker …. and promptly built a villa and Funeral Parlour over the ancestral hovel he was born and raised in. He's got money to burn and lots of parasites ready and willing to help him spend it in Palladino's.

"According to Emilia, he left a Scotch wife and three children back in Glasgow. This is why he hasn't married in Collaquila. Emilia says he had been one of Simonetta's many admirers before the war and still has a yen for her despite what happened when the Goums came. Which, I have to admit is a point in his favour. And from what Emilia tells me, Staffieri has promised to give Simonetta a fancy funeral if she goes before he does."

Giovanni had lost concentration the moment Don Agostino mentioned the Marchesa. His experience from his first and only visit to her palace in Capriati had been traumatic.

"I'm sorry, Don Agostino. Are you saying Staffieri plans to marry Simonetta?"

"Nothing of the sort!" snorted Don Agostino. "You've not been listening, have you? Staffieri has really got under your skin, hasn't he? He's got you worried and not before time, if you ask me. If Emilia is correct and she usually is, then Staffieri, as I've said, is already married. Something which, in my view, is a great pity. Why? Because Simonetta would marry him in a minute if he ever plucked up the courage to ask her. This is all according to Emilia and she's never known to be wrong in such matters.

"You should get your uncle to make enquiries about the family Staffieri abandoned in Scotland and spill the beans in the piazza. For the sake of your reputation, peace of mind and self-respect, you must fight fire with fire. Indifference to what Staffieri is

158

saying isn't the answer and the locals will continue thinking there's no smoke without fire."

Giovanni nodded his head in agreement. He had for some time believed Staffieri was the reason he had been unable to reach the hearts and minds of the locals as much as he had hoped to when he first arrived in Collaquila.

His father had often said that the village belongs to its villagers, meaning they will always back their own against an outsider. In particular, against a foreign born outsider with, to boot, family roots among the despised and odious inhabitants of Milignano.

But Staffieri wasn't Giovanni's only failure if failure it was. In a manner of speaking, alienating the Marchesa Galla Placida Pignatelli del Carretto was the direct consequence of her failed attempt to surmount the constancy of his conduct and intentions.

Some eight months after Giovanni's arrival in Collaquila, the Marchesa had written to Don Agostino requesting the presence of his curate in the nearby town of Capriati. She wanted Giovanni, rather than Don Agostino, to bless a memorial chapel she was having erected to the memory of her second husband, Tenente Ferdinando Umberto Zoccolone, shot by Partisans at the height of their purge on former fascist officials.

The unscrupulous Tenente was executed for having organised private and public beatings of socialist and communist dissidents, for larceny and for misappropriation of property and funds, private and public, on the grandest of scales.

The Marchesa had scarcely turned fourteen when she married her first husband, a lecherous and wealthy octogenarian with all the pomp and circumstance befitting his noble status. It proved to be a brief marriage. But, long enough for her to see off a besotted husband who, according to legend, died while fulfilling his conjugal duties. While the eighty-five-year-old Marquis' desire was boundless, it proved to be fatal when his blood pressure and heart rate could no longer cope with the peremptory demands of his teenage bride.

As for husband number two, the erstwhile Tenente, his fledgeling career as an Officer in the Italian Army had come to an abrupt halt when he was the sole survivor of his regiment's annihilation at the First Battle of Ambi Alaga[1] during the Italo-Ethiopian War of 1895.

It emerged at the Tenente's court martial that while his regiment was being slaughtered in the early hours of the morning by 30,000 Abyssinians- led by the great Ras Mekonnen Mikaèl- the intrepid Lieutenant Zoccolone was otherwise engaged in the former's tent with two of his pre-pubescent wives.

The Fascist Party had given the cashiered Tenente a new lease of life. His dedication to duties sustaining the principles of Grand and Petty Larceny left many scores that could be settled with nothing other than his life.

What had really sealed the Tenente's fate with double-dealing hypocritical Partisans was that, besides having a merited reputation for a string of affairs with a bevy of bourgeois women and their daughters, there were unconfirmed allegations that Tenente Zoccolone had pederastic predispositions.

These facts notwithstanding, Ferdinando had been the first of the many great loves of the Marchesa Galla Placida Pignatelli del Carretto. Her conquests after the former's death had earned her the nickname of La Veuve Clicquot or The Merry Widow.

Sexual promiscuity never undermined the Marchesa Galla Placida Pignatelli del Carretto's pragmatism. Husband number three and four or five would have to be as wealthy as her first husband and no less wealthy than her second.

A colossal wrought-iron fence proclaimed and divided her residence in Capriati from the common carriage track she permitted to pass through her estates. Twin single-arched gates had been fashioned within the fence's wrought iron framework.

At eye-level, each of these gates sported the family escutcheon of the late Marchese Carlomagno Ludovico Francesco Pignatelli del Carretto. Beyond the gates, a monumental marble stairway rose like its inspiration: the *San Miniato al Monte* in Florence.

At the top of the stairway, stood the Marchese's mansion, its Palladian façade elaborately decorated with Homeric bas-reliefs and a profusion of fertility symbols of union and creation. The jewel in its crown was a pair of bronze cast doors depicting scenes from The Festival of Vulcan in which live fish and animals were cast into bonfires as sacrifices in honour of the eponymous God.

The narrow two-storey interior of the palace did not live up to the expectations suggested by the dimensions of the exterior's façade. The Marchese had opted for architectural deception in the pursuit of economy.

The interior's ground floor was dressed in metered squares of black ceramic tiles. Two curving marble staircases, each within touching distance of the lateral walls, were anchored on a colonnade of marble pillars forming a perfect horseshoe supporting the recessed upper floor.

Behind the staircase and on either side of its landing were two separate apartments each of which led into the garden to the rear of the palace. It was into the drawing room of the apartment on the left that Giovanni was being ushered, by the same sullen fop who had opened the gates.

The air in the apartment was heavy with condensation and bouquets of exotic balms and fragrances coming from the bathroom to the rear of the Marchesa's boudoir. Perfumes which disorientated Giovanni's senses making him feel ill at ease with the strange feelings they generated. Feelings which intensified when his eyes wandered to a tapestry dominating the wall to his right displaying two naked back-to-back figures locked in intercourse.

Then he saw her. Through the open doorway of her boudoir, he saw the naked figure of a woman he presumed was the Marchesa. Giovanni stared at her, confused and petrified like one

161

of Medusa's victims. He was transfixed and unable to tear his eyes from this naked woman, sitting on a stool, brushing long wet hair, which hung between her open legs.

When she looked up, the shock he experienced at the sight of her face rescued him from the grip of his excitement: albino eyebrows, narrow serpentine eyes, porcine nose and cavernous nostrils mounted on an acned face and pelican chin which puffed its way to the base of her neck. It was a quasi-hypnotic ugliness which paradoxically lifted the spell which had held him in thrall to her nakedness.

Having distanced himself from the forelegs of the praying mantis, Giovanni looked at her with detachment. A detachment which offended the Marchesa.

Rejection by a man unmoved by the sexuality she believed she exuded was a new experience for La Marchesa Galla Placida Pignatelli del Carretto. In high dudgeon, she retreated to the changing room of her boudoir to consider her options.

In no time at all, the barefooted Marchesa reappeared in the drawing room, smoking a foul smelling Murad through an elongated ivory holder.

She was dressed in a tight-fitting multi-coloured Chinese housecoat, in a fabric of such sheerness that it revealed the nipples of her ample breasts. A yellow cotton towel turbaned her hair with a skill a Sikh would have been proud of.

"Follow me, Reverente, follow me," Giovanni had no option but to obey as the Marchesa led him like the proverbial spider into the web of her boudoir's tiny salon. He knew he had nothing to fear. He had seen, confronted and repulsed the temptations of the serpentine earth-dragon.

"I love sitting in the odour of sanctity, Reverente." The Marchesa patted the brocaded chaise longue as she spoke, inviting Giovanni to share it. She showed no little irritation when Giovanni elected to sit on a matching armchair placed at some

162

distance from the chaise longue. Recovering her composure, she continued.

"How does it feel, Reverente, to be sitting in the uninhibited comfort of a woman's boudoir? As a man and priest sworn to chastity, do you not find its perfumes and odours disturbing? Inviting? Tempting? Exciting?"

"Signora Marchesa," replied Giovanni, quelling the urge to deride the Marchesa's apparent determination to continue with her ridiculous charade, "if you will permit me to be blunt, I find the perfumes of your sitting rooms as pleasant as the smell of sealing wax or the smell of burning incense or," adding less than charitably, "the smell of a wet dog."

"Then let me be equally blunt!" the Marchesa snapped, "The blessing of my late husband's memorial was only an excuse to bring you here. There is and there will never be a memorial or memorials built to honour either of my late husbands.

"I brought you here to inform you that I am displeased, most displeased. Displeased and dismayed you did not see fit to consult me about Collaquila's plans to honour the fiftieth anniversary of Don Agostino's ordination or extend an invitation to chair your so-called Anniversary Committee.

"Had the committee been official, then I'm sure Bishop Pantaleone would have made sure that my expectations would have been met. Need I remind you that I am the Landlord of every farmer who holds a *Tenancy at Will Contract* within the far-flung reaches of his diocese? Contracts which give me the right to order eviction, without notice, as and when it pleases me so to do."

Giovanni sat in silence, in no way overawed or impressed by the Marchesa's angry reactions, not only for having challenged her right to treat him like a contracted vassal but also because he had refused to sacrifice his innocence to her libido by refusing to recognise her *Droit de Jambage* [1].

"As a result of these discourtesies, I am most certainly not prepared to underwrite the expense of the proposed festivities. You will inform this..... this Committee of yours that the proposed Festa will not take place because it will not have my financial support.

"The good people of Collaquila must suffer the consequences of your discourtesies ....insubordinate, unacceptable and unwarranted. My decision is final and irrevocable," adding as she rose to tug the service bell hanging on the wall behind her, "offensive discourtesies which I will refer to my friend, Bishop Cataldo when next we meet."

Giovanni was shown to the door by the same effeminate servant who had admitted him. As he left the Marchesa's palace in Don Agostino's mule-drawn carriage, he wondered how selective Galla Placida Pignatelli del Carretto would be when she informed the Bishop of her contretemps with one of his inconsequential curates.

Later that evening, when the Festa Committee was in full swing, Giovanni announced that unlimited funding was in place to cover the Festa expenses. Since all those present knew where Don Agostino's mule and carriage had been earlier that day, it was assumed that the said funding had come from La Marchesa Galla Placida Pignatelli del Carretto. Giovanni did not choose to enlighten them.

If the good people of Collaquila were to discover the extent of his wealth, they would put two and two together and assume that it included the ill-gotten gains his father had allegedly embezzled from one of their own. This would have given Raffaele Staffieri all the encouragement he needed to continue slandering his father's memory.

But not everything concerning Giovanni in Collaquila had been marred or scarred by failure. Thanks to a shared interest in the poetry of Horace, a warm and genuine father and son relationship had grown between Don Agostino and Giovanni.

164

And this was by no means his only success in Collaquila.

After years of acrimonious back-biting, Giovanni's idea of setting up a secret Anniversary Committee had brought about a miraculous reconciliation between Maria Mangiabambini and Carmelina Capricciosa. With some difficulty, he had persuaded them that their cooperation was indispensable if the parish intended to honour Don Agostino's anniversary.

The Committee had proved to be a master-stroke. It could meet as required after the Evening Rosary Service without arousing the suspicions of Don Agostino who knew nothing of what was in store for him at the end of the month. By including Emilia, Simonetta and the Brigadier's wife, Don Agostino was hardly likely to hear about how his parishioners planned to celebrate the fiftieth anniversary of his Ordination.

Giovanni wanted Thursday, May 28th, the feast day of Sant' Agostino, to be declared a municipal holiday. For this holiday, the Committee needed the good offices of the Mayor. He was flattered into acquiescence for having been taken into the confidence of his erstwhile patients who, up till then, hadn't given him the time of day.

The committee decided that Don Agostino would be told of what was in store when it would be too late to do anything about it. The Committee was Giovanni's priority. Raffaele Staffieri would have to wait.

Chapter Nineteen

Collaquila, Saturday August 24th. 1951

"*Though guiltless, you must answer for your father's sins.* That's how our friend Horace puts it. Not that I'm saying your father was a criminal, but it does seem to be the case that you are being condemned for something your father did or did not do."

These days bringing up Staffieri's attacks on Giovanni's father were becoming a matter of routine with Don Agostino. But his *Big Day* was approaching, so Giovanni made no attempt to steer the old man away from his under-cover project. Anything and everything which delayed discovery of the Committee's existence was to be encouraged.

"So what do you want me to do? Take my collar off and, beat some sense into his skull?? It's never easy with someone like Staffieri who's got it into his thick head that my father swindled him. *Force without wisdom is counter-productive.*"

Giovanni watched the gleam in Don Agostino's face when he quoted from another of Horace's Odes. He discovered months ago that quoting Horace was the best way of side-tracking the old man. Wasn't the Roman Poet himself referred to as *The Master of the Graceful Sidestep?*

"What's more, Don Agostino, you're always telling me to rise above personal misfortunes and the trivialities of our parishioners. Study their lives you keep telling me. Make them a blueprint for what we say and do. Which is easier said than done with the likes of Staffieri. The crux of the matter is that I'm a touch paper for his abhorrent remarks. He won't stop saying what he's saying while I live and breathe in Collaquila. Maybe I should ask the Bishop to send me somewhere else and then ....."

Giovanni said no more. He didn't need to because Don Agostino had dozed off in his armchair. These days Don Agostino seemed to be spending more and more time doing just that. Had old age finally overtaken him? *Many are the discomforts that gather round an old man.*

Giovanni wasn't sure if he was quoting Horace or whether it was a proverb cited by Cicero in his *De Senectute[1]*. He made a mental note to clarify the source of this particular quotation in his next letter to the Bishop.

For some time now, Giovanni felt that the Bishop had shown remarkable acumen in sending him to Collaquila. Regular letters from Venafro surely proved His Grace was keeping a weather eye on his progress.

In his most recent letter, the Bishop had asked for another update on his relationship with Don Agostino and had expressed his deepest disappointment at being unable to join the anniversary celebrations. An important meeting with Cardinal Roccaravindola in Rome was the reason given.

Collaquila, Thursday, August 28th, 1952, Feast Day of Saint Augustine

The scene in the piazza after Mass was chaotic. Around one hundred and sixty men, women and children were shouting, jostling and milling around the red and black striped carnival tents of four gipsy fortune tellers from Venafro and a similar number of market stalls erected by spivs from Forcella, the contraband enclave of Naples.

A dark-skinned fortune teller stood at the entrance to each of these tents, All four were dressed in garish headscarves, baggy sleeved blouses and long multicoloured skirts revealing the hems of soiled petticoats hanging over dirty feet. The odour they emitted was an indelicate combination of fish, onions, cheap perfume, garlic and stale tobacco. Gesticulating, touching,

167

tugging and beckoning, until they lured gullible men and women into their tents of deceit and flattery.

For ten lire, the crystal ball put a gloss on what, to the less naïve, would have been no more than variations of yesterday's domestic arguments: that they would be sad and sometimes happy that a relative, friend or neighbour would irk them or make them laugh; that elderly relatives would soon be moving through the Golden Gates of Paradises and that their enemies would sooner or later be consigned to the fires of Hell.

Contrasting the headscarves, blouses and skirts worn by the barefooted gipsies, were the clean, faded and threadbare clothes and open-toed straw sandals worn by the local hill billies. These were the clothes they wore on Sundays and on those rare days when they had something special to celebrate. Like today's holiday in celebration of the fiftieth anniversary of their parish priest's Ordination. For many, it would be the first time in a generation they had enjoyed an extra day of respite from the toil and drudgery of their hand to mouth existence.

In an uncharacteristically brief sermon, Don Agostino's few words on his namesake were found hard to understand. This Sant' Agostino fellow believed that doing without something completely was preferable to the moderation their own Don Agostino had been preaching for years.

Equally hard to accept was that, according to Saint Augustine, they deserved no praise for doing what was held to be their duty. Many thought that St Augustine's strange beliefs were attributable to drunkenness. After all, was said and done, Saint Augustine was the Patron Saint of Brewers and had been a bit of a lad before he saw the Light.

The controversy caused when Bishop Pantaleone gave his approval for the burial of Colonial Volunteers in Venafro, was reason enough for Don Agostino not to mention that Hippo, St Augustine's birthplace, was in French North Africa and near the Atlas Mountains where the barbarous Goumiers were spawned.

By the time the Angelus rang from the belfry of San Sebastiano, third-rate trinkets, worthless and nearly worthless merchandise had sold like hot cakes. At overblown prices by brash Neapolitan wheeler-dealers plying their trade with entertaining enthusiasm.

And yet, few would have parted from plaster of Paris statues of the Saint they clutched in calloused hands. They would never know that today's effigies of Saint Augustine were yesterday's Saint Bartholomew and would be tomorrow's Saint as listed in the liturgical calendar.

They were determined to eat and drink their fill of the fare paid by the Merry Widow of Capriati from the perceived fruit of her sexual conquests. All were equally determined to stay for the four-o'clock Film Show, to be shown before the sun disappeared behind the Mainarde Mountains. They knew Don Agostino had set the early time for the film show, as he was pleased to put it, *to prevent inappropriate behaviour under cover of darkness.*

By four o'clock most had found a seat on the Church steps. Those with less foresight had to make do with squatting on the piazza's debris and sun-dried goat droppings.

Discussions, arguments or debates were varied and for the most part inconclusive, particularly when focussed on people rather than money or trading. Some considered the labour and upkeep of goats to be hardly worth the bother. Others complained about the fees extorted by Staffieri for butchering their pigs and burying their dead.

Some chewed over rumours of Don Giovanni's personal wealth. They concluded, after much deliberation, that it was a trifling matter. If he had all the money Staffieri said he had then surely he would have bought his own mule rather than borrow Don Agostino's. And surely, if he were as rich as the Count of Monte Cristo, he would have bought an Alfa Romeo or a Fiat.

Eventually, everyone got round to discussing Simonetta Semprepronta. Was she really and truly a reformed woman? Was she suited to the role of a Repentant Magdalene? Would The

169

Undertaker still give her the promised funeral for services previously rendered? Was addiction to sex a curable disease like syphilis? Had Simonetta really taken a fancy to Don Giovanni? Didn't something similar not happen to Mary of Magdalena when she became a follower of Jesus?

'Rome, The Open City', was the film chosen by Don Agostino when he had recovered from the shock on learning that his parishioners wanted to celebrate the fiftieth anniversary of his Ordination. The film show would be followed by a musical performance given by the band from Cisterna di Latina (where the brigands of Monte Lippini came from). They would play until eight o'clock and not a minute longer, to prevent further inappropriate behaviour under cover of darkness.

Of course, Don Agostino had protested how unnecessary the celebration was. But, in the same breath, he insisted that money earmarked for a Fireworks Display should be spent on providing food and drink parcels for parishioners who were too ill to attend the proposed celebrations in the piazza.

"It's not that I don't feel honoured, Giovanni. Of course I do. It's a wonderful gesture from my parishioners. But I think they are taking advantage of the occasion to get a holiday. They've probably got another lined up for my funeral unless it falls on a Sunday. And from the way I'm feeling these days, the additional holiday they crave for isn't too far away.

"And what's all this nonsense I hear from Emilia that the Marchesa is footing the bill? I don't believe a word of it. Otherwise, she would have been calling the shots in this Committee of yours. It's not that she can't afford it. She's loaded and has more money than sense.

"She bewitched the old Marchese. Disgraceful it was! Absolutely disgraceful! Dear God, he married a fourteen-year-old girl when he was nudging ninety. She married a fortune and got her hands on the lot in less than a year. Did you know she was from Trieste and did you know she's a close friend of the Bishop?"

170

"Isn't Trieste the city which inspired the famous song about *La Campana di San Giusto*, the city Horace called Tergestum?"

"Don't change the subject! And Horace never mentions Tergeste. And I don't like the song which sings its praises. More to the point, did La Marchesa try to seduce you? The silly woman thinks she's a *femme fatale*. She sees herself as another Cleopatra. Did you know that Cleopatra was held to be the ugliest woman in Egypt?"

Giovanni thought the better of telling Don Agostino that it was the Marchesa Galla Placida Pignatelli del Carretto's face which had saved him from falling into her clutches.

"She did try, didn't she? Tried and failed. Knew she would. That's why I sent you. I would have gone to Capriati myself to bless the memorial to that useless second husband of hers, but she asked for you specifically. Something which aroused my suspicions. According to Emilia, Bishop Pantaleone was the Marchesa's dinner guest last week. He probably told her about your Committee."

Giovanni looked at his watch. It was two minutes past nine. Don Agostino had retired moments after the band's music had been replaced by the customary evening fanfare of barking dogs, braying donkeys, bleating sheep and the hollow clicking of crickets.

A few of the local worthies had gathered on the concrete bench which lined the façade of Coradino's Barber Shop in the piazza. Giovanni was invited to join the company consisting of the Sindaco, his brother Pasqualino, the Brigadier and Coradino.

The subject under discussion was the generosity shown by the La Marchesa Galla Placida Pignatelli del Carretto's in sponsoring Don Agostino's lavish anniversary celebrations. While Giovanni made no comment on who had met the expenses, he readily agreed that it had cost a pretty penny.

171

"We owe the Marchesa so much. I've lost touch with the number of times, as your Mayor, I've had to go to her cap in hand on municipal matters. Not once, not even once, did I leave empty-handed."

"I'm sure that's true," said the Brigadier, "but thanks are due to Don Giovanni for setting up the Committee which organised today's events. With such success....and I'm not saying this because my wife played a modest part in Don Giovanni's Committee."

Giovanni's heart missed a beat when uninvited, Raffaele Staffieri joined the company. He stood over Giovanni aggressively. He had been drinking since returning from slaughtering and butchering pigs in Sesto Campana and hadn't taken the trouble to wash or change. His breath reeked of wine and his clothes smelled like a butcher's apron.

"That's right, let's all congratulate Don Giovanni for all his efforts today. A worthy son..... of an unworthy father."

A nervous Brigadier made feeble efforts to stop Staffieri's provocations but Giovanni waved them away.

"No, Brigadiere, let him have his say. *In vino veritas, in wine truth.*

The Brigadiere didn't resume his seat beside Giovanni. Sensing trouble, he had no intention of being present when it came. Muttering something about paper-work waiting for him at home, the Brigadiere scuttled off without warning Staffieri to modify his language. He knew there was some substance in the accusations Staffieri had been making about Don Giovanni's father. Silvio Bartolomeo had been among the first of the Blackshirts[1]. Which said all there was to be said about the young priest's father.

"Why not sit beside me, Signor Staffieri, so we can all hear what we've all heard before. Come and tell us all again what my father is supposed to have done twenty years ago." The calmness in

Giovanni's voice and his confidence seemed to wrong-foot Staffieri. But not for long.

"You want to know what your father did in Glasgow? Then I'll stand here and tell you what the dirty rat did."

The R of *rat* was rolled with such venom that it seemed as if Staffieri was clearing his throat to spit on Giovanni's face. Staffieri looked at the Sindaco, Pasqualino, Coradino and Palladino as if seeking the support of fellow villagers, before turning his attention back to Giovanni, who met his gaze without flinching from the flying speckles of saliva.

"Your father lured me to the After-Work Club in Glasgow, which he treated as his personal domain, supported by thugs led by your brother. I had applied to join as soon as I arrived from London. I was offered temporary membership for a year. For months I heard nothing. That is, until I made an offer for Widow Coia's restaurant.

"Two days later I'm invited to the Club. ..... I went, thinking it was about my application for membership. But no..... the high and mighty Silvio Bartolomeo told me that his brother had been trying for ages to get Widow Coia to sell. Then he accused me of cheating her into accepting my offer." Staffieri's voice had become a steady monotonous tone which increased in volume as his anger increased. "Bartolomeo then tells me that it would be in my best interests to sell the business to his brother at the price previously agreed with Signora Coia. And if I didn't, he would arrange for me to have an accident.

"Even after I agreed to sell he had me beaten by your brother and his gang of thugs …. to teach me a lesson he said. To teach me the error of my ways he said. Sending me back home to my mother bruised, battered and pumped up with castor oil.

"I had to sell my business for less than I paid for it. And do you know what? He made me pay the difference between the two offers. £75! The money your father had the cheek to say was for the Club's Building Fund. Building funds my arse! When I know

173

it went straight into his pocket." Shaking with rage, Staffieri exploded into a torrent of abuse.

"That's quite a story," said Giovanni when Staffieri's abuse had run its course, "but I note you are now saying my father bought rather than stole your business. And at a price matching his offer to Widow Coia which must have been a fair one, otherwise, she would have turned it down. Which is not the same thing as saying you were cheated, as you've been claiming to anyone who'd listen. And hardly the daylight robbery you've been claiming it was since I got here. But you haven't told us why you were refused entry into the United States …. before you came back to Collaquila …... to take over your father's businesses. Nor have you told us why you had to leave London in such a hurry …..with enough money in your pocket to buy out Widow Gilda." Giovanni kept his eye on a furious Staffieri, ready to duck in case he lashed out with his fist.

"Keep London and America out of it!" Staffieri shouted, "Your father cheated me! Robbed me of the opportunity of making money from a restaurant everyone knew could be a goldmine. Which is why he wanted it. Not that it did him much good. My restaurant was his one-way ticket to the Arandora Star. God-given revenge for what he did to me..... and just retribution for what he did to your mother!"

This reference to his mother was a new twist in Staffieri's invective against his father. Giovanni had no idea what Staffieri was talking about. That this ignorance was sincere was clearly written on his face. He had no need to ask Staffieri for an explanation.

"Your father thought he knew better than the doctors who attended your mother when she was ill. As she often was, according to my mother who knew her well.

"It was common knowledge she was ill to every Tom, Dick and Harry except your father who thought all she needed was fresh air. Too mean to buy your mother the antibiotics which would

174

have saved her life. Your father was nothing but a thieving rat who killed your ...."

Giovanni's self-control snapped. He leapt to his feet crashing his head against Staffieri's forehead like a sledgehammer followed by an elbow which smashed against Staffieri's nose breaking it with an audible crack. Staffieri's blood spurted over Giovanni's dog collar and the top buttons of his cassock.

Staffieri sagged at the knees before falling backwards, his head crashing with a colossal thud against Coradino's concrete doorstep. Blood and mucus oozed from Staffieri's broken nose. A damp patch appeared at the crotch of his trousers when he lost control of his bodily functions.

The Mayor was the first to react. He bent over Raffaele Staffieri's body, frantically feeling for a pulse at the side of his neck. Shocked by what he had done, Giovanni could only stare at the cross above the San Sebastiano Church's bell-tower.

"I can't find a pulse! I can't find a pulse! I think he's gone! I think he's gone! Can you hear me, Don Giovanni? I think you've killed him!"

Chapter Twenty

"Not much today..... but let's start with a letter to the parish priest of Gallo Matese.... you'll find his details in the Diocesan Manual.... if memory serves me well, it's Don Severino...yes, Severino Rinaldi. Let him know Confirmations will be held on the first Sunday in May of next year. It keeps the peace when we give every parish in the Diocese a chance to set the ball rolling in the Confirmations' Calendar.

"Then there's the official opening of the new church in Acquafondata scheduled for the evening of Thursday 25th October. The old one, the *Stella Maris*, was partially destroyed during artillery exchanges between the Germans and Americans. French Colonials were sent to flush out the German rear guard left to cover the retreat. After which they profaned and desecrated the Stella Maris. They violated and murdered the parish priest on the steps of the altar before turning their attention on the women who were attending the Evening Services of Holy Week. Need I say more when history repeated itself in Collaquila?"

"No, Your Grace, it's all in your *Marocchinate* report."

"On my advice, Papa Pacelli has agreed that it would be in the best interests of all concerned to re-site the Church as far away as possible from the current site of the Stella Maris. Since the new church is in my diocese, the honour of dedicating it with its name falls to me.

"Cardinal Roccaravindola has suggested we call it the *Santa Maria Goretti*. At the end of the day, whatever name is chosen, it must be approved by the Congregation of Sacred Rites.

"The acting parish priest, Don Antonio Bulgari, tells me that work on the dome and ceilings have yet to be completed and that a great deal of additional funding is required. I'm sure I can count on your family's generosity to meet the shortfall. It's a heaven-sent opportunity to postpone the opening until Thursday 22nd of November, the feast day of Santa Lucrezia.... the name I've chosen for the new church.

"I'll leave you to deal with the Architect to work out the extent of the additional funding required. Now, tell me, Giovanni, what have you got for my attention this morning?"

"A letter from the University of Naples arrived this morning, Your Grace, asking for confirmation of your annual engagement with its Historical Society on Wednesday 21st November."

"Ask, no, tell them to change it to a later date. We must give our full attention to the rescheduled opening of the new church in Acquafondata. However, you can also inform Professor what's-his-Name that the subject of my talk will be: *The Samnite Struggles of the Matese.* There's a file somewhere in your desk marked 'Mons Tifernus' .... bottom right-hand drawer...know anything about it?"

Giovanni Bartolomeo wasn't sure whether Bishop Pantaleone was referring to Mons Tifernus or the file itself, so he didn't commit himself. "No, Your Grace, I'm still not up to speed."

In fact, Giovanni Bartolomeo had studied Tofanelli's turgid notes in detail and knew of every single bird to be found in the Matese Mountains: Golden Eagles, Short-toed Eagles, Bubo Eagles, Eurasian Eagles, European Honey-buzzards, Falcons, Moor-hen, Ducks, Lapwings, and Woodcocks and so on to the point of indifference. However, Giovanni knew that when His Grace addressed the History Society in Naples, the Bishop would sound like an authority on the Samnite Tribes and Fauna of Southern Italy.

The Bishop smiled broadly. He always found it satisfying when he was able to parade the depth of his knowledge to less gifted

177

listeners. However, in Giovanni, he had found a kindred spirit who relished the discovery and acquisition of esoteric facts.

Taking Giovanni as his Secretary was the best thing he had done since negotiating the location of the French Military Cemetery in Venafro. Of one thing he was certain: when he became a Cardinal, he would take his encyclopaedic Secretary with him. Giovanni's days as a curate were numbered.

Since His Grace had rescued him from the mess left behind in Collaquila, Giovanni felt he had a duty to repay his Bishop's unexpected magnanimity with every means at his disposal. If this meant spending days researching boring historical matters then so be it. It would be his way of repaying the Bishop for his leniency in not suspending him for having inflicted grievous bodily harm on one of his former parishioners in Collaquila.

While Giovanni had qualms about what he had done to Raffaele Staffieri, he regretted having to leave Don Agostino with whom he had forged a genuine friendship in the short time he had served as his Curate. Poor Don Agostino. On the morning after Giovanni's clash with Staffieri, he had ridden to Venafro on his trusty mule to plead his Curate's case with the Bishop. When His Grace heard what had happened, he had no alternative other than to remove Giovanni from Collaquila.

On the day of Giovanni's departure, Don Agostino was in tears. He and all the local worthies were assembled in the piazza to share his misery. Countless others added to the confusion generated by Giovanni's immanent banishment. Even Raffaele Staffieri was there, an abject figure with bandaged head and nose.

Staffieri had to make a public spectacle of his plea for forgiveness: on his knees, kissing the hand which had pole-axed him. Besides withdrawing the charges of assault and battery made to the Brigadiere, this public humiliation was the additional price he had to pay if he wished to continue serving the needs of the good people of Collaquila.

As laid down by Canon Law, Giovanni knew that the Church's punishment for common assault and battery was a suspension from priestly duties. He had no idea of its duration or where it would be served. He would find the answer when he was carpeted by a highly concerned Bishop.

Bishop Pantaleone had indeed been concerned. Concerned, not so much about Giovanni's welfare but with the possibility that the scandal would reach the newspapers. Civil Charges against Giovanni would have to be withdrawn. Otherwise, a Court Appearance and a jail sentence loomed on the horizon for the brother of a Servant of God. Something Bishop Pantaleone could not permit. His Red Hat was in the balance.

On his way to face the music in Venafro, Giovanni asked Michele il Brigante to make a detour to Milignano. He wanted to confer with his aunt and uncle. To clarify and amend the gossip which had preceded him: that their nephew had attempted to kill Collaquila's Undertaker for insulting his parents and that he was to be unfrocked.

While Michele il Brigante was spreading the news of how he had rescued Don Giovanni from an angry crowd of goat-loving hill billies collectively screaming for his blood, Ettore Bartolomeo was informing his nephew about his father's dealings with Staffieri and the extent of the family's commitment to Mussolini.

"Here are the facts about our dealings with Staffieri in Scotland. You were nine years old at the time. To save Staffieri from deportation as an undesirable alien, our Embassy in London had him dumped on us in Glasgow on the understanding that he did nothing to attract the attention of the City of Glasgow's Constabulary.

"Shortly before Staffieri's arrival from London, we made a verbal offer of £225 for Gilda Coia's restaurant. It was a generous offer because we realised, even if she didn't, its potential for development.

"Then along comes Staffieri with an offer of £300 which the old

179

lady, naturally enough, accepted. To say the least, this really upset your father.

"Since we had more than enough money to outbid any offer Staffieri could possibly make, I was ready to top offers made by Staffieri. But your father said no. To Silvio, it was a matter of principle and money had nothing to do with it. So he invited Staffieri to a meeting in the Casa. The outcome was that Staffieri accepted our offer of £225 and volunteered to pay the difference of £75 into the Party's Building Fund."

"So in effect, it cost Staffieri £75 to sell the restaurant to my father for £225?"

"Put it that way if you like. On a point of principle, we were not prepared to pay a penny more than our original offer to Signora Gilda."

"So, at the end of the day, Staffieri was outsmarted, which must have rankled. He's been kicking himself all these years for accepting an offer he could easily have refused. I knew my father wasn't a thief, which is why I did nothing about Staffieri's accusations. Until his comments about my mother."

"Your mother's health was always delicate, even before she left Milignano to join us in Sarzana[1] where Roberto was born. Let me explain to save you the bother of asking questions.

"National Conscription followed Italy's declaration of war against the Central Powers in 1915. Your father and I reported as directed to Army Headquarters in Cassino. From there we were posted to the regimental headquarters of the *Brigata Ligure* in Sarzana.

"Your mother at the time was sixteen and...," adding with hesitation, "....and pregnant. Within a week, she and your aunt Bianchina had joined us. With your mother's dowry, we bought an apartment overlooking Piazza Cavour."

"And Aunt Bianchina accepted this situation?"

"Let me put it this way, Giovanni. Silvio was the apple of her eye which meant she paid scant attention to his flings with the Borelli sisters and the Postmistress who were her friends.

"When she realised how serious Silvio was about your mother, she stood by him. What I can tell you now is that while we were on the Piave Front[1], Bianchina was with your mother when Roberto was born and looked after both of them. Just as she looked after your father and me when our parents died.

"When the war was over, Bianchina and I returned to Milignano while your parents settled in Sarzana before moving to Scotland to get away from the backlash caused by Matteotti's disappearance. Your mother was expecting you when she arrived in Glasgow."

"Where my father allegedly caused my mother's death?"

"Absolute nonsense!" declared Ettore indignantly. "As I said, your mother's health was always poor. She was poorly when you were born and ever more so when Lucrezia followed three years later.

"She didn't trust the Doctor who attended her. She claimed his examinations were invasive. This was why my wife was present whenever he called. Your father called him *Dr That-Will-Be-Five-Guineas Please.*

"In the weeks before she died, he diagnosed Meningitis. Your mother thought she was pregnant and wouldn't permit an internal examination to confirm one thing or the other. Nor would she take the antibiotics he prescribed in case they harmed the baby she thought was on the way. There was nothing Silvio or Maria or any of our friends could do to persuade your mother to take the antibiotics.

"Silvio adored your mother and grieved for her. She was dead three years before his fondness for Irma's mother turned into something closer. Which explains your father's soft spot for Irma."

When Giovanni stood shamefaced in Bishop Pantaleone's study, his apprehension evaporated as soon as the Bishop began to speak.

"It's my fault, Giovanni. I should have known better than send you to a backwater like Collaquila. I should have kept you here with me.... to make better use of your talents. Brought up in Scotland...the culture clash....your father's politics. All mitigating instances."

Bishop Pantaleone had been apologetic regarding his reasons for sending Giovanni to Collaquila. He explained, with characteristic sophistry, that it had all been done in Lucrezia's best interest. Arguing that a softer option might have been construed as nepotism by the Congregation of Sacred Rites. By way of remediation for the Bishop's error, Giovanni was to be installed as his Acting Private Secretary with immediate effect.

"I know you are still working on the Samnites, Giovanni, but we must prioritise the Wine-Tasting event. Remember to contact Dottor Ferrara about the date and venue. Now let me see...." While the Bishop was consulting his desk diary, he absent-mindedly began to hum the words of the drinking song from the *Cavalleria Rusticana* Opera[1]. "Yes! Let's say Wednesday 17th October....no make it the Tuesday of the same week...the 16th. The date itself will make an interesting topic of conversation."

Giovanni made no comment. Apart from the fact it was the day he entered the Pontificale Seminary in Naples, the date meant nothing to him.

"It's a date I'll always associate with Herman Goering[2]. We know Goering cheated the hangman by committing suicide on the 16th October 1946. However, few historians know that three years earlier...Goering met Generalfeldmarschall Kesselring[3] in Milignano on the same date.

"Why? Probably to confirm its strategic position as a back-door

182

route to Rome via Frosinone. And if I'm not mistaken, the 16th of October is also the date you began your studies for the priesthood in the Naples' Pontificale."

"It was indeed, Your Grace. I must say I knew Goering met with Kesselring in Milignano. Something the locals still boast about. That's about all ...except..." Giovanni hesitated.

"Perhaps you were going to say Kesselring is still alive and serving his sentence in a Westphalian prison...... after Mr. Churchill intervened to save his neck?"

"In fact, your Grace, I was going to say that General Kesselring was educated at the University of Padua where he studied the Arts."

"You must stop hiding your light under a bushel, Giovanni. You are a mine of information for somebody so young and inexperienced. But, in point of fact, I digress. The visit sealed Milignano's fate. And with hindsight, we can say it caused the unspeakable death of your sister. Who knows, my dear Giovanni, perhaps by the Grace of God, we can make amends? But let's wait and see. Regarding the venue for our Wine-tasting, I hope you didn't mention it to Zanzarella."

"No, Your Grace... I didn't mention it to Doctor Zanzarella because I knew you wanted to announce the news at next week's meeting of the Archaeological Society. He has no idea of the Marchesa's bequest …."

"Good.....good" interrupted the Bishop. "No doubt he would be flogging his theory about the existence of a Roman Amphitheatre on the site of Venafro's Municipal Cemetery?" Giovanni nodded.

"I thought so. And no doubt he took you to the alleged site?" Giovanni nodded. "I thought so...there's more chance of finding El Dorado. Still, in point of fact, old Zanzarella means well.... and he has unearthed some extraordinary finds in Ancient Roman terracotta pottery. I look forward to seeing the delight on his face when I tell him about the Civic Museum. And all thanks to the

Marchesa's generosity. Have you written to her, Giovanni?"

"Yes, Your Grace...the letter is in your OUT tray for signature."

"That's fine. No need to post it. I will deliver it personally later this evening. She won't make the next meeting of the Archaeological Society because she leaves for Buenos Aires on Saturday with marriage in the pipeline. Let's hope that it's third time lucky. Her first two husbands brought her nothing but ....money!"

Giovanni laughed, although he was worried at the prospect of meeting the Marchesa again. The Bishop seemed to read his mind.

"There will be no need for you to come with me, Giovanni. I've asked Michele to drive me to Capriati. This will let you put the finishing touches to my speech for Ferrara's wine-tasting....and how is it progressing?"

Giovanni reached into the briefcase at his feet, hoping the Bishop wouldn't see the relief on his face. With the Marchesa emigrating to Argentina to marry her millionaire from the Pampas, it was highly unlikely he would ever see her again. Unless she came back to hunt for rich husband number four.

He handed Pantaleone a single sheet of paper summarising the main points for the Bishop's encounter with Stefano Ferrara. "I'm sorry Your Grace. This is all I've managed to draft so far."

"Your final paper, Giovanni, will no doubt uphold the principle of quality at the expense of quantity. It's a great pity the Marchesa will also miss our wine tasting junket.....although her absence won't upset you too much...unless I'm very much mistaken." Giovanni blushed, but elected to say nothing in mitigation.

"She feels aggrieved, Giovanni. She's mightily upset with you ...for omitting to invite her to chair the Ordination Committee you set up for the Don Agostino Anniversary. The Marchesa asked me who footed the bill for the colossal expense involved in

184

running the celebration. She was more than a little put out when I told her you had footed the bill. You did foot the bill for the Celebrations, Giovanni?" The question was put to him with one of the Bishop's penetrating looks, indicating he knew the answer.

"I thought so," he continued when he observed Giovanni's embarrassment. "Still, it's thanks to her parting gift to the Archaeological Society, that we have solved two of our problems, spiritual and temporal respectively. Her gift of the villa she maintained in Caserta, gives me the opportunity of transferring the Sisters of Saint Claire...vacating their convent here in Venafro…and making it available for the proposed *Pantaleone Civic Museum.*

"Zanzarella will have a perfect setting for the pottery, statues and sundry bits and pieces he has been digging up within the near and far-flung reaches of my diocese."

"Will you or the local authority be running the Museum, Your Grace?" asked Giovanni, anxious to draw the discussion away from the Marchesa.

"It's titular Curator will be Zanzarella. In point of fact, I will be running the Museum...with municipal funding and your kind contributions until the State takes over, as it undoubtedly will in the due process of time. Until then, I will maintain an element of control on how the Pantaleone Museum operates, to establish best practice regarding its administration.

"Now where was I, Giovanni? Ah, yes, my speech for Ferrara's wine tasting event. Let's have a look at what's what.... let's see if I can teach Ferrara another lesson." The Bishop smiled laconically. "I'll read it aloud....you always get a better idea when it's read viva voce: *Bacchus loves the hills*," began the Bishop in a declamatory voice which he believed was best suited to dramatic monologues, "*Bacchus loves the hills and the Salento Peninsula....so beloved by the Greeks that they named it Oenotria...the Land of Wine.* Virgil's words always have a nice ring to them, don't you think Giovanni?

185

"I want you to dig up all the facts you can find about the wines great men enjoyed and promoted in Ancient Roman Times....together with a résumé of their present-day reputation....have they stood the test of time?...Things like that."

"Like Mamertinus, Your Grace, the wine favoured by Julius Caesar? These days it's called Mamertino and is still produced in the neighbourhood of Messina, or Messana as the Romans called it"

"Exactly, Giovanni!" replied Pantaleone, unaware that Giovanni was gently making fun of the Bishop's love of trivialities. "Ferrara will relish information like that...particularly after our discussions on Santa Maddalena...or St Magdalener as he prefers to call it.... the wine promoted by a teetotaller like Mussolini."

"If it pleases Your Grace," suggested Giovanni, tongue in cheek, "I could add that Italy's fascination with wine started long before the Greeks ....or the Romans for that matter."

"Another splendid idea, Giovanni! Let's hit Ferrara with all the facts you can find on the cultivation of wine by the Etruscans three thousand years ago in the hills so beloved by Bacchus. By Jove, Giovanni, we've really got the wind in our sails here....and you could throw in something about Orvieto......how the Etruscans were the first to grow vines on the volcanic rock on which the town is built."

The Bishop laid Giovanni's draft sheet on his desk and sat back. Giovanni knew that a little homily on Etruscan Civilisation was on its way.

"You know, Giovanni, the Etruscans were such practical people. When they dug into the tufa, it was for two reasons. The first being the obvious one the world knows, digging tufa for their ambitious building projects.

"The second reason and this is what fascinates me, because, as they dug, they constructed multi-level wine cellars. The first level for crushing grapes....the middle level for fermentation and the lowest level for storage."

Giovanni doubted whether Ferrara or anybody else would be remotely interested in why the Etruscans spent their lives digging tufa wine-cellars in Orvieto. He was tempted to gild the lily by suggesting that he might wish to say something about *The Miracle of Bolsena* but thought the better of it. However, the Bishop was up to speed with Giovanni's thinking.

"And of course Giovanni, when you mention Orvieto, it would be right and fitting to mention the fourteenth century Eucharistic Miracle of Bolsena[1]. Right, Giovanni. I think you now know the ground I would like you to cover for my speech." Giovanni stood up, thinking the Bishop was about to dismiss him. He was anxious to join the *Santa Maria Maggiore* Festivities in Milignano.

"No, no, Giovanni ...don't be so anxious to get started on my speeches. There are still one or two matters I want to clear up with you before I leave for Capriati." Pantaleone pointed Giovanni back into his chair.

The Bishop made two piles from the papers and documents he had on his desk. He pushed the larger pile towards Giovanni and asked him to deal with it. "As for this lot," he said pointing to the smaller pile, "I'll sign them... you send them....and remember to use sealing wax on the confidential Latin documents addressed to Cardinal Roccaravindola.

"One last thing, Giovanni. When you visit Milignano later today, ask Don Pietro if he can accommodate Ferrara when he gets here from Bolzano...it will be for a few days...It's a great pity your Aunt can't put him up....Ferrara will be disappointed. Don Pietro's cuisine isn't quite up to your Aunt's high standards...you say it's because she has a young lady staying with her?"

"Yes, Your Grace...Irma Pacitti...she's an old friend of the family."

"Ah yes, Giovanni, a friend of the family indeed. In point of fact,

187

is she not the young lady your brother was once betrothed to.... someone you yourself stepped out with? If memory serves, she and her husband were at your Ordination Dinner. A comely young woman...Ferrara seemed much taken by her."

"She's been having serious disagreements with her mother-in-law, Your Grace... I'm sure things will turn out well in the end. She's having problems re-adjusting to village life and culture...Like me, she was brought up in Scotland."

"Quite so, Giovanni, quite so. These things take time.....one final matter, Giovanni. Earlier this afternoon, I had a 'phone call from Cardinal Roccaravindola bringing me up to date with progress regarding your sister's case.

"Preliminary investigations have been held up because the Postulator dealing with Lucrezia's case, my good friend Monsignor Konrad Schmalzgruber has retired to his family estates in West Germany.

"According to the Cardinal, the post is soon to be filled. We must have patience. After all, the process for the beatification of St. Maria Goretti took forty years. And compare this interval to the canonisation of the Scottish Jesuit, John Ogilvie, on-going since he was beatified in 1929 after his hanging, at Glasgow Cross, three hundred years earlier.

"The Cardinal mentioned that there has been an enquiry about your brother Roberto...from an Irish priest. Apparently, they got to know each other when he served as an Army Chaplain in the Australian POW Camp where your brother was interned. Do you know anything about him, Giovanni?"

"He must be the Army Chaplain Roberto wrote to me about. I remember his name..Fiachre Fahy...because it has a connection with a French Cheese....Brie Cheese to be exact." Giovanni braced himself to hear everything the Bishop knew about French cheeses.

"Saint Fiacre...an Irish hermit....patron Saint of gardeners and cab-drivers who gave his name to the horse-drawn carriages they drive to earn a living. You know Giovanni," continued the Bishop with slow knowing nods, "unless I'm very much mistaken, I have a notion that His Eminence will seek to appoint this Fahy individual as Konrad's successor. Why else, I ask you, would he mention the Postulator's job in the same breath as informing me about an enquiry concerning your late brother?

"Where his Eminence is concerned, I don't believe in coincidences. Come what may, the Congregation of Sacred Rites cannot appoint Konrad's successor without consulting me as the sponsor of your sister's case. Cardinal Roccaravindola can recommend whomsoever he likes. The final decision rests with me.... unless of course, Roccaravindola gets his own way by going behind my back to His Holiness. And if I know the old fox, I'm sure he has already done that.

"And a word of advice, Giovanni. Join this evening's Santa Maria Maggiore festivities in Milignano by all means but make sure you get back here afterwards. I don't think it would be wise for you to stay overnight with Ettore and Maria. We can't have tittle-tattle about you and your old flame getting back to Cardinal Roccaravindola."

Chapter Twenty One

"Your Grace, the Monsignor has arrived." Giovanni showed Fiachre Fahy into Bishop Pantaleone's study. With formal introductions over, he made to withdraw.

"No, no, Giovanni ….stay if you please. I'm sure the Monsignor will be pleased if you stay." As he spoke, Pantaleone stood behind his desk, hand outstretched with palm downwards waiting for Fahy to approach and acknowledge his ecclesiastical status. With an enigmatic smile, Fahy bent over the Bishop's amethyst ring making sure it made no contact with his lips.

Fahy, a lover of Dublin's Guinness Stout and the Black North's[1] Whiskey, was superstitious by nature. Knowing that the amethyst gemstone was held by the Ancient Greeks to be a remedy for drunkenness, Fahy could not make contact with a stone which could blight the pleasure he took in drinking his favourite beverages.

"This is a pleasant surprise Monsignore....a pleasant one indeed. According to my good friend, Ippolito, you were supposed to get here earlier in the week. Still, better late than never."

"Your Grace is kind......we Irish are an unpredictable race. I suppose having been ruled for centuries by the British has a lot to do with it."

"Yes, Monsignore, unpredictable but adventurous. Did not your own name saint, St. Fiacrius, forsake his country to build hospices in France for pilgrim travellers?"

"He did indeed your Grace; he left his adopted County of Kilkenny to do missionary work among the barbarians in France.

A bit like your own name saint, your Grace, San Cataldo di Taranto- or St Cathal of Taranto as we Irish prefer to call him. An Irishman who converted your Apulian ancestors from paganism."

"And a splendid job he did too, but let's get back to your namesake. An adopted Irishman you say, Monsignore?"

"Yes indeed, Your Grace. Fiacrius was from Scotland. The son of a Dalriadan King who left his rights of succession behind him to become a monk in my beloved Ireland."

"Where his name became associated with a French cheese, Monsignore?"

"Or figs perhaps Your Grace?" Fahy asked, tongue in cheek.

"Only if served with Brie, Monsignore," parried the Bishop.

Fiachre Fahy laughed at Cataldo Pantaleone's inane suggestion before explaining the reason for his laughter. "Let me explain, Your Grace: St Fiachre specialized in urology and proctology. Ergo, my dear Bishop, haemorrhoids were called '*The Figs of Saint Fiacre*." This time the laughter came from the Bishop.

"Which probably explains," countered the Bishop when he had stopped laughing, "why we don't call our children, Fiacro. After all, who would wish them associated with that part of the body where the eponymous figs are cultivated?"

During the subsequent laughter, Giovanni remained in the background like an unwanted extra, taking no part in the verbal skirmishing between the Bishop and the Postulator. Sensing his discomfiture, Fiachre Fahy glanced sympathetically at Giovanni, wondering why the Bishop had asked the young priest to remain.

Whatever the reason, this young man would surely have to withdraw. There could be no valid reason for the presence of a third party in a confidential discussion about the possible beatification of the Servant of God, Lucrezia Bartolomeo.

"You're thinking Monsignore.... there is a family resemblance?" the Bishop asked when he realised he no longer had Fahy's

191

attention. However, judging from Fahy's reaction, Pantaleone knew the Monsignore had been thinking no such thing. He decided to remain on the same track. This would leave him with the advantage surprise always provided. Roccaravindola's Irish bloodhound had to be prevented from taking the initiative.

"Come, come, my dear Monsignore. You see no resemblance between this young man and the gentleman Cardinal Roccaravindola was enquiring about.... on your behalf?"

It pleased Fahy to pretend he still had no idea who Giovanni was. He decided to let the Bishop show his hand in the game they were playing.

"You don't? Then let me introduce you to Giovanni, Roberto Bartolomeo's brother, brothers of the Servant of God, Lucrezia Bartolomeo."

Bishop Pantaleone's revelation was delivered with all the panache of a magician pulling a rabbit out of a hat. "I understand," resumed the Bishop, keeping what he thought was the initiative, "that you met Giovanni's brother while serving as Army Chaplain in an Adelaide POW camp."

"Life is full of surprises, Your Grace. Come to think of it, there is a faint resemblance...across the eyes. But I would never have guessed without your kind and considerate help. Roberto used to say Giovanni was more like his mother while he was like his father. Temperamentally speaking."

Fahy's voice took on a more serious tone. "From what His Eminence tells me, I have been led to understand young Giovanni had been appointed to serve as a curate in the parish of......" Fahy broke off to consult a small leather backed notebook bearing the Papal Crest, "....Collaquila, I think......" turning a few more pages for effect, "yes, Collaquila. Then why Your Grace is Giovanni with you here in Venafro? Unless ….unless you invited him here to save me the bother of visiting the said parish of Collaquila?"

"In point of fact, Monsignore, Giovanni's been here since the 31st August. Giovanni.....take this correspondence and deal with it at your leisure. Meantime, let me have a few minutes with the Monsignore." Pantaleone handed Giovanni a sheath of documents and letters. "I'll ring for you in due course." Pantaleone held up his hand to restrain Fahy from saying anything until Giovanni closed the study door.

"The young man's presence here in Venafro....given the circumstances...could be embarrassing."

"Embarrassing? Embarrassing for whom and for what, Your Grace?"

"Let me explain, Monsignore," he began, although he had no intention of doing. "It was always in my mind to make Giovanni my Secretary as soon as his predecessor retired. However, I had to bring forward his appointment when Monsignor Tofanelli passed away a few months ago, Requiescat in pace."

Pantaleone looked at Fahy expecting him to comment but Fahy remained impassive and silent. Pantaleone was being evasive and trying to conceal something which was clearly repugnant.

"In point of fact, I sent Giovanni to Collaquila to keep him out of reach of the Press.... until the Church's intentions with regard to his sister's case are made public. It is imperative that Press interest in the boy is not misguided...imperative to protect him from hacks who might....who would...make capital out the tragic deaths which befell his father, his brother, his Aunt and of course his sister....they could, once they started digging, exaggerate, for example, the importance of Giovanni's brief betrothal to a young lady who, as it so happens, is presently residing with his family in Milignano."

Fahy maintained his silence. He was waiting for Pantaleone to say why Giovanni was no longer serving as a curate in the parish of Collaquila. Cardinal Roccaravindola had been correct about the Bishop of Venafro. Pantaleone was second to none when it came to winding facts into a delicate tracery of the finest

193

sophistry. Fahy hesitated to use the word 'devious' to describe the Bishop's behaviour. The word tortuous would have been more appropriate.

"Unfortunately, my dear Monsignore, in point of fact, most unfortunately, Giovanni encountered a problem with Collaquila's Undertaker. The wretched man harboured a grudge against Giovanni's father for some business transaction which went wrong years ago in Glasgow.... you know about Silvio Bartolomeo's PFN[1] background?"

Fahy made no reply. Any information the Bishop had to offer about Lucrezia Bartolomeo's father, over and above what he already knew, could wait.

"Of course you do. This Undertaker fellow, by name, Staffieri Raffaele, was refused a visa to the United States and blamed Silvio Bartolomeo for leaking information about his criminal activities when he lived and operated in London."

"Your Grace, with all due respect *...and there isn't much of it left...* what exactly did Giovanni say or do in Collaquila to merit his removal? Silvio Bartolomeo's behaviour in Scotland is well documented. In this respect, the British Home Office has been most cooperative when our Nuncio in London made the necessary enquiries. Currently, the Cardinal Ponens and I are investigating Silvio Bartolomeo's behaviour in Sarzana.....where Roberto was born. We now have reason to believe that Giovanni's father was one of the ring-leaders in the rioting which took place there in 1923."

Fahy could see he was ruffling Pantaleone's feathers as he began to churn out what he knew about Silvio Bartolomeo.

"In point of fact, I wasn't aware of Silvio Bartolomeo's activities in Sarzana. But, to be frank, I cannot understand what this has to do with Lucrezia Bartolomeo."

".... *in point of fact my eye and Molly Malone*. In point of fact, Your Grace, you yourself brought Silvio Bartolomeo's name into

194

our discussion when I was looking for an answer as to why Giovanni was no longer serving as a curate in Collaquila. But I don't deny that the Servant of God's father will be part of my investigations into her family background. No stone will be left unturned. All must be revealed which has to be revealed about her family and friends before Lucrezia Bartolomeo's case, as a Servant of God, can be processed to a satisfactory conclusion. This means knowing exactly what happened in Collaquila. So, with all due respect, Your Grace, may I ask you, again, to inform me what Giovanni Bartolomeo did or said in Collaquila."

Fahy said no more. There was no need. Pantaleone had finally realised that with Monsignore Konrad Schmalzgruber out of the equation, he could no longer hope to influence the Congregation of Sacred Right's decision to proceed with Lucrezia Bartolomeo's case. It was time to admit defeat.

"Giovanni assaulted Collaquila's Undertaker.....within an inch of his life....in full view of witnesses following the most extreme of provocations. His assault, no matter the said provocations, made Giovanni's position in Collaquila untenable. There, you have it now Monsignore, to the letter, chapter and verse."

"Have civil charges been submitted to the Procurator by the local Police?"

"Charges were withdrawn by the Undertaker, Raffaele Staffieri before I had Giovanni removed two days after the assault. The request for withdrawal of the charges was made by the parish priest and conceded forthwith by Staffieri. In full view, I must say, of those who had heard the said provocations and witnessed the attack."

"Should Giovanni not have been suspended as the Laws of the Church demand? And, more importantly, may I ask why Cardinal Roccaravindola was not informed of the situation?"

"In point of fact, I fully intend to inform the Cardinal Ponens...*small wonder the British found the pig-headed Irish so intractable*...once I finally decide to make Giovanni's transfer permanent. Under normal circumstances, any such incidents of assault would be dealt with at Diocesan level. However, since he is the brother of Lucrezia Bartolomeo, it naturally behoves me, in the circumstances, to inform the Cardinal Ponens when next we meet of Giovanni's unfortunate misdemeanour. But feel free to inform the Cardinal beforehand if it pleases you so to do."

Bishop Lorenzo Cataldo Pantaleone was uncharacteristically flustered. He had underestimated Monsignor Fiachre Fahy. He was finding the Irishman less than courteous in failing to show him the respect due to a man in his position. He would seek him out when he became a Cardinal and put him in his place. His retribution would be merciless.

Monsignor Fahy surveyed the Bishop's discomfort impassively. He knew he was dealing with a dissembler. Which meant that all submissions hitherto made by the unscrupulous Bishop Cataldo Lorenzo Pantaleone to the Congregation of Sacred Rights had to be re-examined with the greatest of care. Nevertheless, the Bishop could not be completely marginalised. Fahy still needed the former's cooperation.

"I cannot comment on what occurred in Collaquila until I have completed my investigations and spoken to the parties and witnesses concerned. This means that I will have to visit Collaquila as soon as possible. I intend speaking to Collaquila's Brigadier....and the Procuratore in Cassino, to find out if the matter reached his ears officially or unofficially. In these matters your help will be invaluable. All the more so, because, together, we will, of necessity, be going over the ground covered by Monsignor Konrad Schmalzgruber. May I inform His Eminence that I will have your fullest cooperation? I must add, Your Grace that your reports and those of my predecessor have been invaluable and will be used as a point of departure in my investigations."

"How can I be of service, Monsignor?" Pantaleone sounded genuine enough. But Fahy believed the Bishop was being as sincere as a hangman's apology to the condemned before he sprung the scaffold's trapdoor.

"Thank you, Your Grace, for your kind cooperation. In Milignano, I intend speaking to the parishioners who remained behind during the artillery exchanges between the Germans and the Allies."

"As you please, Monsignore....as you please....though I don't see the point. Lucrezia Bartolomeo's martyrdom is universally undisputed by the good people of Milignano who have nothing but respect and sympathy for the tragedies which have afflicted the Bartolomeo family ....including what happened to Giovanni in Collaquila."

"Nevertheless, I must interview everyone known to be connected with the Servant of God, from the time she arrived in Milignano to the time she met her tragic end some four years year later. Your report on the circumstances of her death is based on the hearsay of four women, namely the Borelli sisters. Hardly sufficient, wouldn't you agree, Your Grace?" Pantaleone, infuriated by Fahy's assertion, held his tongue with great difficulty.

"I intend therefore to question....no, interrogate...Don Pietro regarding his relationship with the Bartolomeo family and hope to discover why Bianchina and Lucrezia Bartolomeo were not evacuated to Frosinone with all the other women and children in the parish of Santa Maria Maggiore."

"If you must, you must, Monsignore. In point of fact, I can see no benefit in dredging up details of Don Pietro's past. My own report comprehensively deals with the matter..."

"Yes, yes, yes!" This time Fahy made no attempt to hide his irritation. "The Cardinal Ponens thinks there should be a closer examination of Bianchina Bartolomeo's character....the custodian of the Servant of God. In this respect, I must discover why Silvio Bartolomeo saw fit to entrust his daughter's welfare to Bianchina Bartolomeo if he was aware of his sister's alleged indiscretion with Milignano's parish priest. The Cardinal Ponens thinks

Bianchina Bartolomeo is a key figure in any assessment of Lucrezia Bartolomeo's worthiness to be honoured by the Church."

"In point of fact, Monsignore, it's all in my report, Monsignore Fahy, it's all in my report."

"On the contrary, Your Grace, the emphasis in your report is on Don Pietro's defects as a parish priest rather than on the merits or otherwise of the other party involved, namely Bianchina Bartolomeo, in the unfortunate relationship....assuming there was a relationship.... and that this relationship was sexual. How long did the alleged affair last? The report doesn't say. Were there any witnesses? The report doesn't say. Aspects which are glossed over in all of my predecessor's preliminary reports, which, as it so happens, read like copies of your own reports. But as Postulator, I can make no assumptions. Facts are paramount, not assumptions."

"My prostate tells me it's time for a break."

Fahy made no objection to the Bishop's abrupt request for a pause in the proceedings; even if he believed the reason was opportunistic and contrived. Nevertheless, the temporary absence of Pantaleone gave him a chance to study his notebook and tick off areas already discussed.

Two important areas had still to be covered: who were the American soldiers who had arranged the funerals for Lucrezia and Bianchina Bartolomeo? Who were the women who had prepared the bodies for burial?

Before discussions resumed, Monsignor Fahy requested the presence of Giovanni Bartolomeo.

"........in point of fact, Monsignore, there is in my view a simple reason why the Americans took an interest in Lucrezia. Like Giovanni, she spoke English. As did her aunt, even if it was somewhat fractured. Bianchina was, if nothing else, over-protective with Lucrezia, as I'm sure Giovanni will attest."

"Yes indeed, Monsignore, my father used to joke that they were like Conjoined Twins. Aunt Bianchina never let Lucrezia out of her sight from the moment she arrived in Scotland after my mother died. My father had no qualms about leaving Lucrezia in her care when he took me with him on my first visit to Italy, fifteen years ago."

"Thank you, Giovanni. I'm sure Monsignore Fahy will agree it's highly unlikely your aunt behaved any differently when your father sent them over here shortly before war was declared. From what I understand, Lucrezia was a quiet girl and unaware of how beautiful she was. The image of her mother I'm led to believe. She had, I am also led to believe, a schoolgirl's crush on her father's friend, Artemio Ferrara. In this respect, we have it on record that her guardian, Bianchina Bartolomeo, made it known to all that Lucrezia was spoken for and that Artemio Ferrara was the man in question."

"It's all true, Monsignore. It was no secret my father would have welcomed Artemio into the family. He did nothing to discourage the admiration Lucrezia had for his friend, despite the age difference of some twenty years or more."

"I know the Monsignore doesn't like assumptions, but I'm sure Giovanni would agree that his father might have asked Artemio Ferrara to keep an eye on both daughter and sister when they were in Milignano. This would account for Signor Ferrara's frequent visits to Milignano before he took refuge in the Abbey of Montecassino, for reasons I have yet to discover."

"You might also like to know, Monsignore, that Artemio's brother, Stefano, attended my Ordination last year. In fact, you will meet him later this evening. He's staying with Don Pietro. Stefano Ferrara runs the family wine business in Bolzano and organised a wine-tasting here in Venafro last Tuesday."

The Bishop gave Fahy one of his characteristic fixed smiles. He was pleased to have neatly turned the conversation to polite inconsequentialities in which he was a skilled performer. He objected to the Irishman's fixation for incontrovertible facts.

"Do you like wine, Monsignore?" Bishop Pantaleone's rictus smile was once again in evidence as he changed the subject.

"I'm no expert on wine, Your Grace. My favourite tipples are whiskey and Guinness. I leave comments on wine to my friend Seamus O'Fainnaide who is considered a connoisseur in such matters."

"An oenophile like his friend Cardinal Roccaravindola, would you say?"

The Bishop was fishing for information but Fahy refused to comment on anything which could be construed as a criticism of Cardinal Roccaravindola's reputation as a bon viveur.

"Well, no matter. But I'll send Ippolito a few bottles of the pre-war Santa Maddalena that Stefano Ferrara brought last week. I know they will be a welcome addition to his well-stocked cellar. A wine which no doubt will remind him of those balmy days when he wined and dined at the official State Banquets attended by the Duce and our Emperor-King. In point of fact, it's the wine we drank at Giovanni's ordination dinner.

"Monsignore," said the Bishop changing the subject abruptly, "for as long as you are here, you will be my guest. This will give you the opportunity of getting to know Giovanni. Not to mention all the others on your must-see list. An extensive one from what I gather this morning."

"Thank you, Your Grace. I accept your kind offer. But, before doing so, I must contact the Hotel Pavonello in Cassino where I've checked-in until Monday morning."

"The owner is a friend of mine. I'll speak to him about your reservation and have your luggage sent here. But in point of fact, I think you have something else on your mind? Am I right in saying so, Caro Monsignore?"

"You are as ever perceptive, Your Grace. I was wondering why

Ferrara is staying with Don Pietro rather than at the *Pensione Borelli* where his brother stayed whenever he visited Milignano."

"In point of fact, Stefano Ferrara intended staying with Giovanni's Aunt and Uncle but they already have a young lady staying with them. It was Stefano Ferrara's decision not to stay with the Borelli sisters. I have no idea why. Perhaps Don Pietro will shed some light on the matter? Don Pietro has invited Stefano to join Milignano's pilgrimage to Monte Cassino Abbey where his brother Artemio died during the bombing. It leaves tomorrow morning. Giovanni's going too. Why not join the pilgrimage? Most of the women on your *must-see* list will be in the party.

"Meanwhile, I'll leave you with Giovanni while I attend to matters requiring my personal attention. No doubt Giovanni will invite you to sample his Aunt's superb cuisine at dinner this evening? I'll have Michele Verrecchia, another one on your *must- see* list, standing by to take both of you there ….and back again."

Bishop Pantaleone nodded his head with apparent satisfaction, his face beaming with a fixed smile until he closed the study door behind him. Then his expression changed to one of malevolent disdain. *"Sanctimonious Irish Parvenu,"* he muttered to himself. He had underestimated the intemperate Irishman. But all was not lost. He would put him in his place. He could only do this, logically enough, by being seen to be cooperative, in order to assuage the suspicions of the Postulator's Grey Eminence in Rome. Once the Process of Beatification began, the Irishman would no longer have a locus within the Congregation of Rites. He would deliver his *coup de grace* when he became a Cardinal.

"It's a pleasure speaking the language of our Anglo-Saxon masters, Giovanni. I take it you don't mind switching....unless you have the Irish?"

"Some schoolboy French, but no Erse and happy to settle for

201

English albeit with a Scottish accent."

"It's not that I mind speaking Italian. In fact, I love it, even if it's a strain minding my Ps and Qs when I'm with intellects like His Grace."

"I share the feeling, Monsignor...." "Please call me Fiachre, Giovanni ...like Roberto used to do."

"Fiachre, then it is...I too know what it means to mind the Ps and the Qs. It was how I felt when I arrived here after the war. Always terrified of making mistakes. Made me tongue-tied at times. But tell me why you are planning to leave on Monday. Why so soon?"

"For no reason other than that old Italian proverb: *a visit's just like fish. After three days it stinks*. But there's no limit on the number of three day visits I care to make. Just you sit yourself where I was sittin', while I try the Bishop's chair. Not that I see meself as a Bishop. Didn't see meself as a Monsignore either for that matter, but there you have it: *God moves in mysterious ways, His wonders to perform, He plants his footsteps on the sea, and rides upon the storm*. A 'phone call from me friend Seamus enquirin' about Roberto was all it took to set the ball rollin'. And here we are now glory be, united by a Providential interest in your brother."

Monsignor Fahy's relaxed conversation confirmed Giovanni's initial impression of the affable Irishman. He could understand why Roberto spoke so highly of him in his weekly letter from Adelaide. The Monsignor's arrival in Rome was indeed providential. Giovanni was sure that with Fiachre Fahy at the helm, Lucrezia's cause was in safe hands.

"Do you remember this?" Giovanni asked, placing a make-shift cross, made from two pencils and a boot lace, on the Bishop's desk.

"Sweet Star of the Sea as me friend Seamus would say. How could I forget somethin' I made meself? I went for days without a lace on me left boot. Ten short years ago...seems like yesterday. I can still see Roberto, as plain as I can see you now: sittin' in the hospital, no more than a sick bay with four beds, scarcely having the strength to swat the flies and mosquitoes. I can still hear his breathless coughs. After the Arandora sank, he was in the water for hours before rescue arrived. And what do the Brits do? Instead of sending' him to the nearest hospital, to their eternal shame, they pack him into the murky hold of the Dunera Prison Ship, lungs fillin' with pus and send him all the way to Australia. Diabolical it was!"

"I think you will be pleased to know that Roberto was carrying your make-shift cross in his breast pocket when he died. As you know, Fiachre, his letters were censored. but Roberto was able to tell me what the Aussie Military wanted me to know Namely, that when he was examined on arrival at Port Adelaide, Doctors discovered he had *Silent Pneumonia*. This meant they were accepting no responsibility for his condition and passed the buck to the British Home Office in London."

"I tried many times, to no avail, to have Roberto transferred to a civilian hospital in Adelaide. Permission from the Home Office in London never came.....hardly surprisin' from heathens who approved the execution of injured Irish patriots propped up in wheelchairs.

"Roberto never stopped broodin' over his treatment on the Dunera. He refused to go into detail. And it goes without sayin' that he worried about you and his 'wee sister' which is how he referred to Lucrezia."

"Roberto never said anything directly about the Dunera because he couldn't. But he often talked about a book you lent him 'The Count of Monte Cristo'. Of how its hero was locked up in the Château D'If.... plotting revenge against the men responsible for putting him there. After what happened in Newcastle, I suppose he might have been trying to tell me something."

"Easy to say with a fair degree of hindsight, Giovanni. Maybe we underestimated him and maybe he overestimated your ability to read between the lines. We'll never know for sure one way or the other. Even so, we shouldn't be blamin' ourselves for what happened in Newcastle. You know, Giovanni, I used to worry meself sick. Punishin' meself for not bein' able to get closer to Roberto and help him to make peace with his demons. During all the time he spent in the Camp, he must have been like Montecristo, nursing his wrath to keep it warm, if I can borrow a line from Scotland's answer to Oliver Goldsmith[1]. As an Irishman, I should have recognised the extent of Roberto's suffering.

"However, to be sure, God will be merciful to Roberto and grant him all the mercy his soul deserves. I wasn't able to do much for Roberto. Let's see what I can do for his brother and sister. How does that grab you, Giovanni? You don't say much, do you? Plannin' to join the Trappist Monks?"

Giovanni laughed at the absurdity of the suggestion which he had often heard from Don Agostino during his stint in Collaquila. He was tempted to say that Fiachre Fahy did enough talking for both of them, but felt the better of it.

"I'm just glad to have put a face to the priest who was kind to my brother." Giovanni was close to tears as he spoke. Memories came flooding back of how he had felt when identifying Roberto's body in Newcastle's Police Mortuary. With some effort, he managed to control his emotions

"To be sure Giovanni, let your tears flow. I have to say, it came as a shock to me when I found you here in Venafro. God moves in mysterious ways indeed. But tell me, how long have you been here?"

Fahy asked his question knowing the answer. He knew that when Giovanni regained composure he would answer with characteristic precision, giving him the opportunity of responding with some levity. He was not to be disappointed.

"I've been with the Bishop, here in Venafro, for one month and twenty days to be exact."

"One month and twenty days of House Arrest, includin' promotion for unpriestly behaviour in Collaquila? Hardly punitive is it, Giovanni?" Giovanni looked at the Monsignor with surprise before smiling broadly on realising that he was being teased.

"Forgive me Irish sense of humour, Giovanni. In my view, sending you to Collaquila was part of His Great Design for you and Lucrezia. Look at it this way Giovanni: if you hadn't knocked the stuffin' out of Collaquila's Undertaker, I wouldn't have met you here today, and if I hadn't met your brother in Australia and gone to my friend Seamus in Rome then he would never have got in touch with Cardinal Roccaravindola who would never have contacted Bishop Pantaleone. And Bishop Pantaleone would never have been able to make the connection with you, your brother and your sister and his bleedin' Red Hat. But that's as far it goes. I mean to do my job without fear or favour."

"That's good enough for me, Fiachre. I believe you will do what's to be done with integrity. To do what's best, not just for me or Bishop Pantaleone or even Cardinal Roccaravindola, but for my sister Lucrezia, may she rest in peace. I really believe, with all my heart, that your appointment as Monsignor Schmalzgruber's successor is providential... the be all and end all of the Great Design you were talking about."

"Well then me boyo, my journey on behalf of the Servant of God begins today when you take me to Milignano for dinner with your old flame. Your brother never mentioned he had been engaged to your fiancée..... but he never stopped talkin' about Milignano ... ...like Seamus and meself always going on about Kilfenora County Claire bein' some kind o' earthly paradise, where we hope to spend our retirement. But I mustn't tempt providence, me with a bad ticker and all."

"You're right, Fiachre, about the risks of tempting providence.

205

My Dad and Roberto planned to join Lucrezia after the war....
and I was expected to follow after graduation and marry Irma in
the Santa Maria Maggiore. I take it that you'll be starting your
journey of discovery in Milignano with Don Pietro?"

"More or less, but I'll start my journey, literally and
metaphorically, with your driver, Michele Verrecchia. Reading
between the lines of Konrad Schmalzgruber reports, Michele
seems to be the eyes and ears of Milignano. Of the good, the bad
and the make-believe.

"I understand Michele knew your father from their schooldays.
But while I'm with Don Pietro, I want you to get Michele to help
organise meetin's with the women who prepared Lucrezia and
your aunt for burial. I need to find out why voices regardin'
Bianchina Bartolomeo's death are so muted. After all is said and
done, she suffered the same fate as your sister."

"When I arrived from Scotland I also believed their
circumstances were similar. It was Don Pietro who told me that
Bishop Pantaleone was pursuing recognition of a case which
excluded my aunt in favour of Lucrezia. Maybe 'recognition' isn't
the right word....but I got the impression it was something
Bishop Pantaleone was adamant about. At first I didn't feel
confident enough to ask Don Pietro why my aunt's case had been
marginalised. Before I entered the Pontificale, I plucked up the
courage to press him for an explanation. He said he would think
about it.

"A few days later Don Pietro asked me to join him, for the first
and last time as it so happened, on his daily constitutional to the
Campo Santo, where his parents are buried. Near Lucrezia and
Bianchina as it so happens.

"It began to rain as soon after we set off, but he didn't seem to
notice or care. By the time we returned, soaked to the skin, he
had told me the whole story."

*Pietro Verrecchia and Bianchina Bartolomeo had been
sweethearts during their elementary school days. Pietro was the*

206

brightest in the class. At the insistence of the parish priest, his parents agreed to send him to the Abbey Boarding School in Montecassino, where free Secondary education was available to gifted boys with or without a vocation for the priesthood.

Less than a year later, Bianchina's parents died in a cholera epidemic which followed the 1908 earthquake and days after her thirteenth birthday she was left with the responsibility of raising her younger brothers Silvio and Ettore. A responsibility which put paid to her dreams of marrying Pietro Verrecchia.

As for Pietro Verrecchia, taking into account Bianchina Bartolomeo's responsibility regarding her brothers and to please his tutors and mother, he took Holy Orders although their affection for each other remained as strong as it ever was.

By the time Don Pietro returned to Milignano as parish priest some ten years later, the marriage-that-never- was had become part of village folklore.

Giovanni paused. He had reached a critical point in Don Pietro's story. He needed to think clearly before articulating his thoughts.

"Don Pietro was a little flustered at this point in his account of what happened. His embarrassment was heart-rending, but he felt he had to tell me exactly what happened.

Bianchina was in the Santa Maria Maggiore changing the altar cloth. She had volunteered to do the washing and pressing of the sacred linens. That morning she was upset because her brother had asked her to look after his daughter after his wife died. Bianchina didn't want to leave Milignano but felt sorry for her brother who had always been the apple of her eye. Her tears kindled compassion and regret in Don Pietro when she told him of her planned departure. One thing led to another and the impropriety took place in the sacristy much to their mutual shame. Bianchina left for Scotland two days later, vowing never again to return.

"I'm sure Don Pietro will confirm what you've said, Giovanni.

207

Now, what can you tell me about the Americans who arranged the funerals in Don Pietro's absence? I understand Bishop Pantaleone wrote to the soldiers involved but got no reply. I can say, however, that Cardinal Roccaravindola is presently making enquiries on my behalf through the Vatican Diplomatic Corps to verify if the three soldiers concerned survived when they moved out of Milignano. If they did survive, I intend to hear what they have to say. If the Bishop has no objections, you could come with me to the United States. If you care to that is.... and the Bishop gives permission. I know you can afford it. A priest of some considerable means I understand."

"I have no money problems if that's what you mean," replied Giovanni, "as you obviously know. And no doubt you might like to know that, besides my father's money, I also inherited Lucrezia, Roberto and Aunt Bianchina's money. And yes I would love to go to America. I'm sure His Grace will give his permission."

"I'm sure he will, but everything depends on Cardinal Roccaravindola's enquiries at the Pentagon. Now tell me about tomorrow's visit to Montecassino. I understand Artemio Ferrara's brother is going."

"Artemio Ferrara is buried in the Abbey with other civilian casualties. Artemio, as you know, was my father's friend and business partner, which is probably one of the reasons why his brother Stefano came to my Ordination. I gather Stefano has a private matter to discuss with the Abbot which is why he accepted Don Pietro's invitation to join the pilgrimage."

"It seems his brother was temptin' providence by seekin' refuge in Montecassino a few days before the Armistice. God moves in mysterious ways indeed. But, to be honest, I'm looking forward to meetin' Stefano Ferrara tomorrow.

"There seems to be no end to what happens in this great metropolis of yours: what with Vintage Wine Tastings, an Archaeological Society, a Pantaleone Museum of Roman

Antiquities and a French Military Cemetery, is there anything left of interest in the Bishop's Diocese?" Fahy's flippancy flew over Giovanni's head.

"Come to think of, Fiachre," said Giovanni seriously, "there's a painting in the *Chiesa Del Purgatorio* which, according to His Grace, is Fedele Fischetti's *Madonna and Child*. However, for some reason, His Grace won't listen to my advice and have it authenticated. I don't have the expertise to gainsay anything the Bishop has to say on Fine Arts, but I've looked into the painting's history and I'm convinced it's the work of Fischetti's son, Alessandro."

Monsignor Fiachre Fahy had never heard of Fidele Fischietti or for that matter of his son Alessandro. He smiled at Giovanni's modesty regarding his knowledge of Italian Artists. He liked Giovanni Bartolomeo. He was highly intelligent and well-educated. The qualities which had persuaded Bishop Pantaleone to take him under his wing, No doubt Giovanni's intelligence and personal wealth would serve as indispensable props for His Grace's ambition.

Chapter Twenty Two

Milignano's Annual Pilgrimage to the Abbey of Monte Cassino, Sunday 19th October 1951

The recitation of The Mysteries of the Rosary[1] was well under way when Monsignor Fahy and Don Giovanni Bartolomeo boarded Michele's bus at the Venafro's Frosinone-Cassino intersection.

Their arrival did not interrupt the prayers. Don Pietro, sitting behind the driver, with Stefano Ferrara in the window seat beside him, pointed over his shoulder towards the wood slatted bench reserved for them at the rear. The gentlest of taps on Michele's shoulder was all it took to set the bus off with a bone-shaking shudder. As the bus bounced and swayed over the pitted roadway, the two priests pulled and hauled their way from bench to bench, with Giovanni nodding greetings to the faces he recognised.

The relentless and uninterrupted recitation of the Faithful continued, as ever oblivious to Michele driving. Their fervour untroubled by the bus' speed along an uneven and rising road, unperturbed by the gnashing and grinding of the lower gears which erupted each time Michele took his preferred option of speeding around bends with characteristic determination rather than losing precious momentum by slowing down.

Don Pietro always insisted that the journey to the Abbey of Montecassino was an integral part of the pilgrimage. In no way was it to be undertaken as a sightseeing opportunity. Rosary beads were mandatory. This imposition had weighed heavily on a reluctant Stefano Ferrara, sitting with the allegedly indisposed Rosaria's rosary clasped in his hand. Don Pietro's abuse of the dictum, *when in Rome, do as the Romans do*, had put paid to any objection Stefano might have had about carrying a rosary which belonged to Don Pietro's sex-starved Housekeeper.

Stefano Ferrara's inclusion on the pilgrimage, traditionally the preserve of women and the clergy, had raised no eyebrows in Milignano. Michele had spread the news of Stefano Ferrara's reasons for a return visit to Milignano ….. recalling that the latter had been a guest at Don Giovannino's ordination and was the brother of the man who had taken refuge in the Abbey six months before the bombing ...... brothers who were both under investigation by the Irish Monsignore from Rome sent by Papa Pacelli: to make Don Giovannino's sister a saint; to clear up the turmoil Don Giovannino had left in Collaquila (where he dished out a merited beating to a disreputable Undertaker) and to secure Don Giovannino's promotion as the Bishop of Venafro's Secretary. The same Bishop who had tried to have Don Pietro sacked over you-know-what with you-know-who .... may she rest in peace....the same Bishop who had permitted the French to bury Moroccan degenerates in Venafro.

The Way of the Cross...... Milignano's pilgrims had reached the fourth Sorrowful Mystery of the Rosary when they caught their first glimpse of the Abbey's ivory coloured shell in the distant hills. In the limpid October morning sun, it sat imperiously on a defoliated platform of volcanic rock looking like a gigantic wedding cake.

But *The Eye of God*, as St Benedict called his monastery, was not the only distraction for the faithful concentrating, as best they could, on the repetitive prayers and responses led by a dogged Don Pietro. Particularly when Michele reached the peripheries of the bombed city of Cassino and had to slow down to avoid the boulders and rubble strewn here and there over the road. Prayers faded into silence when the bus began to snake its way into the chaotic womb of the construction site from which would rise the new town of Cassino.

Working on the Sabbath until noon was not an option for tradesmen and labourers paid by the hour and day. Their faces, hands, caps, bandannas, clothes and boots, all generously splattered or caked with dried cement was proof enough of work done that day.

Milignano's pilgrims, silent and agog, stared at a motley collection of tents and makeshift shacks squatting in the background. In the squalor of these makeshift dwellings lived wives and women of the construction workers with their respective brats.

Via Casalina, Cassino

"There are two ways up to the Abbey. The first begins at the traffic lights you see in front you. It covers a distance of about eight kilometres," Don Pietro paused for effect before continuing, "For those who choose to walk, there's the ancient Santa Scolastica[1] mule track which starts at the drinking well behind our bus.

"My parishioners always take the arduous mule track which they feel is part of the pilgrimage. If this mule-track was good enough for the monks and their mules, then it's good enough for us. Take your time. Stay close and climb in Indian file behind the Borelli sisters who know the way. It's half past eight. All going well we'll meet for lunch in the Abbey's main car park no later than the noon Angelus Bell. Whatever you do and wherever you go after lunch, remember our bus for the return journey to Milignano leaves at four o'clock."

When Don Pietro re-boarded the bus, he found Michele sitting behind the wheel, smoking another of his black market Chesterfields, neutralising the smell of perspiration left by the women. Behind him sat the forlorn figure of Ferrara, his eyes fixed on Irma's buttocks as she made her way up the mule track.

At the rear of the bus, Giovanni and Fiachre were lamenting the fact that there were as yet no transatlantic passenger flights from either Naples' Capodichino or Rome's Ciampino. As things stood, a sea voyage to New York was more than likely. A prospect which horrified Giovanni, given the nightmare of the Arandora Star disaster and the horrors endured by his brother on the Dunera.

Don Pietro was explaining the banalities of the one-way traffic system to the Abbey. Something to do with faulty calibrations in the first two of the seven horseshoe bends under construction when he was brusquely interrupted by a verbal volley from a frustrated Ferrara.

"You of all people, Don Pietro, should have been advising some of the women to stay with us, namely the less hardy, and those not used to toiling in the fields with the sun bearing on their backs and heads hour after hour after hour."

The sharpness of Ferrara's comments pricked Don Pietro's susceptibilities. Don Pietro disliked criticism, warranted or unwarranted. Especially when it questioned his organising skills, of which he was extremely proud. In particular, he disliked criticism coming from Northerners like Ferrara.

However, before putting Ferrara in his place, he felt he had to get rid of his nephew, Michele, the champion of Milignano's gossiping classes. "Do me a favour Michele and find out when we are likely to get the green light to the Abbey. That's a good lad."

Michele made a show of being pleased to comply with his uncle's request. He would have loved to have seen and heard Mr High and Mighty from the South Tyrol being put in his place. Now, he would just have to invent the details when giving a report to his cronies in Milignano, of how the sleazy South Tyrolean pisspot had received his just desserts for having the gall to challenge Don Pietro's authority.

As soon as his nephew was out of earshot, Don Pietro rounded on Ferrara, his voice as venomous as a nose-horned viper when hissing its rage.

"However arduous and exhausting the climb surely is, Dottor Ferrara," Don Pietro fumed, spraying the latter's face with saliva, "my parishioners, having come here as penitents, will tackle it willingly with courage, fortitude and determination. A hardship they are pleased to endure to obtain the spiritual benefits the Church offers to those who undertake a pilgrimage like today's." The extent of Don Pietro's fury stifled Stefano Ferrara's into silence.

"As a Northerner you obviously don't or can't understand that this hardship is an integral part any pilgrimage undertaken south of the Tyrol Valleys ..." at which point Don Pietro added, with gratuitous malice, "and let me remind you, Dottor Ferrara, that you are here today neither as a pilgrim nor as a champagne salesman. You are here as a guest of provincial yokels like us from the so-called backwaters of Southern Italy......"

Ferrara said nothing after Don Pietro had vented his spleen. The former's body language creating the impression that he had been put in his place like an errant schoolboy. In reality, Don Pietro's outrage had given Stefano food for illogicalities...... Irma was one of the penitent pilgrims Don Pietro was blathering about..... therefore it was reasonable to suppose that she could be seeking forgiveness.....for something she hadn't done........ and for something she wanted to do. With him in both cases.

Ferrara's illogicalities gave way to excitement when he spotted Irma's swaying buttocks on the Santa Scolastica Mule Track. A light breeze caught the hem of her dress showing much of her bare and sinuous legs above the knee.

While Don Pietro sat in silent contemplation, apparently satisfied with his retribution, Ferrara's eyes were fixed on Irma's thighs as she climbed beyond his line of vision. Missing what for him would have been a moment of ecstasy when a whispering wind lifted her frock to reveal lily-white underwear.

214

Stefano asked himself if the old man sitting next to him knew his interest in Irma was far from platonic. Don Pietro seemed to be doing everything that could be done to keep them apart. Like boarding him in his dreary presbytery where he had to put up with the rustic cooking of his buxom housekeeper and the odious attentions of her precocious brat.

Like making sure Irma sat nowhere near him during dinner last night; like making sure he sat nowhere near her on Michele's bus. Giving him a window seat as far away as possible from the intoxicating fragrances of her voluptuous body.

Then, like a bolt from the blue, it dawned on Ferrara. He was astonished he hadn't thought of it sooner: he had made a bigger impression on Irma at the Ordination Dinner than he had dared hope. Had it been an impression big enough to send her running in despair to Don Pietro's Confessional Box to seek absolution for her adulterous yearnings?

It made more sense of the stupid story the old goat had told about a bell during last night's dinner. It made more sense of Don Pietro's surprising invitation to stay in his presbytery rather than with Ettore and Maria where Irma was staying.

In Stefano's fevered mind, it all added up. It gave substance to the hitherto vague impression he had that there was a conspiracy afoot to keep him from being alone with Irma Pacitti. Why else had she been chaperoned wherever and whenever they met during his stay in Milignano? If it wasn't Maria Bartolomeo, the Postmistress or Don Pietro's shifty Housekeeper, then it was one or other or all of the gorgons whose company he had been forced to endure at the ordination dinner. Not for one moment did he believe the story that Irma had to be chaperoned to protect her from the undesirable attention of her estranged husband, the legendary one-legged goalkeeper of Milignano.

The more he thought about it, the more Stefano was convinced of the reasons behind the infantile story about the bell he heard during last night's dinner in Ettore's house. And what other reason could there have been for the unpleasantness which sprang from a light-hearted discussion on the relative merits of Italian and German Lyric Operas?

When this discussion was winding down, the Irish Monsignor mischievously suggested that the late and great Irish tenor, John McCormack[1], was a better singer than Gigli[2]. The Irishman had taken the lack of reaction as agreement. He was astonished that Opera Lovers could hold that a living legend like Gigli could be unfavourably compared to a dead singer whose only claim to fame was that he could sing twenty-four wonderful notes in the one breath.

To make matters worse, the Irish mischief maker suggested that his compatriot was a heaven-sent gift to Verdi's *Rigoletto*[3], as opposed to a second-rate Titta Ruffo [4]. Remarks which the Irishman knew had no substance because McCormack was a tenor while Tita Ruffo was a baritone. However, these remarks caused Don Pietro to betray a deadly dislike of *Rigoletto.*

Like a man possessed, Don Pietro had ranted about the crude and vulgar immorality of the Duke of Mantua's attitude to women. Married women in particular. The inference that he, the Beau of Bolzano, was like the licentious *Duca di Mantova*, did not offend Stefano. On the contrary, he felt flattered by the comparison.

However, for the time being, Stefano Ferrara was ready to admit that he had been out-manoeuvred. He should have seen the light while Don Pietro was delivering his *Parable of the Bell.*

Perhaps Bishop Pantaleone could be flattered into having another wine tasting? The promise of a case or two of Mammertino 1951 was sure to massage the Bishop's ego when he discovered it was currently being marketed as Julius Caesar's favourite wine. Come what may, wine-tasting or no wine-tasting, he would have his way with Irma Pacitti. As sure as night followed day, *Fortune favoured the Brave* [5]

However, Stefano Ferrara had an ulterior motive for remaining on the bus with the three priests: he needed their goodwill to make contact with the monks regarding his brother's fate whose name had not been included in their official list of 229 civilian casualties. He needed the support of the three priests if he wanted to discover the reason for this omission. In his will, Artemio Ferrara had left every cent of his considerable wealth to the Benedictine Order. Stefano felt cheated and hoped the Abbot would not only explain his brother's decision but also make restitution.

From what Stefano had read in the *Corriere Della Sera,* the monks were extremely sensitive about the number of civilians killed during the bombing and hostile Press coverage in London and Washington had exacerbated this sensitivity. It held that Papa Pacelli could and should have done more to ensure the evacuation of the civilians who had taken refuge in the Abbey prior to its bombing. Just as the same hostile Press claimed he had done little or nothing to prevent the Jewish Holocaust in Nazi Extermination Camps.

He believed the monks would be all the better disposed to meeting him if he were accompanied by three priests, one of whom had Vatican connections. However, come what may, with or without their support, he was determined to find out why his brother had bought himself a refuge in the Abbey. At his expense.

Fahy's reasons for accepting Don Pietro's invitation to join the pilgrimage were more straightforward than Ferrara's. Fahy was visiting the Abbey as a representative of the Congregation of Sacred Rites. As such, a meeting with the Abbot was guaranteed. He needed to know what, if anything, there was to know about Artemio Ferrara's interest in Lucrezia Bartolomeo. Cardinal Roccaravindola had briefed him on the questions to be asked in order to circumvent, if need be, the confidentiality of the Confessional. And once he delivered the Cardinal's letter to the Abbot, he was sure he would obtain the latter's fullest cooperation.

For his part, Giovanni had been encouraged to join Milignano's pilgrimage by Bishop Pantaleone for two reasons. The first reason was that the Bishop needed someone to keep track on a meddlesome Postulator who was sniffing around as Roccaravindola's bloodhound. The second, was to exploit his interest in illuminated manuscripts, which had recently been returned to the Abbey from the safety of the Benedictine Mother House in Rome.

The Archaeological Society would surely be impressed with the Bishop's paper on '*The Illuminated Manuscripts of Monte Cassino Abbey'.* He would be able to impress members with the fruits of Giovanni's detailed research on the Abbey's 500 incunabula. And during his performance, he would reveal the part he had played in providing packaging materials and transport for their transfer to Rome.

As for Don Pietro, his pilgrimages to the Abbey were a much-needed source of revenue and guaranteed him the warmest of welcomes from the Monks. It was a welcome Ferrara intended to exploit if it helped him meet the Abbot. Somehow, he knew he would have to mollify Don Pietro before he could seek this indispensable support.

"You know, when I come to think of it, Don Pietro, pilgrim penitents make similar sacrifices the world over. In France for example.... my brother told me that while serving in Paris with the Foreign Ministry- its headquarters are close to the Sacre Coeur.- he used to see pilgrims climbing the 300 steps to the Basilica on their knees in all kinds of weather.

"Let me say, Don Pietro, I regret being less than appreciative of the courage and willingness shown by your parishioners' in tackling the mule track route to the Abbey. I should have thought twice before speaking out of turn. To show there are no hard feelings, I would ask a favour of you, Don Pietro ..."

A moment of hesitation followed, before Ferrara drew the anticipated response from Don Pietro. With Christian fortitude,

Don Pietro was about to turn the other cheek.

"A favour you say? Tell me how I can be of assistance? I'm intrigued to know what this favour might be, so don't keep me in suspense, Stefano." Don Pietro looked at Stefano, a vague smile creasing his mouth. He had called Ferrara by his Christian name for the first time since their fraught exchanges during last night's dinner.

During their present exchanges, Giovanni and Fiachre had looked on with misgivings. They believed Stefano to be a glib and shameless liar. However, since Don Pietro appeared to have taken Ferrara's overtures at face value, they braced themselves for more of Stefano's devious machinations.

"Don Pietro I would like you ….. Giovanni and the Monsignore for that matter.... to accompany me when I meet with ...." Stefano looked at the name written on an envelope, "Don Martino Matronola."

"That's the name of the monk I wrote to at Giovanni's request," replied Don Pietro, "Don Martino was the late Abbot Diamare's Secretary and one of the six monks who remained in the monastery despite being advised to leave by Von Weizsacker, the German Ambassador to the Holy See."

"How on earth did the Abbot and his monks survive the bombing?" Fahy asked Don Pietro. He had seen countless photographs of the Abbey flattened by The Flying Fortresses[1] and was surprised that any of the monks had survived the bombardments.

"They were in the crypt below the High Altar," replied Don Pietro. "The one containing the tombs of St Benedict and St. Scolastica."

"With your help, Don Pietro, I hope the monks will agree to see me. Maybe they'll tell me why my brother wasn't listed among the civilian casualties. Something, in my view, that doesn't add up."

219

Giovanni and Fiachre were no longer listening to Ferrara's exchanges with Don Pietro. While Fahy was having a catnap, Giovanni was thinking about how Fiachre would react to his obsession about reading and touching the *Placito Cassinese¹* in his view the most famous document held in the Abbey's Archives. This was what he hoped to do once he had completed his researches for the Bishop's next meeting of the Archaeological Society.

It never crossed Giovanni's mind that his enthusiasm for sharing what he knew about the Placito with Fahy would lead to a misunderstanding when an apparently refreshed Fahy reopened his eyes after his catnap.

"Now that you're awake, Fiachre, I'll fill your head with everything you need to know about the Placito Cassinese." Giovanni stopped in his tracks. A look of displeasure had spread across Fahy's face. He had no idea what had caused Fahy's sudden mood change. When the answer came, it was chastening.

"I know you don't mean to be patronisin'. It's something I refuse to accept from half-baked scholars..... WASP gobshites who have a tendency to underestimate the Irish. Tainted by narrow-mindedness which festers in their Universities ......where you'll find little mention that the Irish language has the oldest vernacular literature in Western Europe."

"I'm sorry, Fiachre, it seems I've offended you. Although I don't quite know how or why."

"Well, for a start, this *Placito Cassinese* you're blathering about is what we dumb Irishmen, refer to as the *Placito Capuano*. A Document which is said to contain the first words recorded in the emerging Italian language of the tenth century." Giovanni said nothing. He felt he had got his just desserts for underestimating Fahy's intellectual capacities. "Generally speaking, Italians never give the Irish credit for St Brendan's discovery of Newfoundland a thousand years before Amerigo Vespucci, Cristoforo Colombo and Marco Polo saw the light of day. But I'll leave the *Navigatio*

Sancti Brendani Abbatis[1] until, appropriately enough, we set sail for the Americas."

Giovanni realised he should have been more circumspect when sharing what he knew about the Placito. Fahy's hyper-sensitivity regarding his Irishness was something he would have to keep in mind in future discussions. The next time he raised the matter he would have done his homework on the *Navigatio Sancti Brendani Abbatis.*

Chapter Twenty Three

The Abbey Basilica of Monte Cassino

At the Sanctuary, nearest the High Altar, dust sheets were removed from a solitary pew by a uniformed Custodian. It had been placed there for the benefit of Abbot Ildefonso Rea, who sat there to view the progress of the reconstruction work. Usually on Sunday afternoons when manual labour was not permitted.

The custodian invited Monsignor Fahy, Don Pietro, Don Giovanni and Dottor Ferrara to accommodate themselves on the Abbot's pew while he delivered letters from Cardinal Roccaravindola and Bishop Pantaleone respectively together with Stefano Ferrara's business card to the Abbot.

Thirty minutes later, they were still waiting to hear if or when Abbot Ildefonso would see one or any of the four visitors. This delay left them with ample time to study the intricacy of the scaffolding which stretched from floor to ceiling around and above the High Altar: five galleries of platforms extending to the walls on either of its sides. The overall effect suggesting the work of a deranged architect.

The High Alter and cupola were obscured by canopies hanging from the platform galleries. A red sanctuary lamp could be seen flickering between the tubular uprights. In acknowledgement of the presence of the Eucharist, the three priests knelt in silence. Not so Stefano Ferrara.

Restless and impatient, Stefano had no intention of kneeling or sitting in what to him was no more than a building site. Where madcap steeplejacks jumped from one platform to the next like demented grasshoppers. The thought that his brother's remains might be buried in the rubble under the concrete floor never occurred to him.

222

Hanging around, while hoping to see the Abbot, made Ferrara feel like the proverbial beggar at the gate. He took some satisfaction in the probability that his arrival had sent the monks running for cover.......*Come what may, I'm not leaving here... until I find out what the hell Artemio was doing in the this mausoleum ......and giving monks what by rights is mine. Things don't add up. I smell a rat if you....*

Stefano Ferrara's malevolence was interrupted by the arrival of a Benedictine whose habit had seen better days. The monk's closely cropped grey-black hair betrayed the approach of late middle age. He smelled vaguely of onions and mothballs. Deposits of dandruff on his cowl gave him the appearance of an impoverished country curate. In an Italian accent betraying his Neapolitan roots, the monk was reading aloud from Stefano Ferrara's business card:

FERRARA WINERIES BOLZANO

SUPPLIERS TO THE PAPACY

MANAGING DIRECTOR

DOTTOR CLAUDIO STEFANO FERRARA

"Dottor Ferrara, your brother often spoke of your business acumen, which he claimed more than matched his own. Forgive the delay in coming to meet you. Abbot Idelfonso had to be briefed on the details regarding your brother's admission and, of course, his tragic death." The monk returned Stefano's card before introducing himself. "Matronola, Martino Matronola." He shook hands with each of the four visitors, starting with Stefano who was nearest. I must inform you all that the Abbot is permitted to meet with visitors on matters of a personal nature to the community." This said, he turned his attention to Fiachre Fahy, "Monsignor Fahy, Abbot Ildefonso will meet with you in your capacity as Postulator. After reading His Eminence's letter, he contacted him on matters he will discuss when you meet. Perhaps you might care to wait in the apse until his Secretary comes for you?"

Fahy nodded in agreement. He guessed Stefano's business card, rather than Roccaravindola's letter, had thrown a stone into a bottomless pool.

Don Martino turned once more to Stefano." Since I had the honour of being present when Brother Artemio was admitted to the Abbey, Abbot Ildefonso thinks it would be right and fitting for me to take you into our confidence." Stefano was flabbergasted. Calling Artemio, Brother, meant that the monks had extorted every cent his brother had in return for the sanctuary they gave him in their doomed monastery.

Exercising consummate diplomacy, Don Martino found the perfect way of removing the superfluous presence of Milignano's parish priest. "Abbot Idelfonso has been made aware of your letter enquiring after Dottor Ferrara's brother for which he thanks you. He also thanks you for once again bringing your parishioners to our Abbey and fully appreciates you will be anxious to re-join them as soon as possible. He asks you to convey to each and all his thanks for what he knows will be their generous contributions to our Building Fund. He hopes that when you return next year, the reconstruction work will have been completed and the Abbey restored to its former glory."

Don Pietro was both relieved and surprised. He felt relieved, not only because young Stefano had been favourably received, but also because he was able to take his leave without appearing to be discourteous. Nevertheless, like Stefano, he too was struck by the news about Artemio apparent vocation.

Having provided Don Pietro with the means of a dignified departure, Don Martino turned his attention to Giovanni. "I know that it was at your request Don Pietro made enquiries about Brother Artemio a few months before you entered the Pontificale. Having read Bishop Pantaleone's letter, Abbot Idelfonso is happy to grant you the freedom of our libraries. My assistant, Don Faustino, will be pleased to escort you there in due course. He will remain at your service and provide you with the necessary requisites to examine those same inconabula[1] which His Grace, Bishop Pantaleone, so jealously helped to despatch to our Mother House in Rome prior to the bombing on February 15th 1944."

As befitted Abbot Ildefonso's heir apparent, Don Martino Matronola concluded the formalities with impressive self-assurance. Before escorting Don Pietro, Giovanni and Stefano from the Basilica, Don Martino exchanged a few more words and a handshake with Monsignor Fahy. This done, he led the three men from the gloomy Basilica into the brightness of the warm October sun and down the semi-circular stairway leading to the Bramante Cloisters [1]. Its surface had been re-laid, for the most part with the granite slabs dislodged by the bombing. The old and the new slabs making it look like a patchwork quilt.

The Bramante Cloisters' Courtyard and Loggia del Paradiso

The Cloisters were enclosed on each side by the reconstructed Bramante Arches which supported the partially completed Loggia Del Paradiso. Still to be added were its balustrades. Clearly seen in the distance from the far end of the Loggia were the Pantano Hills which loomed over the town of Venafro and the communes of Milignano and Collaquila.

Don Martino paused and waited for a moment near the octagonal well at the centre of the Bramante Cloisters Long enough for a monk to approach and stand respectfully by his side. Don Martino turned to Giovanni.

"My assistant, Brother Faustino. Once he has escorted Don Pietro to the entrance garden, he'll take you to our libraries. From His Grace's letter, we understand you were born in Scotland. You might wish to examine the Celtic manuscripts gifted to the Abbey by brother monks from the Iona Community. They spent seven years in the Clonmacnoise Monastery[1] before visiting our Abbey. Afterwards, when you have completed your researches, you might care to join Dottor Ferrara and me in the Students Refectory where we will share the Lord's Bounty."

As he followed Brother Faustino to the library, Giovanni was thinking of what Don Martino had said about the Clonmacnoise Monastery. He would of course mention the matter of the Scottish connection to Fiachre. As tactfully as possible. And certainly not before discussing the possible impact, of Artemio Ferrara's admission to the Benedictine Order on his sister's case for Beatification.

Abbot Idelfonso Rea's Study

".......that's why I had to keep you waiting, my dear Monsignore. Once I read His Eminence's letter, I discussed its content with Don Martino, my predecessor's Secretary. After which I rang His Eminence. And yes, in answer to your question, it was Don

226

Martino who liaised with Ambassador Ciano about Brother Artemio's intentions to join our Order. As we speak, Don Martino is briefing Dottor Ferrara about the how, why and when of his brother's decision to join our Order."

"I understand the need for confidentiality, Abbot Idelfonso. However, I need to know when the notion of joining the Benedictines was first mooted. Timing is important, given Brother Artemio's close association with the Bartolomeo family and in particular with the Servant of God, Lucrezia Bartolomeo."

"According to Brother Artemio, his disenchantment with the Fascist regime, having served it faithfully since the March on Rome [1], started after he arrested the alleged fugitive, Titta Ruffo, for illegally re-entering the country from the United States.

"Signor Ruffo, who I believe is currently living in Florence, had refused to sing in Italy after the assassination of his brother-in-law, Giacomo Matteotti and not before his native land had recovered from its Fascist affliction.

"Strange, is it not Monsignore, that Signor Ruffo should be remembered more for a resounding silence rather than for the exceptional quality of his basso profondo voice.

"An international outcry followed Ruffo's arrest for what was in effect a self-imposed exile. In the wake of this outcry, Brother Artemio felt he was made the scapegoat when the Fascist Government was trying to save face over the arrest. It was the beginning of the end as far as Brother Artemio was concerned." Fahy waited patiently for the Abbot to reveal what else he knew about Artemio Ferrara. Questions he wanted to ask could wait.

"Brother Artemio also told us that he had sent for his trusted friend Silvio Bartolomeo to help deal with Arturo Toscanini's anti-fascist propaganda in Bologna. Signor Toscanini's severe thrashing was signed and sealed when he refused to play the fascist anthem *Giovinezza* in the Teatro Comunale as was prescribed when Mussolini or members of his Inner Cabinet entered a public auditorium. It was an act of calculated defiance from Musical Director Toscanini who had been warned, well in advance, that Foreign Secretary Galeazzo Ciano, and his wife, Mussolini's daughter, would be in joining the audience at some point during the performance."

"That's an interesting development," interrupted Fahy, "since Silvio Bartolomeo was supposed to be in Glasgow at the time."

"According to Cardinal Roccaravindola," the Abbot continued, "it appears that Artemio Ferrara's disillusionment with Mussolini echoed those of his boss, Ciano, whose political ambivalence had enraged Ribbentrop, the German Foreign Minister. We can only assume that Mussolini made his son-in-law Ambassador to the Holy See for his own safety. At least until he buckled under German pressure and had him executed on a trumped-up charge of treason.

"However, Monsignore, I can tell you that it was Ciano, in his capacity as Ambassador to the Holy See, who informed my predecessor of Brother Artemio's spiritual aspirations.

"At the time, we were unaware of the extent of his personal wealth. We knew of course that he had a majority holding in the family wineries which supplied the Vatican and the Royal House of Savoy. We had no idea of the assets he had accumulated from various commercial activities in association with his business partner, the Servant of God's father."

"Was Ferrara's wealth handed over to your Order before his admission?"

"Let me remind you, Monsignore, that Benedictines take a vow of poverty on entering the Order. But, as I've said, we had no idea of the extent of Brother Artemio's vast wealth until he joined our order. Therefore, in answer to your question, his wealth was not taken into consideration when we appraised his request for admission to our Order. However, I must and should say that Brother Artemio's liquid assets made a heaven-sent contribution to our Building Fund when it was most needed."

228

"My dear Abbot Idelfonso, I apologise for my bluntness."

"No need to apologise, my dear Monsignore. These are questions a Postulator must ask and have answered to his satisfaction. No stone can be left unturned in your quest to know all there is to know about everything which concerns, directly or indirectly, the Servant of God, Lucrezia Bartolomeo, the, sister of the young man who is, as we speak, is studying in our Libraries. Working diligently on behalf of the same Bishop who first brought Lucrezia Bartolomeo's case to the attention of the Holy Father.

"So, my dear Monsignore, it is right and fitting that you should know Brother Artemio's made provision for Lucrezia Bartolomeo in his will. The Foreign Office sent our Mother House in Rome a copy of Brother Artemio's last testament. Stefano Ferrara's lawyers having demanded and received possession of the original.

"Allow me to read verbatim the words of the provision relative to the Servant of God: *to the daughter of the late Bartolomeo Silvio ......Bartolomeo Lucrezia.... resident in the parish of Santa Maria Maggiore, Milignano....... a substantial but unspecified sum of money......the amount to be decided at the discretion of the Benedictine Order ......on the occasion of the said Bartolomeo Lucrezia's marriage, ...as and when approved by her guardian, Bartolomeo Bianchina, sister of the late Bartolomeo Silvio.....formerly a resident of Milignano........ Signed and witnessed ....Count Galeazzo Ciano, Italian Ambassador to the Holy See and Count Dino Grandi, President of the Chamber of Fasci etc. etc.....*

"Finally, my dear Monsignore, I think you should also know that the Benedictine Order will defray all expenses incurred on behalf of the Servant of God, Lucrezia Bartolomeo. Our arrangement will of course remain strictly confidential and at the discretion of Cardinal Roccaravindola as Cardinal Ponens of the Congregation of Sacred Rites."

229

Chapter Twenty Four

The Abbey of Montecassino

Office of Head Librarian, Don Martino Matronola

Stefano Ferrara had subjected Don Martino to a ferocious interrogation regarding what he believed was his brother's decision to buy his way into the Benedictine Order.

Don Martino had remained calm throughout the exchanges and kept to his script: the Abbot Primate in Rome had been contacted by the Italian Ambassador to the Holy See about Artemio's wish to enter the Order; Monte Cassino had been Brother Artemio's preference because of his interest in the welfare of the Bartolomeo family who lived within the neighbouring diocese of Venafro; it was Brother Artemio's wish to provide a dowry for Lucrezia because of a promise made to her father regarding her marriage prospects; the Order had no idea of Brother Artemio's wealth until after he was admitted.

By the time Don Martino had finished dealing with the circumstances leading to his brother's death, Stefano could no longer contain his anger.

"If my brother joined the order, then why was he the only monk to perish in the bombing? When the bombing started, why wasn't he sheltering in the crypt with you and the others? Explain that if you can."

In the face of Stefano's anger, Don Martino bowed his head and said nothing. At least until the former had said his piece.

"Artemio should never have been permitted to leave the safety of the crypt, assuming he was there in the first place. Was it to save a few hundred good-for-nothing vagrants? Riff-raff scum who opted for free board and lodgings in the Abbey rather than honest toil in neighbouring farms?"

Don Martino continued to hold his silence. There would be a better time to inform Stefano Ferrara that Brother Artemio had pleaded with Abbot Gregorio for the chance to persuade homeless brothers and sisters to leave the Abbey using the Mule track to Via Casalina. The last thing Stefano Ferrara would have wanted to hear was that his brother had been given a free hand by the Abbot to use all means at his disposal, excluding force, to persuade the civilian refugees to leave the doomed monastery.

"And you didn't say why those good-for-nothing parasites were encouraged to doss in the Abbey. Something here doesn't add up. Take me back to the Basilica. I want to see the crypt for myself. It could be," he continued illogically, as if the truth had struck him like a bolt from the proverbial blue, "that Artemio thought the crypt was big enough to provide shelter for everyone ... and not just for the privileged few. This would explain why he might have herded those misfits into the Basilica for a roll call, before leading them to the crypt. Which is more than people like them deserve. And all the more reason to take me to the Basilica so that I can see the crypt and judge accordingly."

The extent of Stefano's senseless assertions about the crypt's capacity had Don Matronola shaking his head in disbelief. He knew that Ferrara would realise the extent of his self-deception when he visited the crypt. He beat a retreat as soon as he and Stefano Ferrara reached the stairway which led into the Basilica.

While Stefano Ferrara was examining the low-vaulted crypt, he stuck to his absurd assertion that it could accommodate two hundred and thirty men women and children. As far as he was concerned, work-shy Southern scum were used to living in cramped and filthy conditions. The provision of sanitary facilities for people like them was not a matter for serious consideration by anyone whose opinion mattered.

However, in no time at all Stefano found the low vaulted ceilings made the tiny crypt unbearably claustrophobic. After several minutes, he had an overwhelming need for fresh air. And where better than the courtyard of the Bramante Cloisters at seventeen hundred feet above sea level?

In the rush to fill his lungs with fresh air, polemics regarding the fate of flea-bitten refugees were banished from Stefano Ferrara's preoccupations. When he reached the Courtyard, he found dozens of noisy pilgrims milling around in what was supposed to be a Zone of Silence.

Strolling between the statues of St. Benedict and St Scolastica, in the direction of the promontory balcony at the far end of the courtyard, the air Ferrara breathed into his lungs was as fresh and as cool just as he had hoped it would be when fleeing from the crypt.

Nearing the balcony, Stefano saw four enormous rumps displayed indecorously over the parapet wall. Stefano had seen those hindquarters too many times not to recognise their owners, Irma's chaperones, Prima, Seconda, Terza, and Quarta Borelli. They were leaning over the parapet to get a better view of the of the Polish Cemetery on the plateau below.

Irma had to be in the vicinity. All was not lost. He was roused at the thought of seeing Irma again. He looked at his watch. It was half past one. Three and a half hours to go before Michele drove took them back to Milignano.

Then he saw her standing near the Octagonal Well at the centre of the Courtyard. "Let's hope you don't do to me what Beatrice did to Dante[1] ..... and deny me a greeting," he began when he was within touching distance. "How fortunate for me to meet you below the Loggia del Paradiso." Irma smiled. She had no idea who Beatrice was but guessed that whoever she was, she had given this Dante fellow a hard time.

When Irma noticed Stefano's excitement it made her ears, neck and upper chest blush and quicken her heartbeat. As had happened at Giovanni's ordination dinner. To the extent that it

232

made her head for Don Pietro's absolution. She dreaded her next visit to the Santa Maria Maggiore's Confessional Box.

Irma never ceased to wonder how a Plain Jane like her, with no figure to write home about ...who spoke pidgin Italian.... a caterpillar with no hope of turning into a butterfly...could possibly interest a handsome, educated, rich and sexy man like Stefano Ferrara.

"Have you been to the souvenir shop?" Stefano asked when he was close enough to catch the sweetness of her breath. "These monks don't miss a trick. The way in and out of the Abbey is through the Souvenir shop."

"Later I go with no chaperones," Irma pointed at the Borelli sisters who were staring at them from the courtyard's balcony with a look of disapproval.

"Go over and tell them you plan to seduce me in the Souvenir Shop," he said, acknowledging the sisters with a disarming wave, "and you'll meet up with them later, after you've had your way with me in the crypt."

As Irma joined her four officially appointed chaperones, she smiled at the flattering absurdity of Stefano Ferrara's remarks. Chance would be a fine thing. The possibility, however remote, made her blush with excitement.

When Stefano wandered into the crowded Souvenir shop, the first thing he noticed, besides the absence of Irma, was the absence of monks and custodians. Honesty boxes, for Dollars, Pounds and AM Lire respectively, were bolted left, right and centre of the sales counter. The monks knew visitors would err on the side of generosity for souvenirs showing no prices. They were thieves and hypocrites and nailing honesty boxes to sales counters showed there was no honour among thieves.

To pass the time until Irma arrived, Stefano flicked through open cardboard containers of black and white picture postcards. Some

233

of the postcards showed aerial views of the Abbey before and after the bombing, looking like wedding cakes before and after being smashed by a sledgehammer.

The Abbey of Montecassino, before and after its bombing by 250 *Flying Fortresses* of the US Army Air Corps.

One postcard, in particular, caught Stefano's attention: a tombstone sitting on the Abbey ruins bearing the inscription: 15th February 1944, RIP. A paradoxical reminder of how he planned to sue the Benedictine Order for misappropriation and embezzlement of his late brother's assets.

Apprehensively, Irma looked around for familiar faces when she arrived at the Souvenir Shop. She relaxed after checking there were no familiar faces among the visitors. Failing to spot Stefano, she elbowed her way to the long narrow counter littered with trays of religious mementoes wedged between the honesty

234

boxes. She had no real interest in postcards or plaster figurines and tin medals of San Benedetto and Santa Scolastica respectively. Picking two effigies and two medals at random, she placed a 1000 AM lira banknote in the honesty box clearly earmarked for US dollars. Suddenly, she felt the thrill of Stefano standing closely behind her.

"Tell me, Irma," said Stefano, cupping the point of her elbow as he steered her from the Souvenir Shop, "what was Don Pietro trying to say when he performed his party piece about the bell during last night's dinner?"

"Don Pietro tell story for warning to me." Irma spoke with hesitation. She stumbled over the Italian words, unable to connect them with the necessary grammar. This didn't bother her when she spoke to Don Pietro or Mauro, or anyone else in Milignano for that matter. But with Stefano, it mattered a great deal. His Italian was polished, educated and captivating. And notwithstanding her poor Italian, Stefano had taken a real shine to an ordinary girl like her. Don Pietro knew how she felt about Stefano Ferrara. From the moment she laid eyes on him at Giovanni's ordination dinner.

"Maybe his story is one of those old chestnuts he trundles out to keep people like me away from attractive women like you."

Much to Irma's amusement, Stefano began to mimic Don Pietro's Southern Italian accent, with particular emphasis on the first two of the five vowels, opening and closing his mouth like a fish as he did so: " ....*AND WHEN* SHE *CAME* TO *CONFESSION* .... *WHAT DOES SHE SAY? SHE SAYS: LISTEN TO THE BELL ......DING DONG.... LISTEN TO THE BELL.....DING DONG...MARRY HIM MARRY HIM ....DING DONG.....* Months later she runs back to Don Pietro asking him what she should do because her husband was beating her.....and Don Pietro says: *LISTEN TO THE BELL, MY CHILD......DING DONG...... LISTEN TO THE BELL: CAN'T YOU HEAR WHAT IT' SAYS? ....DING DONG... IT'S SAYS DING DONG......YOU'RE STUCK WITH HIM! ......YOU'RE STUCK WITH HIM! ...DING*

235

DONG.....YOU'RE STUCK WITH HIM!"

Irma's unladylike laughter rang out as she and Stefano made their way through the exit gate. Neither of them noticed a brass plaque on the left gate pillar. Had they done so, they would have learned that the pillar contained the mortal remains of Abbot Gregorio Vito Diamare, born Naples 1865, died Sant'Elia Fiumerapido 1945.

Turning left, they strolled towards the bus park at the edge of a cement and sand depository. A charge of excitement raged through Irma's body each time she inadvertently bumped against Stefano Ferrara's shoulder.

"Why not take your souvenirs back to the bus? Then we can walk to the Polish Cemetery if you like" Irma brushed aside Stefano's suggestion about the cemetery She had no desire to view where Dumb Pollacks were buried. Besides, Don Pietro and his precious parishioners would be there. And Don Pietro was the last person she wanted to meet at this particular moment of mounting excitement.

"There's a restaurant not too far down the hill. We could go there.... or are you worried as to what people might say if they see us together?"

"I no care what them say. They know nothing...hear nothing..... make things up. No hungry....tired after long climb. Need rest."

"In that case, we should get back to the bus. I'll keep you company until the others get back in time for departure."

To their relief, there was no one on the bus. Michele had been drawn the curtains on the side and back windows. With hands on her waist, Stefano steered Irma to the rear bench where earlier she had sat between the Borelli sisters.

"Just sit back," he said huskily, "stretch your legs over my knees and relax until the others return."

Pushing back her dress, Stefano caressed Irma's knees, slowly

236

pushing them apart. As he inched his way to the soft flesh of her inner thighs, he gently removed dank strands of hair which had fallen over her face and placed them behind her ears.

Irma's lips parted but murmured words of protest turned to groans. Arousal had reached the point of no return when his fingers touched and explored her wet lips. The awareness of his excitement thrilled her. Her heart pounded as the passion of Stefano's kisses and caresses intensified. She offered no resistance when Stefano entered her knowing that it would induce the ecstatic torment of rhythmic muscular contractions.

Stefano drew deeply on a Toscano as he assessed the dissatisfaction obtained from his latest conquest. He had enjoyed the hunt and the chase, but the kill had been disappointing. The hapless woman had made him feel like a bull servicing a flea-bitten cow in heat. Her one-legged husband was welcome to her. She should have listened to Don Pietro's stupid bell.

"Have you seen Irma?" The question interrupted Stefano's reflections. He chose not to answer and continued to smoke with the air of a shepherd who had kicked a dog for tormenting his sheep. From the overpowering smell of Borotalc, he knew that the repugnant Borelli sisters had arrived.

"Have you seen Irma?" the sisters repeated in unison. Turning to face them, he nodded towards the bus. He watched with disgust as four enormous spheres of flesh boarded the bus. Inside, Ferrara knew they would find a wanton tart crying over curdled milk.

The worldly-wise sisters, whom Don Pietro had charged to chaperone Irma, put two and two together before deciding they had arrived in good time to prevent a randy Stefano from ravishing Mauro's wife.

When Michele finally appeared, Stefano asked him to convey his thanks to Don Pietro for his hospitality and good offices in helping him to confront the monks.

"The information received this morning about my brother means that I must get back to Bolzano as soon as possible to consult my lawyers. Perhaps you could help me, Michele," he added, "to wangle a lift down to the station in time for the 16.35 to Bolzano? I'll fill you in on what transpired in the Abbey earlier today."

Michele led the way to the red traffic lights which faced a row of waiting vehicles. He wondered what the little Northern stronzo could possibly add to his Uncle's account of how Brother Artemio had swapped a Black Shirt for a Black Habit.

Chapter Twenty Five

Vatican City, Saturday 25th October 1951

Like the Stazione Termini, the Via della Conciliazione is another of the legacies left to the City and to the World by Benito Mussolini. Its reconstruction followed soon after the historic Lateran Pact[1], which brought reconciliation between the Kingdom of Italy and the Vatican City.

The unhindered view of Via della Conciliazione from St Peter's Square to Castel Sant'Angelo did not exist when Fiachre Fahy left the Irish College for Adelaide in 1935. Palazzo Jacopo da Brescia, built for Giacomo Bartolomeo in the sixteenth century, although derelict, had still to be demolished.

Under leaden skies, Fiachre Fahy strode along the Via della Conciliazione trying to remember the location of the dilapidated and abandoned eyesore which once stood at the confluence of Borgo Nuovo and Borgo Sant' Angelo.

Nobody lamented the Palazzo's demolition in 1937. Its removal provided an awesome view of the road which joined the Vatican State to the Capital City of Rome.

"Sweet Star of the Sea, *Pustulator* Fiachre Fahy," Seamus had exclaimed, "Here in Italy, nobody but the Brits carry a brolly in the month of October when the Romans are still sunbathing in Santa Marinella[2]. I'm sure you've lost more than the unmentionables on yer head forgettin' that serious rain don't fall in Rome until the month of the Holy Souls[3]."

O'Fainnaide's words reached the limits of absurdity when the heavens unleashed a downpour and water cascaded from the brim of Fahy's hat to the front of his raincoat whenever he looked at where he put his brogues when they confronted a puddle.

Shoes, socks and turn-ups were saturated as Fahy splashed through the torrential rain which pranced on the pavement with the vigour of marching infantrymen. Behind the curtain of rain, the blurred view of St Peter's Basilica was still as impressive as ever.

When Fahy crossed the thin ribbon of Roman travertine which marked the confines of the Capital, he was in the forecourt of St Peter's Square. At that moment, the downpour became heavier. There was a pinkish glow in the sky from streaks of lightning as thunderclaps reverberated around the damp and grimy colonnades.

As Fahy crossed the rain swept square, such was the intensity of the downpour, he was unable to raise his eyes to glance at the familiar statues on the lintels above Bernini's columns.

He moved under the colonnades, sharing a temporary shelter with a stray dog. It looked at Fahy fearfully before slinking off as the lightning and the thunder claps returned with a vengeance. The dog was forgotten as Fahy walked over the flooding cobblestones into Via di Porta Angelica.

When Fahy reached Porta Santa Anna, he showed his pass to a solitary Swiss Guard. It was examined carefully and closely and long enough for the rain to obliterate the ink on Fahy's name. When the guard stepped aside to let him enter, Fahy glanced at his rifle. He had had enough Army training to know that in weather like this the traditional Halberd would have been more efficient than a rifle barrel exposed to heavy and persistent rain.

Fahy remembered that American infantrymen in the rain-swept Liri Valley had solved the problem of keeping rifle barrels dry by finding another practical use for army issue condoms.

Given Papa Pacelli's dogmatic views on contraception, it was unlikely that Swiss Papal Guards would have been permitted to improvise with similar ingenuity.

At the junction of Via del Belvedere and Via del Pellegrino, Fahy thought he could still hear the rain drumming on the Swiss Guard's helmet. Moments later, he reached the Church of Santa Anna dei Palfrenieri in Via del Pellegrino. This was Cardinal Roccaravindola's Church and had been since he received a Red Hat from Pius X1. It was a stone's throw from the Offices of the Congregation of Sacred Rites which shared a common entrance with the *Osservatore Romano*, the Vatican's official newspaper.

A series of thunderclaps followed him into the imposing building. Two impressive black marble stairways, one on either side of a massive metal lift-cage, faced Fahy as he paused in the white marble hallway.

Heading for the lift, Fahy walked across a mosaic of the Papal Keys and Tiara. The lights flickered several times. Fearing a power failure might trap him in the antiquated lift, Fahy took the left-hand stairway. The other stairway had a brass plaque on its third riser: ***OSSERVATORE ROMANO.***

While climbing the stairway, streaks of lightning flashed through the stained glass window on the half-landing. Images of Bela Lugosi[1] ran through Fahy's head with a hooded Seamus O'Fainnaide lying in wait at the top of the stairway singing his favourite Cole Porter song: *Shoes! Go on carry me there, I'll build a stairway to Paradise and build a new step every day.*

"See to the Monsignor's hat, E-U-genio!" were the words which interrupted Fahy's daydreaming when he entered the headquarters of the Congregation of Sacred Rites. His approach had been spotted by Cardinal Roccaravindola's look-out.

"Your hat, Monsignore," requested Eugenio, looking at it sympathetically. Fahy removed the sodden trilby making sure the arrangement of his hair was undisturbed. Catching his reflection on a book-case, he saw that the strands *needed no strategic readjustment* as Seamus would have put it before their pact.

Fahy watched Eugenio holding his trilby like a dead fish with the tip of his index finger and thumb before hanging it in the hallway's cloakroom.

241

"We hope the size of our office draws attention to our position as Cardinal Ponens rather than to our limited stature." As he spoke, the Cardinal placed a hand on Fahy's shoulder testing it for dampness. "Dry. Your trench coat has taken its punishment with admirable ease.

"Pah! How many times were our shoes in a similar condition when the Grand Canal burst its banks? Hundreds of times! But the condition of your shoes makes it imperative for us to dispose of our business as soon as possible, Monsignore. After which our Berlina will convey you to the San Isidoro. We must insist on this."

"I've experienced worse weather in Australia, during army manoeuvres in the country's western landmass the likes of which the Australians call *The Wet*."

"If you say so, my dear Monsignore, if you say so." The Cardinal was making the familiar chopping gesture with his hand. "However, we have no desire to encourage pneumonia in the line of duty. Pah! Now that the Good Lord has sent you to us, we must look after you. Think how Cataldo would react if you were taken from us. But please, accommodate yourself beside your Cardinal Ponens.

The Cardinal pointed to one of the two Louis Quinze chairs facing his oak-panelled desk. When Fahy walked to his chair, he noticed a plump, red velvet cushion lying on the floor behind the Cardinal's desk. The Cardinal offered an immediate explanation.

"The cushion on the floor is not for praying purposes, Monsignore. Not that we have no need of prayer when we are but a stone's throw from our day of reckoning. Pah! The cushion is to support our short legs. It reduces the distance from terra firma when we sit on this chair behind a pretentiously large desk ... which comes with the territory, we are sorry to say. But no more procrastination. You will be anxious to return to the wonderful cooking of the blessed Salvatore."

Monsignor Fiachre Fahy pulled a bulky envelope from the inside pocket of his jacket and laid it on the Cardinal's desk.

"Pah! More reports. We note you have been busy since your return from Montecassino and Milignano. For now, what we want from you are the salient points it contains ... to whet our appetite, so to speak. Otherwise, we would have asked you to mail your report and your extremities would not be morphing into Ducks' Feet.

"We prefer to hear from you in person." His Eminence leaned over and pressed a button on the surface of the desk. Within seconds Eugenio appeared at the door.

"Pah! What kept you E-U-genio?" said the Cardinal with mocking irony. "Take the Monsignori report and summarise it for me as soon as you can. This means we want it yesterday. Get Benedetto to bring coffee and a bottle of Stock Medicinale[1] and 'phone Ambassador Devlin's Secretary for an update on the two kegs of Guinness we ordered for the San Isidoro.

"And E-U-genio, have Benedetto bring our Berlina to the Via del Pellegrino portal to convey the Monsignore to the San Isidoro. Now, go away like a good lad and let us get on with our business."

The Cardinal waved his Secretary away with a friendly gesture. He removed his sapphire ring with a 'puh' and placed it on the desk.

"Removing my ring will confirm the informality of our discussions and allow me to dispense with the linguistic burden of the *pluralis maestatis* [2] which goes with the territory. So, my dear FA-I give me the essence of your report."

"Your Eminence let me begin by saying that visiting Milignano, as you suggested, was an absolute necessity. I'm astounded that Monsignor Schmalzgruber never understood the need to do so."

"Pah! The truth is that our Teutonic friend did not gainsay Cataldo on being told it wasn't necessary. He was in awe of Cataldo and fearful of his rapport with Monsignor Roncalli,

243

knowing that both had Papa Pacelli's ear. But, please continue, my dear FA-I."

"As a result of my enquiries in Milignano, I find that a visit to the United States is indispensable."

"It's a necessity I anticipated. I have since been in touch with the American Emissary to the Holy See, a benign Irish-American called Bernàrd FL-E-E-N. On our behalf, FL-E-E-N made enquiries about the three Americans named in the deposition submitted by Milignano's parish priest. Only one of them survived: Sergeant Johannes Nielsonsson ...."

"A stroke of luck! Because he's the one who organised the funerals of Lucrezia and Bianchina Bartolomeo. The two others being dead couldn't reply to Bishop Pantaleone's letter, but this Nielsonsson could have done so but didn't."

"Hardly surprising that he didn't because Pantaleone wrote to the three of them in Italian, as you no doubt noted from the carbon copies in Schmalzgruber's file."

"Could it be he ignored the Bishop's letter because he's got something to hide?"

"That's not for me to say but for you to find out. We must be cautious, my dear FA-I."

"I'll soon know if he's got something to hide when I confront him. A Colonel should know how to deal with a non-commissioned officer."

"One of the reasons why I thank the Good Lord for sending you to me in my hour of need."

"Your Eminence, if you don't mind, I would prefer to get back to Nielsonsson later."

"As you wish, my dear FA-I. The floor is yours."

"Thank you, Your Eminence. I informed you last Monday evening that Giovanni Bartolomeo had his appointment as

Secretary confirmed by Bishop Pantaleone. I have to say the young Giovanni has proved to be most cooperative and helpful during my investigations.

"A report from Collaquila's Parish Priest says he has the makings of a fine priest. He shows great promise, except for ..."

"Except for the blind spot he seems to have for Pantaleone? Is that what you were going to say?"

"Putting it that way, Your Eminence, we could say that he has two blind spots: one for the Bishop Pantaleone and one for his sister."

"The young man's blind spot for Pantaleone is understandable. Cataldo pulled him out of a hole he dug for himself in Collaquila. As for the alleged blind spot for his sister, please explain, my dear FA-I."

"Giovanni has no doubts whatsoever that his sister will be beatified. Unlike Pantaleone, he assumes my job will be to edit Schmalzgruber's report, dotting its 'Is' and crossing its 'Ts'. Unlike Pantaleone, he doesn't see me as a threat to his aspirations for the Servant of God."

"Are you saying that young Giovanni, brilliant as he is, has still to ask himself why Cataldo has taken such a keen interest in his welfare? Why he was honoured with a private ordination ceremony in the village where his sister was violated? Why a criminal assault was overlooked? Why no civil charges were brought? Why the church in Acquafondata is to be dedicated to Santa Lucrezia? And finally, why Cataldo made him his Private Secretary?"

"Of course he has, Your Eminence. He knows that what the Bishop has done for him is tied to a mutual interest in his sister. Giovanni is also well aware of the fact that Bishop Pantaleone sees Lucrezia Bartolomeo as a means of getting his hands on a Red Hat.

"For his part, Giovanni sees his sister's beatification as a means of re-establishing his family's good name. To put it more crudely, Your Eminence, he sees Beatification as a pay-back for the tragedies which have befallen his family.

"In my view, he tolerates the Bishop not only for extricating him from the Collaquila mess, but also because it keeps him closer than he should be to the Congregation of Sacred Rites' investigations. As I've said, and as you know this from the Bishop's reports, Giovanni is by nature a quiet lad and modest about his intellectual brilliance. But he must never be underestimated. Still waters run deep and in Giovanni's case, they run to unfathomable depths."

"And of course, my dear FA-I, we must never forget that violence runs in the family: Silvio, Roberto and now Giovanni. Just bear in mind that when you think you know somebody, it's like saying the sea ends on the horizon.

"I understand from Cataldo that the violence in Collaquila is linked to Giovanni's father's behaviour in Scotland. Cataldo claims he removed Giovanni from the scene of the crime to keep everything in house. Given the interest of the Press in the circumstances of Lucrezia's death and its aftermath, between you and me, I would have done the same."

"Nevertheless, as you say, Your Eminence, the incident in Collaquila throws unfavourable light on the family's tendency to violence. This brings me to what I learned about Giovanni's father during my discussions with Abbot Ildefonso."

"There's no real need to do so. Remember, my dear FA-I that I also spoke with the Abbot on the day you visited his Abbey. And again this morning before you arrived. It seems that Stefano Ferrara intends to sue the Benedictine Order for misappropriation of his brother's considerable fortune. A strange decision given the repercussions it would have on his business connection with the Vatican.

"Be that as it may be your Eminence, permit me to get back to Giovanni's father. Abbot Ildefonso also informed me of Silvio

246

Bartolomeo and Artemio Ferrara's business activities during their fascist heydays. Details of which are in my report."

"Splendid, my dear FA-I. Now tell me what you know about this Stefano Ferrara fellow?"

"According to Bishop Pantaleone, Ferrara could sell the stripes of a zebra and snow to the Eskimos albeit with a caveat comparing his honesty and here I quote, *to the thief who stole the nine commandments.*

"Reading between the lines, we know that Ferrara blotted his copybook in Monte Cassino, Your Eminence. It is a rather unsavoury episode. Since it has nothing to do with our investigations, it has not been included in my report."

"Monsignore! Monsignore! You flatter me by trying to spare my blushes. There is no need to protect me from hearing the unsavoury. Anything you have to say could not possibly compare to what I learned from victims of the *Marocchinate*. An objectionable euphemism indeed when referring to the atrocities committed by the Goumiers.

"As Your Eminence wishes. The unsavoury matter in question concerns a young lady who was betrothed to Giovanni and before him to his brother, Roberto. Currently, she is estranged from her husband and lives with Giovanni's Aunt and Uncle in Milignano.

"It seems the young woman found the mule-track route to the Abbey rather demanding. On advice from her chaperones, the Borelli sisters, she agreed to recover on the bus which drove them to the Abbey. According to her chaperones, Stefano Ferrara found her sleeping and .... and tried to take advantage of her."

"In other words, Ferrara tried to violate her. Did he succeed in your opinion?"

"Hard to say, your Eminence. It is alleged that she woke up in time to fend him off. The point here is that she was, as the story goes, saved by the timely intervention of the four Borelli sisters.

247

The same sisters who prepared Bianchina and Lucrezia for burial."

"Please continue, my dear FA-I. I have a feeling that we've not heard the last of the ubiquitous Borelli sisters."

"Undoubtedly, Your Eminence, but if I could get back to Ferrara. All we know is that he subsequently took off from the Abbey without as much as a by-your-leave to Don Pietro, who had been his host in Milignano and one of his sponsors with the monks. He claimed he had an urgent need to consult his lawyers. Which he did, as we know."

"And what of Don Pietro and his alleged relationship with Lucrezia's guardian?"

"You will find details of this relationship in my report. Suffice to say that there is an admission of a single act of folly which took place days before Bianchina Bartolomeo left the country to look after Lucrezia when her mother passed away in Scotland.

"According to Giovanni, his aunt was rather strict as a guardian. Not that she needed to be because Lucrezia was reserved and shy just like her brother ..... until his fall from grace."

"And Don Pietro?"

"He is held in great esteem by his parishioners. When Bishop Pantaleone tried to conclude the disciplinary process set up to deal with Don Pietro's indiscretion, he couldn't find a parishioner willing to file a formal complaint against him.

"It's common knowledge that Bianchina Bartolomeo and Pietro Verrecchia planned to marry once he had completed his studies in the Abbey School. Even today, there's a lot of sympathy associated with the circumstances which put paid to their wedding plans.

"What is irrefutable is that the women of Milignano trust Don Pietro without reservation. To such an extent that they refused to be evacuated to Frozinone without him.

"Pah! My dear FA-I, it's Fro-SI-none ….not Fro-Zi-none.

"I sit corrected, Your Eminence. Fro-S-inone. But for Don Pietro, the women and children would have been in Milignano when it was caught between the devil and the deep blue sea. It also accounts for his absence during the so-called *Marocchinate*."

"Then why, tell me, did Lucrezia and Bianchina Bartolomeo and the Borelli women not leave for Frosinone?"

"Good question, Your Eminence. Lucrezia refused to leave without her aunt who in turn refused to travel with Don Pietro. For obvious reasons. As for the Borelli sisters, German Officers were billeted in their Pensione. And as the story goes, they remained behind to look after their interests. When the Germans left, French Officers took their place.

"However, as Postulator, I must be circumspect when I investigate the part they played in preparing Bianchina and Lucrezia Bartolomeo for burial."

"We have no interest in hearsay, my dear FA-I. Tell me, what are the facts about Lucrezia's relationship with Artemio Ferrara?"

"According to Giovanni, there was an agreement made by his father that Artemio would look after Lucrezia's interests until he could re-join her in Milignano.

"When the Arandora Star went down, Artemio kept in regular contact with Bianchina and Lucrezia until he joined the Order. In fact he said goodbye to both of them on the day he left for Monte Cassino.

"Despite the age difference, Giovanni said that his father would not have been opposed to Lucrezia marrying Artemio if he so wished. With the proviso that Bianchina moved with them to the South Tyrol where Ferrara has extensive holdings."

"Man proposes and God disposes, my dear FA-I. And we know that Artemio Ferrara kept his promise to Silvio Bartolomeo by making provision for Lucrezia before joining the Order.

"And Silvio Bartolomeo, Your Eminence, sends his daughter from Glasgow to Milignano for safety and God disposes that Milignano becomes a battleground between two armies of occupation. And, as you said, Artemio Ferrara hoped to find peace in Monte Cassino and God disposes that the Allies razed the Abbey to rubble. Blowing him and two hundred refugees to kingdom come in the process."

Fahy was beginning to despair that Benedetto would ever get round to bringing the promised coffee and cognac. For all he knew, Benedetto could be in the Cardinal's car reading the latest edition of Topolino[1].

"Your Eminence, if I may, I would now like to turn to the American and French Expeditionary Forces who took possession of Milignano when the Germans retreated.

"After French Officers moved into Pensione Borelli, on the advice of those same Officers, two of the sisters moved into the Bartolomeo villa. Their presence safeguarded their home from being ransacked by the Goumiers. However, on the day Lucrezia and Bianchina were violated and murdered, all four sisters were entertaining French Officers in their Pensione.

"It seems that Lucrezia was kept out of sight in the cellar. However, when the Americans were undertaking a house to house inspection looking for God knows what, they discovered Lucrezia. Nielsonsson was one of the three soldiers who did so.

"Since Lucrezia spoke English, we can only assume that the Americans kept a weather eye on both Bartolomeo women. According to the Borelli sisters there were no improprieties. They were adamant that the Americans had a paternal interest in Lucrezia."

Cardinal Roccaravindola looked at his watch. Fahy imagined he had remembered the coffee and cognac and that he would be pressing the bell to find out what was keeping Benedetto. He was wrong. The Cardinal had the Borelli sisters on his mind.

"You have spoken to the women who attended to the bodies before burial? The women who apparently saved the Pacitti woman from the improper attentions of the man now suing the Benedictine Order for misappropriation? The same women who entertained first German and then French Officers? The same women who are said to have had an on-going affair with Silvio Bartolomeo and Artemio Ferrara? ...and the Tribes of Judea for all we know. And the same women who swear there were no improprieties between the Americans and Lucrezia Bartolomeo? My dear FA-I, what more is to be said about these omnipresent sisters?"

"Don Pietro holds them in the highest regard and confirms their good standing in the community and, more importantly, their enduring attachment to the Bartolomeo family. Bishop Pantaleone said he was most impressed with the Borelli sisters when he met them at Giovanni's ordination dinner."

"Pah! This makes me more than ever suspicious of the Borelli sisters... Puh! What would Pantaleone know about women? When he was too naive to realise that his great friend, the Marchesa Gala Placida Pignatelli was the biggest whore in the Mezzogiorno since Messalina[1] plied her trade in the streets of Ancient Rome ..... before she swanned off on a busman's holiday to Argentina.

"Pah! Cataldo knows as much about women as I do. Which as it so happens is less than nothing. It's a great pity we can't say the same for Milignano's parish priest who, according to you, holds the Borelli Sisters to be pillars of the community because they provided the necessary funds for the redecoration of the Santa Maria Maggiore.

"Don't you find it amusing that we always refer to these four women as The Borelli Sisters? It makes them sound like a grotesque circus act. Nevertheless, we must examine their statements carefully. These women are too good to be true, but here speaks an old cynic. It all sounds like material for a novel. Puh! Perhaps you might care to write it yourself, my dear FA-I?

251

"Perhaps you might choose to do so after you've written what Se-Amus tells me will be a definitive biography on the work of the Irish Missionaries throughout the world," adding with a smile, "which shouldn't take too long ....then you can write this saga on the Bartolomeo family which we both hope will conclude with a happy ending. However, my nose tells me there might be a few surprises in store when you meet with Yankee Doodle in America."

"This is why I plan another visit to Milignano when I get back from the United States. Visits, I might add, which Bishop Pantaleone thinks are a waste of time and money. A waste of my time and the Church's money, Your Eminence. Since we only have the Borelli Sisters word for what happened to Lucrezia and her aunt, it stands to reason that we need Nielsonsson to corroborate what occurred when they arrived on the scene.

"According to the Borelli sisters, Lucrezia was already dead, a Goumier was lying by her side with his head in two halves and close to a fatally wounded Bianchina. Most important of all, I need to gather detailed information about the condition and respective positions of the bodies."

"We are agreed on this point, my dear FA-I, given that we only have the Borelli Sisters word that Lucrezia died virgo intacta and that Bianchina killed the Goumier who was molesting her niece. Since we know the Goumiers operated in threes, we also need to know what happened to the other two. As things stand at the moment, we can draw no firm conclusions.

"My dear FA-I, let me tell you how easy it is to manipulate facts when it is politically expedient so to do. Take for example the official version of how Mussolini and his mistress met their deaths."

"That he and Petacci, Your Eminence, stood tall when facing execution by Communist Partisans in the streets of Dongo?"

"Exactly. What ha still to be revealed is that Mussolini and Petacci were already dead before being dumped in the streets of

Dongo and that Petacci's clothes had been torn to shreds while she was being beaten and abused by her captors. Before and after she was strangled and shot.

"After which, to cover their tracks, Petacci was dressed in a borrowed blouse and skirt, before being transported in a cattle wagon to Piazza Loreto in Milan. All of which explains the scandal caused by her lack of underwear when she was strung up by the heels.....alongside Mussolini and a collection of fascist diehards.

"So you see, my dear FA-I, we must make sure that there are no versions of the truth which could come back to haunt us after we have made the decision to process the Servant of God's case."

"Meaning, Your Eminence, that Nielsonsson's corroboration is indispensable no matter what Bishop Pantaleone has to say to the contrary? And speaking of the United States, Your Eminence ...."

"Pah! I know, I know. You want me to persuade Se-Amus to change his mind about leaving his students during term time? I've tried without success when I was telling him our business in America couldn't wait until the Christmas break."

"What I was going to say, your Eminence, is that if Seamus cannot accompany me, we should consider Giovanni as a replacement."

"Absolutely not! Not a good idea, my dear FA-I. The boy's presence might influence Nielsonsson. We can't take that chance. The expense involved in sending him to the United States is another matter. From the Church's point of view, it would be unethical to use Bartolomeo money to fund our enquiries, either directly, by drawing on Giovanni's personal wealth or indirectly by getting the Benedictine Order to foot the bill using the Ferrara bequest to the Servant of God. No, leave Giovanni to the tender mercies of Cataldo. Pah! Tell me, was it his idea to invite Giovanni?"

"No, your Eminence, it was mine."

"No matter. Leave the boy with Cataldo. Who knows, Giovanni might come to terms with the cost of his cosy relationship with Cataldo." Cardinal Roccaravindola pressed the bell on his desk.

"Ah, here you are E-U-genio. Ask Benedetto to run Monsignore FA-I back to the San Isidoro and fetch a bottle of *Medicinale* from my cellar for my dear friend, Se-amus. Open another case if

 you have to."

Cardinal Roccaravindola replaced his sapphire ring. A sign that the meeting was over.

"Tell me, E-U-genio, has Laurent Battandier's limo arrived?" Cardinal Roccaravindola rose from his seat and Fiachre Fahy did likewise. "Or is the Cardinal once again showing the Gallic predilection for unpunctuality?" Turning once more to Fahy, "You see my dear FA-I, Cardinal Battandier considers punctuality to be a vice of the working classes and that hoi polloi like us are too easily contaminated by this endemic weakness.

"French Patricians, like Laurent Battandier, flaunt their superiority in the same way as the Sadducees flaunted theirs with the Pharisees. Today we have the misfortune of dining with Laurent. Puh! The disgusting eating habits of the French make us wish we were of the Jewish faith."

"Your Eminence?"

"The French, unlike Semites, eat snails, frogs and sea crustaceans which thrive on human filth. Like us, they eat animals which chew the cud and have cloven hooves. Unlike us, they also eat those parts we Italians reserve for pigswill.

"So today, chez Battandier, we will content ourselves with an omelette made with mascarpone and gorgonzola by pretending to have a stomach upset which will excuses us from partaking one of his so-called *plats soignés* which need a nose-peg prior to and during consumption.

"Santa polenta! Last time it was *Tetines* followed by *Tête de*

Veau. Horror of horrors, what could it be this evening? No doubt another nose-peg job. *Andouillette de Troyes* perhaps? A dish which gives off a stench which surpasses the mephitic and miasmic emanations of *Riz du veau."*

Fahy would have enjoyed sauntering over the Ponte Umberto, admiring the Palazzaccio and looking down on the River Tiber coming to terms with the recent heavy. A scene he often envisaged when standing on one or other of the Bridges over the Murrumbidgee River.

The Cardinal's decision to send him back to the San Isidoro by car had deprived him of these pleasures.

Chapter Twenty Six

Milwaukee, Friday 9th November 1952

The four-hour flight from Ciampino to London had been a vicious winner-takes-all dogfight between colliding turbulences over the Mediterranean Sea.

The flight from London to New York was even more of a nightmare. And all thanks to the unruly behavior of an Italo-American family returning from a visit to The Old Country, where they had boasted to aging parents and old friends not only of how well they were doing in their Manhattan Snack Bar but also their hopes of securing a Harvard education for their twin daughters.

"We always travel first class," persisted the father to Fahy who had been ignoring him almost to the point of rudeness, "Especially when travelling to and from *Sh-poll-eh-toe Perr-oo-gee-ah* where I was born and raised... it's famous for its *Bloody Bridge*," he added proudly.

"The Ancient Roman *Ponte Sanguinario*," interrupted Fahy, showing interest for the first time, "mentioned by Goethe in his Italian Journey."

The blockhead's pride in Spoleto, Perugia, seemed to evaporate when he realised that his fellow passenger knew more about his home town than he did. The genie was out of the bottle. He had no option other than listening to an Irish priest telling him how an Irish mercenary, Paddy O'Riley, had defended Lucrezia Borgia's Duchy of Spoleto on behalf of her father, Pope Alexander V1.

By the time Fahy finished his *tour de force*, the erstwhile Sploletano had taken refuge in sleep. As had his wife and Harvard bound daughters.

The TWA Boeing Stratocruiser to Milwaukee banked to the right over Lake Michigan, making it easier to enjoy the spectacular view of Manitowoc and Sheboygan as it approached Milwaukee's Airport.

A voice from the cockpit, speaking in a distinctive Wisconsin drawl (in which the E's are reversed with the A's), sang the praises of Solomon Laurent Juneau. Until then, Fahy had always associated trail-blazing in America with the likes of Dave Crockett and Daniel Boone. He now knew that Juneau was an *Intrepid Québécois Frontiersman* and a Founding Father of Milwaukee, a name inspired by the Algonquian Indian word *Millioke* meaning 'Good and Pleasant Land'.

Fahy wondered if the running commentary was provided to give him value for the first class fare. On the other hand, it took his mind off the discomfort he felt in his ears whenever a 'plane was reducing altitude.

"...... *cosmopolitan East Side,*" continued the voice from the cockpit, "f*ashionable centre of the Arts. Next we see the densely populated multi-cultural industrial South Side to your far left.....*" Fahy smiled....it was a novel way of describing areas populated by poor, working class ethnic minorities.

"......*we are now making our approach to General Mitchell Field, the Airport of Milwaukee City, and the Beer Capital of the World.....*"

With thoughts of Guinness flashing in his mind, Fahy's attention was drawn to a yachting regatta and a grubby stretch of sand looking like bearded corn cobs.

Fahy tensed as the Stratocruiser thudded on impact with the runway, hurtling forward at an alarming speed until its engines engaged in reverse thrust. He relaxed when the aircraft began gliding over the smooth surface of the runway to the terminal building, where it came to a stop with the inevitable jerk.

As the only first class passenger, Fahy was first to disembark.

While doing so, it occurred to him that he hadn't had a bowel movement since leaving the Irish College on Wednesday morning...... *an Ave Maria and an Our Father to St Bonaventure, Patron Saint of the Constipated, should restore my regularity.*

Poor old Seamus O'Fainnaide. How disappointed he had been when Fahy confirmed the news that his business in Milwaukee couldn't wait until the San Isidoro's Christmas vacations. They had parted at Ciampino Airport on the understanding that he would be back in time for Salvatore's Christmas Dinner: *Agnello e Pesce Arrostito, Cannoli con Ricotta* and *Zeppole di San Giuseppe al Forno.* To be washed down with Ambassador Devlin's Guinness. They had agreed to postpone the drinking of *Mammertino* and *Santa Maddalena*. It was the least they could do if Ferrara persisted with his threat to sue the Benedictine Order.

If Giovanni Bartolomeo was disappointed about missing out on a trip to America he had hidden it well. Fiachre had told him the truth. More or less: Cardinal Roccaravindola wanted him to remain in Venafro to consolidate his position as Bishop Pantaleone's Diocesan Secretary.

At the time, Giovanni had a woman on his mind rather than regrets about cancelled air-tickets. He had done his best to reconcile Irma with Mauro. It hadn't been easy in a climate where tongues were wagging about what happened or almost happened or didn't happen on Michele's bus in the Abbey.

The motives behind the Borelli sisters' probable *mise en scène* did not matter to Giovanni. Whatever way he looked at it, Irma was the injured party and Ferrara was an unmitigated scoundrel.

As Fahy headed for Luggage Retrieval, he spotted a boyish looking priest holding a placard close to his chest. As he approached the mop of blond hair, he was sure the placard would have his name on it.

"Monsignor Fahy?" enquired the lad when his blue eyes fell on Fahy's scarlet bib.

258

"In person, young man." shaking his outstretched hand, "Let me collect my valise and *I'll be with you in two ticks,* or as we say in Irish, *Nì mé dhá mheandar leis.*

"Let me take your valise, Monsignor, and introduce myself: Tomas Tomczacs, Secretary to His Grace, Archbishop Henry Hynek. Welcome to the Great Lake City of Milwaukee. The Archbishop regrets he couldn't meet you personally. His Grace left yesterday morning for a meeting with Monsignor Roncalli and Bishop Pantaleone in Paris.

"The Archbishop has arranged for you to stay in St. Joseph's Convent. We use it as a Guest House for distinguished visitors like you. It's a pleasant establishment, quiet and unpretentious. There, you will find you have much in common with the Mother Superior. Her Convent is on the South Layton Boulevard and conveniently placed for Cedarburg...where your man Nielsonsson owns and runs a repair garage and filling station.

"Mr Nielsonsson is expecting you on Monday morning, but don't count on it." Noting Fahy's irritation, Tomczacs explained. "He's an army reservist, on standby and ready to leave if called on for the war in Korea."

Fahy was too tired to comment on Uncle Sam's latest military adventure and was glad the Archbishop's Secretary seemed hell-bent on monopolising the conversation....*Giovanni could take a leaf out of Tomczacs' book any day....what could I have in common with the Mother Superior ....did His Eminence know about Pantaleone's visit to Paris.... what on earth was Pantaleone up to now....meeting his mentor in Paris was understandable.... but how did Henry Hynek figure in his Grand Design....if the Cardinal doesn't know then Giovanni would...young Tomczacs needs a haircut........*

When the Archbishop's black sedan pulled up inside the Convent Complex, Fahy was impressed by the convent's Italianate doorways and windows crowned by twin towers separated by an

259

octagonal dome. He followed Father Tomczacs into the convent thinking he was being led to his billet. Instead, he found himself in a chapel marginally bigger than Cardinal Roccaravindola's Office. Apart from the Carrara and Prato marble altar and terrazzo flooring, the interior was decidedly Germanic.

"The mosaics above the altar and on the walls were created by artisans from Innsbruck." It was the voice of Sister Mary, Mother Superior of The Society of the Holy Child Jesus. Warm, friendly and unmistakeably Irish.

Sister Mary smiled as she approached. Notwithstanding her sixty-five years, her teeth were as white as the cincture girding her waist and her eyes dark like the large ebony beads on the rosary hanging from her neck. If first impressions mattered, then Sister Mary was a woman to be reckoned with.

"I'll be lookin' after the *Mon-sing-yor-ray* now young Father Tomas, so we won't be detain' you any longer from yer dooties." Her soft Irish-American accent suddenly as Irish as the Book of Kells.

"I'd better be off then, Monsignor, before Sister Mary has me ejected. You'll have the use of the Archbishop's stand-by during your stay. It's parked in the garage. Sister Mary has the Diocesan 'phone number when you need to call me to take you to the Mitchell. If time is at your disposal, I would be pleased to show you the best of what Milwaukee has to offer."

He shook Fahy's hand and bowed, first to the altar and then to the Mother Superior before marching off with relief etched on his face. Fahy pursed his lips into a smile.... *he'll be heading for the nearest Barber Shop.... and not before time*.

Sister Mary was from Dunfanaghy in County Donegal. Born and bred there and fifteen when her parents emigrated fifty years ago. Neither of her parents had been offered employment in the new C of E Bally Bowe Primary School. Both had been overlooked because of their support for Home Rule and its eponymous Political Party.

Campaigning for Legislative Independence and Land Reform, in a rural protestant parish like Gweedore, was hardly likely to endear them to the Titled Anglican Landlords who controlled the School Boards.

"'Tis a pleasure to be sure to be sure it is *Mon-sing-yor-ray* to be having you wit' us for such a short time....and as a payin' guest...for which the Lord be tanked as we're needin' the spondulicks. We'll be stoppin' here in the chapel until the Sisters arrive for Compline Prayers."

Fahy was delighted, his fatigue forgotten. Sister Mary sounded like a female version of Seamus. And, like Seamus, she exaggerated her Irish brogue when in the company of a fellow Irish exile.

"From Kilfinora says you... *Cill Fhionnúrach* bein' more precise as I likes to be on occasions like this, *Mon-sing-yor-ray*. And sure now isn't the Holy Father himself the parish priest somewhere near that fine place? You have relatives livin' in the Free State?"

"None, Mother Superior that I know of," said Fahy noticing her moustache for the first time. "I was raised in an orphanage. Me and me good friend Seamus O'Fainnaide. And you, if I may ask, Mother Superior, would you still be havin' kin in the Republic?"

"Me cousin Brigid until last year. Until she up and died before her time and leaves me father's house and garden at the mercy of me renegade cousins.... who've been tryin' to lay their soup-takin'[1] hands on me inheritance ever since.

"But they won't be drivin' me off like them Anglican Spikes did to me father and me mother, God rest their sainted souls. It's me them renegades will be dealing with next year to be sure. They'll find me a different kettle o' mackerels. And you and your friend Seamus can visit me any time. As payin' guests to be sure."

Fahy made no comment, but didn't doubt for a moment that Sister Mary's soup-takin' renegade cousins would get more than

261

they bargained for when their mackerel-snapping cousin got back to claim her freehold in Dunfanaghy County Donegal or as Sister Mary would have it, *Dún Fionnachaidh Chontae Dhùn na nGall.*

Sister Mary looked at the watch on her right wrist. She tapped its face with her index finger, 'It's four o'clock. Me choir of angels should be here any time now...you'll be leadin' the prayers, *Mon-sing-yor-ray.* After which Sister Scolastica will show you to your room.

"You'll be free to come and go as you like. Provided you're in by seven when we bolt the doors. And if you let Father Tomczacs take you on a *Brendan Behan* to McCafferty's Irish Castle then you can sleep it off in the garage."

Early next morning, after a breakfast which Seamus would have described as frugal, Fahy decided to see Nielsonsson that day rather than wait until Monday. By which time, Sergeant Nielsonsson could well be in Korea. Fahy couldn't take that chance.

On advice from Sister Mary, Fahy drove to East St Paul Street, where he parked on the wharf and crossed the foot bridge to North Plankinton Street. There, he caught the eight o'clock barge for the ten minute transit to Cedarburg.

From what Fahy could see, Nielsonsson's garage and filling station was the only one in Cedarburg's Main Street. Shopkeepers ignored him as they set up pavement stalls displaying their merchandise. They knew a potential customer when they saw one.

There was a strong smell of roasting malted barley, hops and yeast in the air. The aroma reminded Fahy of the Guinness Brewery in Dublin. He deduced there was at least one brewery in the vicinity.... *elementary my dear Watson. We are in the Beer Capital of the world....*

Johannes Nielsonsson spotted Fahy as soon as he stepped off the barge at the north end of the Main Street. A stranger dressed in black, with a gleaming white Roman collar could be none other than the clergyman who had travelled all the way from Rome Italy to speak to him about something he would rather leave dead and buried. As it had been, for the last seven years.

Johannes Nielsonsson had kept Dook and Ed's families in the dark about what happened in that Godforsaken hole called *Millanano*. He was in no mood to spill the beans.... *there's nothing this damned English Pastor from Rome Italy can do to make me change my mind.*

Nielsonsson, tall, lean and athletic, stood erect, motionless and po-faced. He watched Fahy enter the courtyard of his filling station where each of its four island pumps was shaped like a beer bottle carrying monochromatic adverts for Pabst Beer.

"I'm the man you're looking for, Johannes Nielsonsson. Ignoring Fahy's outstretched hand, "Come into the Garage. We won't be disturbed, unless somebody stops for gas. Unlikely on a Saturday at this time of day."

Fahy followed Nielsonsson into a cheerless garage. The air was thick with the smell of oil, stale tobacco and body odour. The faintest smell of disinfectant came from what Fahy could see was the wash-room. Nielsonsson closed its door with a slam and ushered Fahy towards a parallelepiped of frosted glass which served as his office. To Fahy's surprise, it was neat and tidy. It contained a small uncluttered desk positioned against the wall, two padded black leather chairs, a calendar advertising Pabst Beer, a Betty Grable[1] Pin-up Poster, telephone and a filing cabinet topped with a large bowl of pot pourri which emitted a vaguely sulphurous odour.

Nielsonsson invited Fahy to take a seat while he stood with his back to the desk, arms folded and a face ready for a no-holds-barred exchange of views.

"I won't shake hands or sit down. My hands and overalls have been overhauling engines since day-break. Didn't expect you

263

until Monday. But Saturday or Monday. Makes no difference to me."

"I won't be keeping you from your work any longer than I have too, Mr Nielsonsson. So I'll get to the point. Let me explain the......"

"Look, if it's about the letters your people sent, I didn't open any of them. I trashed them because..... because I surmised what they contained."

"Then tell me why you think I've travelled here to see you. It's a good place to start, Mr Nielsonsson. Don't you think?"

"You want to know about my buddies...Dook and Ed. You want to know what they did? And upset their folks? Forget it, Pastor. Just forget it." Nielsonsson looked at Fahy defiantly.

"Mr. Nielsonsson, let me explain what brought me nearly five thousand miles from Rome to Milwaukee. You're the only one who can help me to throw light on what I need to know."

"Throw muck more like! Muck on the memories of buddies buried in Cassino's Military Cemetery. No way will I let people like you upset families still grieving over the loss of their sons."

"Mr. Nielsonsson, please hear me out. My only interest concerns the sixteen-year-old girl you and your friends got to know in Milignano. The sixteen-year-old girl to whom you *and* your two friends gave a decent burial."

"It's the same thing!" exclaimed Nielsonsson, his agitation growing by the minute.

"Hear me out, Mr Nielsonsson, that's all I ask. Let me put my cards on the table." Nielsonsson nodded his agreement without concealing his distrust.

"My Church, The Roman Catholic and Apostolic Church of Rome, has set in motion a certain process following Lucrezia Bartolomeo's tragic death. A process we call *Beatification*" A mystified Nielsonsson shrugged his shoulders.

"Let me explain what *Beatification* means to Roman Catholics. Beatification is my Church's recognition of a person's entrance into Heaven and the right of that person to intercede with the Almighty on behalf of those who choose to pray in his or her name."

"In my Church, Pastor Fahy, we believe that if a person has chosen redemption, then that person has the right to Salvation. With no mumbo jumbo obstacles standing in his or her way."

"Be that as it may be, Mr Nielsonsson. However, the process I'm referring to requires a close examination of the life, virtue and moral reputation of Lucrezia Bartolomeo, rather than yours or those of your dead comrades."

"But it still means raking up the past .... Dishonouring the dead. Broadcasting things that are better left unsaid."

"Lucrezia Bartolomeo's interests are exclusively paramount, Mr Nielsonsson. Should the events which took place in the Bartolomeo cellar, involving you and your comrades, prove Lucrezia Bartolomeo to be unworthy of the honour of Beatification....then you have my word that our investigations will go no further. There would be no need to disclose any of your confidences. I can only repeat that if your revelations reflect badly on Lucrezia Bartolomeo then the matter will end here and now."

"There will be hell to pay from Dook and Ed's folks if they ever got to know Johannes Nielsonsson sent their service records down the chute."

Nielsonsson pulled a green-leafed cigar from the breast patch-pocket of his overall, stuck it between his teeth and began to chew it nervously.

"My wife has a smoking ban. She works weekdays. Answers the 'phone and does the accounts. But I'm allowed to smoke in the garage but not in here..." Fahy thought he saw the faintest of smiles on Neilsonsson's hitherto forbidding face.

"Just tell me all you know, Mr Nielsonsson. What you say will remain confidential. I'll be making a few notes which I'll let you read if you so wish before I leave."

"As Medics," Nielsonsson began with some hesitation, "the three of us were part of a bomb-squad detail ordered to sweep the houses after the Krauts left. We found the two Bartolomeo women hiding in the cellar. When we discovered they spoke English the least we could do was to get better acquainted.

"The young one was a good looking broad. Skinny, but a fine piece of Latin tail I can tell you. She looked like a younger version of Rita Hayworth. I took a real shine to her I can tell you, but the old woman wouldn't let her out of her sight. And more so after Dook let slip I was married.....to my first wife.

"We took to visiting them as often as we could. So the Goums kept their distance. Or so we thought. I was well and truly smitten but, I have to admit, she was never anything other than friendly.

"Ed and Dook reckoned we had to find a way of getting the old gal out of the way for me to make first base with the young broad. We didn't have a plan but we were working on one. Get the picture Mr Pastor?" Nielsonsson removed the soggy cigar from his lips and pushed it deeply into the pot pourri.

"Yes, I get the picture, however unsavoury."

"That's a real polite way of putting it, Mr Pastor. A fancy word for immoral intentions, no offence meant, I suppose. We were on our way to see them when we heard screaming coming from the house. By the time we got there the screaming had stopped. They were in the cellar. The old woman was semi-naked with several stab wounds on her back. When we turned her over, there was blood on her face, neck and shoulders. She was still alive. Barely.

"Her dress was in shreds. Her hands covering the mess between her legs. A Goum was lying on his back, his head and shoulders hacked and oozing blood, slime and muscle. A kitchen cleaver was lying at his side. It had blood and fragments of bone tissue on the blade and handle." Nielsonsson stopped, but Fahy waved his hand for him to continue with what sounded like a Medic's preliminary report.

"Two Goums were busy with Lucrezia. She was dead, not that the Goums noticed or cared. She was on her back, legs apart. One was fucking her and the other one was kneeling behind her head giving her a gob job. Neither one nor the other was bothered by our presence, knowing we were under orders not to get involved with the Goums when they were on the rampage.

"We knew there was nothing we could do for the girl. We thought we could do something for the old gal, even though we realised she was going fast.

"Dook and Joe made her as decent as best they could. They helped me cradle her head over my knees. She knew she was dying but was agitated about the girl. She was speaking Italian but one word she repeated over and over again was clear enough: *Reputazione, Reputazione, Reputazione.* She died in my arms, gasping the word *Pietro* before she went. "

"What happened to the two Goums? How did they get away?" Fahy asked as he jotted and bracketed the initials DP and BB in his note book.

"They didn't. We dealt with them. At least Dook and Ed did."

"Dealt with them , Mr Nielsonsson?"

"The two Goums got to their feet after they had changed positions on the girl. Both were leering and looking like cats that got the cream. They stood over the girl's body with their tumescent donkey-dicks hanging between the folds of their overcoats.

For Dook and Ed, the last straw was when they began gyratin' their thighs, beckoning us over to take a piece of the action. That was it, as far as Dook and Ed were concerned. Dook, moving like lightening, floored the nearest black bastard with a Jack Dempsey and broke his neck with the heel of his boot when he hit the floor. Likewise Ed. He went for the other one before he could react and draw his sabre-dagger. Ed knocked him down and kicked him again and again until the cunt's face was unrecognisable."

"And the Borelli sisters? When did they appear on the scene?"

"They appeared just as Dook and Ed were dragging the Goums away by the heels to dump them in the ditch the Sappers had dug for cattle carcasses. They hardly blinked or twitched at the sight and of donkey-dicks, smashed faces and the smell of shit and piss. The women were more concerned about their dead friends.....especially after I repeated what the old gal was saying before she died. After that the four women took over.

"First they washed and dressed the bodies. After that they told us in pidgin English what to say to the Military Police when they arrived."

"The version of events accepted by the Military Police?"

"As far as they were concerned, the dead Goumier in the cellar was killed by his comrades in a fight over possession of the two women. Lucrezia was strangled to stop her screaming while the old gal was being raped. The two Goums hitting the road when they heard us approaching. One more thing, it was sisters' idea to conceal the kitchen cleaver from the MPs. It never occurred to any of us that the Goums would have used their sabre-dagger rather than a kitchen cleaver."

"And the MPs you say, accepted this story full of holes?"

"And why not? Our Officers had made it clear that we were in Italy to fight the Germans and not the French who were our allies. Which meant we were all expected to turn a blind eye to all the looting, raping and sodomising those black bastards got up to when they were let loose by their ringmasters."

Postulator Fahy was still scribbling notes when Johannes

268

Nielsonsson pulled another green-leafed cigar from his pocket, stuck it between his teeth, lit it with a zippo and drew deeply before blowing its smoke into the pot-pourri.

"How did the French react when the MPs returned the dead Goumier to their headquarters?"

"With indifference. To them, the Goumiers were expendable cannon fodder recruited from their Colonies in Africa. As for the two who allegedly escaped, the French choose two Goums at random, rustled up a firing squad, marched them up to the Piazza and had them executed by their own kind.. End of story, as far as they were concerned. Will that be all, Pastor Fahy, or is there something else?"

"One or two things to clarify before you get back to your repairs. Regarding the Goumier you found dead in the cellar, who killed him in your view, Mr Nielsonsson?" "Does it matter who killed the black bastard?" "Of course it does! My remit is to weigh up the possibilities and match them with the probabilities." Fahy consulted his notes before continuing. "You said there was blood over Bianchina's face, neck and shoulders besides the blood on her back from the stab wounds. How do you account for the blood on her face, neck and shoulders?"

"Must have happened when she hacked the Goum who was fucking her niece. This would account for the fact that there was no blood to speak of on the girl's body. How could there be with a Goum lying on her?"

"Mr Nielsonsson did you, either of you friends or all of you kill the Goumier in revenge for what they did to Lucrezia Bartolomeo?"

"Holy shit, Pastor! He was dead when we arrived. If I can tell who killed the other two, why should I lie about the third one? It doesn't make sense."

"It would make sense if one of your comrades killed him. Let me thank you for your time this morning. Rest assured that what you

269

have told me about your comrades will remain between us. It will not be included in my report to Rome."

"Fair enough, Pastor Fahy." Nielsonsson offered Fahy his hand which the latter shook without hesitation. A handshake sealed in grimy oil.

Johannes Nielsonsson watched Monsignor Fiachre Fahy disappearing in the direction of the wharf, a puzzled look on his face. It was impossible for him to understand all the fuss and mumbo-jumbo about three black bucks who had beaten him to the punch for a good-looking sixteen-year-old broad.

When Fahy got back to St. Joseph's Convent Complex he could hear the voice of Sister Mary reading from the Corinthians 13: *If I speak in the tongues of men or of angels, but do not have love, I am only a resounding gong or a clanging cymbal.*

The nuns were having lunch. Not wishing to partake of bread and Milwaukee Cheeses served with sour milk, Fahy slipped unobserved to his room.

He needed to be alone with his thoughts and wanted to study the notes he had taken while they were still fresh in his mind. His morning with the heretic had been most productive, once the ground rules had been established.

Fahy re-read his notes again and again. And each time his eyes fell on a question underlined with emphasis: Why was blood found on Bianchina's face, neck and torso and none on the Servant of God? Something didn't add up.

Of one thing he was absolutely sure. The Borelli Sisters would have to be grilled, individually and collectively, with the threat of Excommunication over their heads, if they didn't tell the truth, the whole truth and nothing but the truth. Monsignor Fiachre Fahy, Postulator of the Congregation of Sacred Rights was looking forward to the experience of dealing with each of the Borelli Quartet in the intimacy of the Confessional Box.

Having brought forward his meeting with Johannes Nielsonsson, Fiachre Fahy felt justified in taking up the invitation made earlier by young Tomas to see the best that Milwaukee had to offer. He looked forward to visiting the Basilica of St Josaphat, the Pabst Mansion and in particular bellying up in McCafferty's famous Irish Castle for 'The Craic' and getting his round in with umpteen noggins of Guinness depending on the number of drinkers doing a *Breandán Ó Beachán* at the Bar Counter. Forgotten was the prospect of spending the night in Archbishop Henry Hynek's stand-by limousine.

Chapter Twenty Seven

Venafro, Sunday 10th February 1952, Feast Day of Santa Scolastica di Norcia

Seamus was right....as usual. I should have left the dirty work to Farinata and Pantaleone.... the Milwaukee trip has burned me out....alternatives...alternatives...what actually happened...didn't happen....could have happened....probabilities....possibilities ....possibilities...probabilities...... draft after draft.... first English..... then Italian ....then Latin.

"I'm surprised me ol' ticker has lasted the pace." The last words were addressed to Fahy's reflection as the Rome-Cassino-Naples express sped south through the Mezzogiorno[1].

He studied his reflection intently. A recent army-style short back and sides had removed a network of cross-overs. Predictably, it provided Seamus with a new target for his banter. He could still hear Seamus' opening salvo, spoken in an exaggerated Looney Tunes' voice:

"Shwewer now Monsswinwowe Wiachwe Wahy of Cwill Fhionnúwach Cwounty Cwaiw, the new haiw-do with its six inch pauwtin' o' bauwdness makes ya wook wike Elmer Fudd."

Excluding Christmas Day, Fahy had worked into the small hours of the morning for nearly two months before submitting his findings to the Cardinal Ponens of the Congregation of Sacred Rites.

Within days, he had received a draft of His Eminence's conclusions on the Servant of God, Lucrezia Bartolomeo. It confirmed that the circumstances connected with the martyrdom of Lucrezia Bartolomeo had altered preconceptions held before his visit to the United States.

Now, more than ever before, Fahy believed there was something apocalyptic about the turmoils endured by the entire Bartolomeo family.

Silvio Bartolomeo, pater familias, arrested for anti-British activities and deported to Newfoundland on the ill-fated Arandora Star and his calamitous decision to send his twelve-year- old daughter Lucrezia to Italy in the care of his sister.

Roberto Bartolomeo, watching helplessly as the Arandora sank to the bottom of the Atlantic with his father on board. And then, within days of rescue, to be deported on the Dunera's infamous voyage to Australia.

Fiachre Fahy hoped that God would give Giovanni Bartolomeo the strength to endure the shattering disclosure that his sister Lucrezia had died defiled in a doomed struggle when defending her honour.

He wanted to tell Giovanni, within the limits set by his remit, what he believed had happened before and after his sister's death. Rather than have the details obscured by the subjunctive subtleties of Latin syntax when His Eminence's missive arrived on the Bishop's desk.

The train slowed down but didn't stop as it clanked through the ruined station of Roccasecca, which like Milignano, had been an area of heavy artillery exchanges between German and Allied Forces.

Roccasecca, according to Bishop Pantaleone, was where Thomas Aquinas was born. And who was he, a humble priest from Kilfenora County Claire, to tell the bold Cathal that the Great Doctor Angelicus was, in point of fact, born a mere six kilometres away in the village of Aquino?

Cardinal Roccaravindola had wanted to post his deposition to Bishop Pantaleone without delay. But, despite impatience to put Pantaleone in his place, he understood why Postulator Fahy had requested a face-to-face with Cataldo Pantaleone and Giovanni

Bartolomeo and why the Borelli sisters had to be interviewed, yet again, to corroborate Nielsonsson's version of the events which had taken place in Milignano eight years earlier.

The outline of Monte Cassino Abbey could be seen clearly from the window of Fahy's Railway Carriage. It was just as spectacular as it had been when first viewed from Michele il Brigante's bus on the day it took him to the Abbey. He could understand why St Benedict had described the monastery as *Oculus Dei*, the Eye of God. ..... *leave everything to Him .....things will work out in the end ....I'll be teaching in the San Isidoro ...... writing my book on the Irish Missionaries ..... and ending my days in Cill Fhionnúrach .....*

The clock hanging from the glazed roof between Cassino Station's two platforms read 10.25. The Rome-Naples Express had arrived thirty five minutes late... *Come back Musso all is forgiven[1]....* Fahy was sure that by the time the train rumbled into Naples' Stazione Garibaldi, Mussolini's ghost would have had even more cause for unrest.

As the train chugged off to Naples in billows of steam, Fahy was scanning the faces of fellow passengers in search of Michele il Brigante. His Eminence had asked Pantaleone to make sure his Postulator was picked up in Cassino, rather than have him wait for the legendary first train to Venafro which would arrive before the next train to Venafro.

"Monsignore! *Dear God he's as bald as a coot!*" Fahy was relieved to hear Michele's voice and pleased that his haircut had gone unnoticed.

"Just follow me, Monsignore ... *his head is shining like a glow-worm's* ....my car's parked at the Station Bar."

The sighting of Venafro nestling in the foothills of the Apennines was eye-catching. Not quite as spectacular as the Abbey on Monastery Hill, but nevertheless striking enough to keep Fahy's mind from fretting about Michele's idiosyncratic driving.

There was snow at the top of Monte Croce, thick and white until it faded into a smudged snowline where semi-transparent igneous rock lazed beneath the rays of a powerful springtime sun.

Fahy had travelled in this direction before but his attention then was taken by the concerns he and Giovanni had shared for Irma Pacitti's traumatic experience in the Abbey's bus park. Had he known then what he knew now about the Borelli sisters, he would have given scant consideration to their claims of having rescued Irma from the lecherous intentions of the *Beast of Bolzano.*

Within two hours of leaving Cassino's Railway Station, Michele's taxi screeched to a halt under the canopy a blighted palm tree dominating the garden terrace of Pantaleone's residence.

"Wait here Michele. I want you to take me to Milignano. If all goes according to plan, you will be driving me back to Cassino in time for the One-Thirty-Five Express to Rome."

When Fahy stepped out of Michele's taxi he was met by Giovanni Bartolomeo's warm handshake and a face beaming with hope and expectation. "It's great seeing you again, Fiachre."

A happy and excited Giovanni blurted his welcoming words in English. Fahy's heart sank.... *I should have been a coward .....left it all to Farinata*. Giovanni's euphoria was going to make his job so much harder. In no time at all, he was in Pantaleone's study, shaking the Bishop's clammy hand and getting one of his trademark thirty-two-teeth smiles.

"Ah Monsignore, "vuns more to de bree-sci," my friend, once more as my honoured guest in the great and ancient metropolis of Venafrum. Let's hope your visit lasts longer than the proverbial three-day- visiting limitations young Giovanni here is so fond of repeating. Please, take a seat. And how was your trip to Milwaukee? Fruitful I trust?"

"Indeed it was Your Grace. And probably as fruitful as your trip to Paris."

"Touché, mon ami, touché. I note that your new hairstyle has put a decided shine on your cerebral sense of humour. But you must be tired after your journey. Perhaps you might care to postpone our discussion until tomorrow?"

"No thank you , Your Grace. I've asked Michele to take me back to Cassino via Milignano after our discussion, but I would be happy to accept coffee and a San Pellegrino."

"Giovanni, buzz Flavio for coffee and a few of his home-made bagels. However, I'm sure Postulator Fahy hasn't come all the way from Rome for a cup of coffee and one of our local specialities."

"No, Your Grace, the pleasure of meeting you again was uppermost in my mind," replied Fahy, with the sincerity of an auctioneer. "In point of fact, I've come to see both you and Giovanni. Informally and on my own initiative …and of course, with the qualified approval of the Cardinal Ponens."

"Ah yes, my good friend, Ippolito Baldassare Roccaravindola. Forever distinguished for his sanctity, his savoir-faire, his fame as a bon viveur and his love of titbits fried in batter. I wonder if he received the case of Vernaccia I sent him last week. He mentioned he would be entertaining our mutual friend Cardinal Battandier. Tomorrow, in point of fact. Ippolito's chef needs the Vernaccia for the eels he will be serving to honour the feast day of Pope Martin IV." Fahy winked at Giovanni. Both knew they were about to be regaled with a needless exposé of Pope Martin's legendary gluttony.

"A Pope whose taste for eels drowned in Vernaccia was immortalised by an Irish Bishop and Saint, Malachy of Armagh: *O God on high, how much our stomachs must suffer on behalf of Holy Mother Church.* But I digress, for which you can blame the late Monsignor Tofanelli who had a habit of providing me with esoteric information. You were saying, Monsignore?"

"Cardinal Roccaravindola will be writing to you within the next few days in his capacity as Cardinal Ponens....."

"Quite so....quite so.... AND?"

".....after he has fully digested the contents of the report I submitted on my return from the United States"

"As he must, Monsignore," said the Bishop.

"Are we permitted to know, Monsignore, the recommendations made in your official report?" Giovanni's indiscreet question surprised Fahy and embarrassed Pantaleone.

"I make no recommendations, Giovanni," replied Fahy with kindness rather than irritation. "My job as Postulator is to gather and collate information pertaining to the circumstances relevant to your sister's death and to highlight factors which could or would affect the Process of Beatification. Only the Cardinal Ponens can make recommendations for consideration by Papa Pacelli acting in conjunction with the Congregation of Sacred Rites."

"Of course, of course. Monsignore, you must forgive my Secretary's inexperience in procedural matters. In point of fact, what Giovanni should have asked for is an indication of the gist of your investigations.

"I assume you made contact with the surviving American soldier? Not that I considered your visit to the United States was in any way necessary."

"It would not have been necessary if Monsignor Schmalzgruber had done so and which would have saved you an equally unnecessary trip to Paris. But, in answer to your question, I did speak to the soldier in question, by name, Johannes Nielsonsson.

"His two comrades were killed in action shortly after their regiment moved out of Milignano. But this you probably know following your meeting with Archbishop Hynek and Monsignore Roncalli in Paris."

"In point of fact, one of two soldiers in question fell in Acquafondata and the other in Vallerotondo and both are buried in Cassino's Allied Military Cemetery."

Fahy paused, unsure of what he should divulge since he wasn't at liberty to lay all his cards on the table. Pantaleone picked up on Fahy's hesitation.

"In point of fact, Monsignore, I'm sure Giovanni would dearly like to have the gist of your exchanges with this Nielsonsson fellow. You could begin, in point of fact, by telling us what he does for living.... were his circumstances such that he had to be offered inducements in exchange for telling his side of the story?"

"He runs a profitable garage and filling station .... and has no need to sell his story for money."

"In point of fact, did this prosperous garage and filling station proprietor ...ah...shed any light on the dark events which took place in Milignano?"

"Yes and no, Your Grace. I don't know how to put this," turning to Giovanni, "other than asking you to tell me, once again, how you think your sister died."

Giovanni hesitated, fearful of committing another *faux pas*, but he continued when Pantaleone gave him a nod of encouragement.

"Lucrezia died defending her honour and her chastity. She died...virgo intacta.... undefiled.....a martyr's death."

"I'm sorry to say, Giovanni, that your sister, resisting to the end, died prior or during violation from the same men who abused and murdered your Aunt. The American soldiers arrived too late to prevent any of the atrocities which took place in the family cellar."

"In point of fact, Monsignore Schmalzgruber found evidence of no such atrocities with regard to Giovanni's sister. The eye-

278

witnesses who saw the bodies, who prepared Lucrezia and her aunt for burial, testified that Lucrezia had not been interfered with and that she died virgo intacta."

"Let me put it this way, Your Grace. If we believe Sergeant Nielsonsson told the truth, and we have absolutely no reason to believe that he didn't, then we have reason to believe that the Borelli sisters have been less than truthful about what happened in the Bartolomeo cellar."

"In my view," retorted Pantaleone, "the Borelli sisters had no reason to be devious. There was nothing in Don Pietro's statement which gave Monsignore Schmalzgruber any cause for concern."

"The Borelli, Your Grace, we have reason to believe, colluded with the three American soldiers to conceal what occurred in the cellar. Everything was said and done to protect Lucrezia's reputation."

Fahy's revelations had plunged Giovanni into a depressing silence while Bishop's Pantaleone's characteristic self-confidence, with considerable difficulty, helped him to withstand the devastating impact of the Postulator's revelations.

The Bishop was deep in thought, eyes fixed on the surface of his mahogany desk, the shadow of a frown creasing his brow. It fell to him to break the silence which had engulfed the room.

"Nevertheless, nothing, absolutely nothing, will have emerged to cast the slightest doubt on the incontrovertible truth that Giovanni's sister met a martyr's death. Even more so now that you have described the savagery and violence she had to endure. Like Santa Maria Goretti, she died rather than surrender her honour."

Fahy felt there was no point in saying that a comparison between the martyrdom of Santa Maria Goretti and Lucrezia Bartolomeo was flawed. Flawed, because the former had survived virgo intacta and had lived long enough to forgive her attacker.

279

"Your Grace, nobody has disputed ....disputes ..... or will dispute .....the martyrdom of Giovanni's sister. In due course, Giovanni will be informed of the circumstances associated with the events which took place in the cellar." placing his hand on Giovanni's shoulder, Fahy continued, "which is why I have come here today, to inform you that things are not quite as they seemed to be prior to my Milwaukee visit."

"A mere formality, in point of fact, since Lucrezia's martyrdom is unchallenged and indisputable. And it was kind of you to come here to enlighten Giovanni and me about how his sister met her death. Vatican correspondence can sometimes be ... how should I put it? ... insensitive. My dear Monsignore, you must stay for lunch. I have some excellent vintages in my cellar to complement: Flavio's cooking."

"I'm afraid not, Your Grace, because I'm not quite finished with what I have to say. My enquiries in Milwaukee also revealed some other circumstances. Circumstances better left for amplification in His Eminence's submission as Cardinal Ponens."

"Other circumstances, Monsignore? What circumstances, Monsignore?" Harshness had returned to Pantaleone's voice.

"Johannes Nielsonsson disclosed details of blood found on Bianchina's face and neck. Something which I can only verify by speaking to the Borelli sisters. It brings into question who killed the Goumier found dead in the cellar when the Americans arrived."

"The Goumier was killed by one or both of his comrades. From what I remember of my Report to His Holiness, these barbarians were always squabbling with each other over the spoils, human or otherwise. Besides, I don't see what this has to with Giovanni's sister."

"We must ask ourselves that if the Goumier found in the cellar wasn't killed by his comrades or the American soldiers, then who killed him?"

"Come, come Monsignore, it stands to reason that he must have been killed by one of his own. It's preposterous to suggest that it could have been Giovanni's aunt."

"What I am saying, Your Grace is that we do not know for sure who killed the Goumier found dead in the cellar....." Pantaleone interrupted Fahy before he could finish.

"Absolute nonsense, Monsignore! Absolute nonsense! It's ludicrous, absolutely ludicrous to suggest a defenceless woman could have found the strength to kill a savage animal with a single blow. Absolute rubbish, rubbish. I cannot and will not listen to any more of such absurdity."

"Be that as it may be, Your Grace," re-joined Fahy in no way put out by Pantaleone's blustering, "Nevertheless, as Postulator, I submit my findings in which I highlight areas open to interpretation. Which is why I must speak to the Borelli sisters. After which I will report back to the Cardinal Ponens as soon as possible. Don't disturb yourself on my account, your Grace. Giovanni will see me to the car." Bishop Pantaleone nodded agreement, but made no effort to rise from his chair. Fahy reciprocated this discourtesy by ignoring Pantaleone's outstretched hand.

Monsignor Fiachre Fahy followed a dejected Giovanni Bartolomeo to the terrace where Michele and his taxi were waiting in the shade of the blighted palm tree.

Out of Michele's earshot, they said their farewells. And it was Giovanni who broke the silence he had held throughout the heated exchanges in Pantaleone's office.

"A martyr's death and yet some undefined ambiguities? From which I may assume what?"

Fahy placed a sympathetic hand on Giovanni's shoulder before replying. "It's not for me to say what Cardinal Roccaravindola as Ponens will decide, Giovanni, once I've reported the outcome of my meeting with the Borelli sisters. But I agree with you,

281

Giovanni there are too many ifs and buts. Just bear two things in mind, my dear dear Giovanni: your beloved sister Lucrezia must have fought tooth and nail defending her honour and that she has fully earned *a posteriori* accolade of martyrdom."

As soon as Fahy and Giovanni left his Study, Pantaleone made a telephone call to his mentor, Monsignor Roncalli in Paris.

The outcome of the conversation was enough to assure Pantaleone that Papa Pacelli was well aware of the great support and encouragement he had given to Monsignore Fahy's investigations on behalf of the Congregation of Sacred Rites and that the Pope had praised the Bishop for his perennial readiness to uphold the sanctity and traditions of Canon Law.

Bishop Pantaleone, as ever solipsistic, assumed that the Pope's recognition of his efforts, in seeking the truth behind the martyrdom of Lucrezia Bartolomeo, meant that a Red Hat was in the pipeline.

All he had to do, as Monsignore Roncalli had advised, was to make use of his undoubted pastoral endowments and help Giovanni to recover from the trauma caused by Roccaravindola's highly probable setback.

His Grace, Bishop Cataldo Lorenzo Pantaleone, had no intentions of losing a brilliant young priest like Giovanni Bartolomeo. Long term, he had every intention of taking Giovanni to Rome when the call came to receive the Red Hat for which he agonised.

When in Rome, Pantaleone would make good use not only of Giovanni Bartolomeo's intellect to further his pontifical ambitions but also his personal wealth which was per se be indispensable in the pursuit of the aforementioned ambitions.

In the short term, as a Cardinal Elect, Pantaleone had to be as understanding as the limits of his ambitions permitted.

The extent of Giovanni's anticipated despair, confusion and insecurity could have serious and negative consequences on both their futures. Therefore, Pantaleone made the necessary arrangements for Giovanni to spend a few weeks as a guest of the Benedictine Order in Subiaco.

There, he hoped his young protégé would come to terms with the spiritual confusion likely to be caused by the misguided Roccaravindola's negative deposition.

Moreover, with Giovanni out of the way, he could inform the Press that it was the thoroughness of his investigations, including a meeting with the Archbishop of Milwaukee, which led to the discovery of the terrible truth lurking behind the death of Lucrezia Bartolomeo.

Chapter Twenty Eight

To His most Illustrious and most Reverent Lordship Lorenzo Pantaleone, Bishop of Venafro:

From Ippolito Baldassare Roccaravindola:

Cardinals Ponens of the Congregation Rituum Sacrorum.

Since, as a result of the investigations undertaken with the highest degree of diligence by our Postulator, certain suspicions do not seem to be able to be removed from the Servant of God, Lucrezia Bartolomeo; We are sufficiently convinced that there must not be any further continuation of the Cause of Beatification.

For the situation rests as follows: it is not solely a case of a Virgin of the Faith sexually violated and shamefully put to death; but also a case involving the killer of a certain soldier not of the Faith. Wherefore, there is placed in doubt whether blame should in any degree be attributed to the Servant of God, Lucrezia Bartolomeo or to her aunt or to some unknown person.

Since this is the case, We are certainly persuaded as follows: should any argument be advanced by the Advocatus Diaboli whereby the hands of Servant of God, Lucrezia Bartolomeo may be demonstrated as being stained with blood, it cannot in any way whatsoever be possible for the actual beginnings of Beatification to be undertaken; for the Servant of God must not be involved in any such suspicion.

Since therefore the Servant of God, Lucrezia Bartolomeo, cannot be confirmed as being devoid of this blame or suspicion (even if her martyrdom is placed in the least doubt), We decree that there be an immediate cessation of the cause of Beatification.

From this, Our Opinion, there can be no departure nor can any appeal to the contrary be made by anyone.

Given in Rome under the Seal of the Cardinalis Ponens on the 10th Day of February, 1952

[1]See Appendix 1

****

Benedictine Monasteries of Subiaco, Tuesday 26th February1952

Giovanni Bartolomeo had read the five paragraphs in Roccaravindola's letter so many times that he knew each of them by heart. Every sentence in each and every paragraph of its elegant Latin. Five short paragraphs which demolished the expectations he had cherished for his sister Lucrezia since the day he entered the Pontificale in Naples.

Although dated February 10th, two copies of the Cardinal Roccaravindola's letter arrived five days after Fiachre Fahy's last visit to Milignano. Bishop Pantaleone had noticed this apparent irregularity and, ever the solipsist, believed it was part of a plot to discredit him in the eyes of the Pope and deprive him of a Red Hat. As for Giovanni was concerned, the date of the letter was inconsequential given that it didn't affect or alter its conclusions.

For the first time in since his arrival in Subiaco, Giovanni took the letter from its impressive silvery grey envelope. He wanted to reread the words which had extinguished his hopes for Lucrezia's beatification.....*we are sufficiently convinced that the cause of beatification must not proceed.....nobis satis constat de causa beatificationis non esse procedendum.*....not completely convinced. but sufficiently convinced .....

It had not been only a matter of a virgin being subjected to an act of sexual violation and wickedly put to death but also a question of who killed the infidel found in the cellar with Lucrezia and his aunt. There was no hard evidence about who had killed the Goumier. Only suspicions, possibilities and probabilities.

If the Devil's Advocate[1] could claim, as he most certainly would....that the Servant of God's hands could be tainted with blood....*sanguine infectas demonstrentu.*....then the initial steps towards beatification could not be undertaken. The Servant of God must not be open to any suspicion. He could not ignore what the Cardinal stated in his letter. There was the possibility that Lucrezia could have had a hand in the death of the Goumier in question.

His sister could never be free from this burden of suspicion, even if her martyrdom was not in doubt.

Suspicion was reason enough to quash the cause of beatification.....*de causa beatificationis desistendum*. Even if Lucrezia was a martyr- *etiamsi martyrium eius minimo in dubio ponitur-* she could never be a saint.

Whether the Cardinal's decision was fair or not was irrelevant. Nothing could be done to redress the situation....nor could any appeal to the contrary be made by anyone. It was final, Rome had spoken and the case was closed...

Giovanni refolded the letter and returned it to the envelope. Its Papal seal, a white dove on a blue escutcheon, was still intact.

When he had last spoken to Fiachre Fahy, it was fairly obvious that his submission to the Cardinal would put paid to Lucrezia's chances of beatification. Giovanni bore Fiachre no ill-will for doing his duty as a Postulator on behalf of the Congregation of Sacred Rites. From his friend he expected nothing less.

Something which couldn't be said for Schmalzgruber whose negligence had been brutally exposed by Fahy's visit to Milwaukee. It was the German's dereliction of duty which had inadvertently fed Giovanni's expectations regarding Lucrezia's cause for Beatification.

Unlike Bishop Pantaleone, Giovanni couldn't or wouldn't say that Fiachre knew of the Cardinal's final decision before he came to see them on the 10th of February. Understandably, the Cardinal Ponens' letter could only be despatched once Fiachre Fahy had returned to Rome with the expected confirmation of Nielsonsson's testimony from the Borelli sisters.

The circumstantial evidence Fiachre had spoken of had weighed heavily on the Cardinal's decision not to proceed with the case for beatification: *DE CAUSA BEATIFICATIONIS NON ESSE PROCEDENDUM.*

****

Monastery of San Benedetto, Tuesday 26th February 1952

Don Ovidio Passarella, Giovanni's designated Father Confessor and Spiritual Adviser in Subiaco, was a friend of Bishop Pantaleone and had been made aware of Cardinal Roccaravindola's decision which honoured the letter of Canonical Law and how this had affected Giovanni's psychological and spiritual resilience.

During the first week of Giovanni's Spiritual Retreat, Don Ovidio had avoided raising the subject of Roccaravindola's letter. Discussions had centred on why St Benedict had taken refuge in Subiaco during a crisis of conscience.

In the second week, Don Passarella and Giovanni had concentrated on the most personal and impassioned of St Paul's rhetorical Epistles: the second letter to the Corinthians. Giovanni had been in no mood to draw comparisons between himself and St Benedict because they had both taken refuge in Subiaco.

Nor did he feel inclined to argue that the Second Letter to the Corinthians was, as far as he was concerned, the most incoherent of the thirteen letters written by St Paul. Unshakable Faith, according to St Paul, would sustain through hardship, suffering and humiliation. Easy to say but difficult to accomplish.

Don Ovidio's was explaining why he had opted for monastic life after the death of his wife. Both had been teachers of Mathematics at the University of Bologna. The profound simplicity of Benedictine philosophy, he claimed, had lifted him from the depths of despair and enabled him to find peace.

"I don't want to join the Order if that's what you are driving at, Don Ovidio!" declared Giovanni, interrupting Don Ovidio with determination rather than rudeness. For that matter, I don't want to remain a priest. Not now. Not ever ...... loyalty to my sister's memory is paramount."

Passarella seemed unperturbed by Giovanni's interruption. He was expecting it.

"It's a mistake, Giovanni, to think that, as your Father Confessor and Spiritual Adviser, I am only concerned with the metaphysical. The emotive forces of Nature.... human and animal must be confronted. If the problem concerns a woman ...." Don Ovidio looked at Giovanni sympathetically, pushing his squat nose further into his face as he rubbed it with his index finger. An action which drew attention to the diastema between Don Passarella's upper teeth. "About this woman, Irma Pacitti. Bishop Pantaleone tells me you were once very close."

"In a manner of speaking, we still are. I've known Irma for years. Her mother was a friend of my father and they came to an arrangement for us to marry. We simply weren't suited....

288

temperamentally." Giovanni could see from the expression on Don Ovidio's less than handsome face that he was dissatisfied with his answer.

"Don Ovidio, with respect, Irma Pacitti has nothing to do, at least not directly, with my decision to leave the priesthood. She did, however ..." Don Ovidio interrupted him with a conciliatory gesture, a smile softening his pugnacious face. "No Giovanni, there's no line of enquiry in that sense. I just want to know of anything which might have affected your emotional state after the Cardinal's letter arrived. Please be patient with me. Now tell me about this woman. Irma Pacitti. Were you in contact with her after she moved in with your Aunt and Uncle in Milignano?"

"She moved in with them when she separated from her husband. My Aunt felt sorry for her. She and Irma's mother were friends in Scotland. I think my Aunt felt in some way responsible because she had helped to arrange their marriage. There was a temporary reconciliation between Irma and her husband.....before she decided to rejoin her brother in Glasgow."

"I understand she was pregnant," said Don Ovidio sympathetically, "which hardly seems a good reason for a return to Scotland. Unless she had been unfaithful during the separation?"

"And you think I might be responsible?"

"Giovanni, Bishop Pantaleone informed me your Aunt Bianchina, may she rest in peace, was once engaged to the parish priest of Milignano and ...." Giovanni blushed at Passarella's inference.

"Irma, Don Osvaldo, thinks the father of her child could be Stefano Ferrara. I know this for sure because she told me. He took advantage of her while she was recovering from the physical demands of taking the mule track route to the Abbey of Montecassino. Something she did to please Don Pietro."

Giovanni looked Don Ovidio in the eye, "I'm sure the Bishop

informed you of the unsavoury details regarding what happened in Montecassino. And yes, my crisis of conscience is caused by a woman. But it's not Irma. The only woman in my life was and is my sister. She was the main reason I became a priest ...the guiding light of my vocation."

Passarella held his silence for a few moments before replying. "You were fond of Irma Pacitti? Bishop Pantaleone tells me you took her departure for Scotland very badly. Can you explain why?"

"I felt that I had let her down."

"As a man or as a priest?"

"As a friend! As a friend, Don Ovidio. As a friend, for goodness sake! When she came to me in need of advice, I let her down.

"She came to see me in Venafro on the day after I got the bad news about my sister. She wanted to know if she should tell her husband Ferrara might be the father of the child she was expecting. A doubt which added substance to the tittle-tattle circulating about what happened or didn't happen between her and Stefano Ferrara in the Abbey's car park."

"Incidentally, Giovanni, I'm sure you will be interested to know that this Ferrara individual withdrew his writ when our lawyers informed him of Signora Pacitti's pregnancy."

"I don't really care what Ferrara does. It's what he did that matters. I advised Irma to tell her husband what happened in Montecassino.

"I told her she couldn't keep this from her husband for the rest of their married life. That's the insensitive advice I gave her. Ironic, isn't it, Don Ovidio? I told Irma not to live a lie while I was living my own lie as a priest. Living a lie ...... from the moment I set foot in the Seminario Pontificale."

"Come come, Giovanni. As a priest and a friend, was there any other advice you could have given the young lady?"

"She came to see me as a friend and I gave her the advice of a priest. She wanted reassurance from me that living with a lie could save her marriage. Not to mention her reputation. And what do I do? I tell her it would be wrong to deceive her husband. And this despite the fact that he had no doubts that he was the father of the child. A great friend I turned out to be in Irma's hour of need."

"You are judging yourself too severely, Caro Giovanni. Your advice to the young lady was the only advice any honourable man, priest or friend, could have given..... she came to you because her conscience was troubling her more than the fear of losing her reputation as an honest woman. Perhaps, you gave her the advice she wanted to hear and perhaps it helped her to make the decision she wanted to make and did make. So, my dear Giovanni, you must not confuse honesty with worldliness."

"I don't follow, Don Ovidio."

"The world's way is always the easier way because it condones moral cowardice. A world which permits you to do the right thing for the wrong reason and vice-versa. In simple words, it condones a lack of honesty. Irma faced up to this reality and so must you, my dear young man."

"This is why I cannot remain a priest, Don Ovidio. My allegiance should be to God. Where it should have been from the start. It wasn't. This undermines my honesty and the credibility of my vocation."

Passarella said nothing. He was thinking it might be better to give Giovanni some respite to consider his options. "I suggest a change of scenery might be what's needed here, Giovanni. In the meantime, *we will see and we will reflect, videbimus et cogitabimus.* Until our next meeting tomorrow, I suggest you visit the monastery of Santa Scolastica. Don't be put off by the scaffolding across its facade. The inside is in good order. I'm sure a scholar like you will find its library of interest.

"I've asked Don Osvaldo, a visiting monk from Spain to take you to its library, just as we did for you in Montecassino. He'll be the perfect tonic needed to revive your spirits."

Monastery of Santa Scolastica

After lunch, Giovanni took Don Ovidio Passarella's advice and visited the nearby Santa Scolastica Monastery, situated half-way down the hill which separated it from the Monastery of San Benedetto. The work of rebuilding the former's façade was in full swing. It had been damaged by maverick Allied bombing during the razing of Montecassino's Abbey.

On arrival, Giovanni was greeted by Don Osvaldo, a monk on Spiritual Retreat from the *Abbey of Santa Maria de Monserrat* in Catalonia. Brushing aside Giovanni's half-hearted protests, he insisted on giving him a guided tour of the monastery before heading for its library.

For the first time in weeks, a semblance of a smile creased Giovanni's face as he listened to the elderly Benedictine prattling in a strange mixture of Spanish, Italian and English.

"Ay de me golli-gosh! See what the Anglo-Sassone de ruda comportamento has done to this bello monasterio. Non contento with the bombardario of Montecassino he has también bombardariod the monasterio dedicato alla hermana of Santo Benedetto. Man the destructor! Man el destructor!"

Having taken time to peruse a history of Subiaco prior to his departure from Venafro, Giovanni soon discovered that the old monk knew a great deal less than he did about the history, content and architecture of the Santa Scolastica Monastery.

Through the skylight windows above the corridors leading to the library, Giovanni saw plumes of red and gold streaking the evening sky as the sun moved steadily down towards its overnight accommodation behind the Simbruini Mountains.

On the way, Don Osvaldo stopped beside a faded fresco.

Giovanni assumed that he was about to make a comment on the latter. He was mistaken.

Don Osvaldo stopped to stroke an inflamed chilblain on his big toe with loving care and attention. While doing so, Giovanni read the inscription at the bottom of the fading fresco. It referred to its subject as James III, King of England, Scotland and Ireland (1701 to 1766). The fresco was unsigned. The artist having no desire to lend his name to a work of art which failed to reach the height of his mediocrity.

"Of no importancia! Of no importancia!" declared Don Osvaldo dismissively when he noticed Giovanni's interest in the fresco. "A minor paintura .... by a minor artista."Giovanni laughed at the old monk's disparaging comments.

Don Osvaldo beamed with pleasure at the laughter he had provoked. Passarella would be pleased when he reported Giovanni's amusement.

"Did you know, Don Osvaldo," said Giovanni tongue in cheek, "that the gentleman on the fresco was never crowned as King of England, Scotland and Ireland and that he and his son, Bonnie Prince Charlie, are buried in St Peter's Basilica?"

"Papa Borgia est interrar in the Vaticano. Ergo, no grande sorpresa mia who is interrare in the Vaticano. But vamos padre...to the biblioteca donde demonstrare tesoros in manos del convento. En particolar una versiòn of Lactantius."

The mention of Lactantius reminded Giovanni of Don Agostino and Collaquila. Both were still on Giovanni's thoughts when Don Osvaldo led him into the Santa Scolastica Library and made for Lactantius' masterpiece.

Don Agostino had a copy of *THE DEATH OF PERSECUTORS* among his precious collection. Giovanni closed his eyes and in his mind, he could hear the voice of Don Agostino..... *and in this masterpiece, the author writes..... sometimes crudely.... about the deaths of the Christians' Persecutors.... among them*

Nero and Diocletian and God's judgement of them ......

Don Agostino, with borrowed wisdom from God knows where, used to say that books were the telescopes, sextants and the charts prepared by wiser men to help us navigate the dangerous seas of human life.

Giovanni knew that all his experience of life had come from books and that they had not provided him with the knowledge needed to help him deal with the Staffieri, Ferrari and Irmas of this world. St Benedict was described as being *knowingly ignorant and wisely unlearned, scienter nescius et sapienter indoctus.* Giovanni knew he could never dream of earning the right to such a judgement, because, unlike St Benedict, he had no personal experience of life.

Notwithstanding Don Ovidio's experience of life, he had failed to understand his reasons for wishing to leave the priesthood. Despite what Don Ovidio said or inferred, Giovanni's decision to leave had nothing to do with a subconscious desire to have known Irma in the biblical sense.

When he met Don Ovidio in the Sacro Speco, Giovanni was determined to put paid to Don Ovidio's apparent obsession with Irma.

Monastery of San Benedetto

Giovanni climbed down three sets of spiral stairways leading to the Sacro Speco, the holy grotto where St. Benedict had prayed for enlightenment. There, looking like a retired pugilist, he found the portly figure of Don Ovidio.

"Peace be with you, Giovanni."

"And also with you, Don Ovidio."

"Please sit here ...beside me," Passarella beckoned Giovanni

294

over to a niche on the rock face of the cavern.

"You seem convinced that your vocation is a sham because you became a priest to help promote the case for your sister's beatification."

The abruptness with which Passarella opened the discussion took Giovanni by surprise. He had been expecting more probing about his past and present relationship with Irma.

While waiting for Giovanni's response, Passarella put his hands inside the pockets of his scapula. A sure indication that he was prepared to wait, for as long as was necessary, for Giovanni's response to his opening gambit. Giovanni, however, took Don Ovidio's cue with assurance.

"Even if Monsignor Fahy's visit in February prepared me for bad news, my doubts began when Cardinal Roccaravindola's letter arrived a few days later. It was like a bolt from the blue. The letter made me feel my calling had not been from God. I had become a priest for the wrong reason ... not to serve Him but to serve my pride and self-esteem. To fill a void created by a sequence of deaths which wiped out my family like the cholera epidemic did to my grandparents."

"And so you now feel you can atone for your perceived dishonesty by leaving the priesthood?" Giovanni nodded but said nothing.

"Would you agree that one of the universal signs of honesty is a sense of horror regarding transgression?" Again Giovanni made no comment.

"I'll take your silence as a yes. And this sense of horror brings in its wake a need for reparation following any such transgression?" Giovanni sat in silence. His body language betraying the weariness caused by all the doubts he felt were undermining his vocation. He held his silence.

"You have no guilt to expiate, my dear Giovanni. What you need is a cure for your honest presumption. A cure which will permit you to become more accessible to a realistic sense of responsibility."

"How or where do I find such a cure, Don Ovidio?"

"First thing you must do is to realise that even a healthy soul like yours can be momentarily closed to God when it becomes complacent with what it mistakenly perceives as a lack of honesty."

"So what you are saying, Don Ovidio is that I should be welcoming the doubts I have?"

"Why be afraid Giovanni of thinking it is a weakness to have doubts? Didn't Christ himself have doubts in the Garden of Gethsemane and on the Cross? Did not John the Baptist himself have doubts about the identity of Jesus?

"Don't be like the centipede that couldn't begin its search for sustenance because it was unable to decide which leg to move first. I ask you to consider the words of St Ignatius: *scruples are good for a time, purifying the soul, but they should not be protracted because then they become unhealthy.*"

"Are you now saying my reactions to the Cardinal's letter are unhealthy?"

"More or less, Giovanni. Now tell me if you still think of your sister as a martyr for the Faith?"

"Of course I do. As does the Congregation of Sacred Rights: ***martyrium eius minimo in dubio ponitur.***"

"So why the doubts? Did your sister not die with her honour intact, fighting to preserve it? Isn't this something to be proud of? Does it make you less proud of her because she may or may not have had blood on her hands when defending herself and possibly your aunt, so heroically?

"Torturing yourself for what happened to Lucrezia would be as absurd as blaming your father for sending her to Italy in the first place. Or indeed, blaming your father because it was his friendship with Artemio Ferrara which brought his brother into our lives. You might as well say you became a priest to protect yourself from the Evil Eye."

Don Ovidio had been brutally frank and for the most part convincing. Giovanni would need more time to consider the doubts he would be taking back to Venafro and to discern what was false and what was true, which, according to Lactantius, was be the first sign of wisdom.

From the depths of Giovanni's soul came the words which Don Agostino had attributed to his namesake[1]: *our doubts are like traitors which often make us lose the good we could obtain because we don't have the courage to try.*

"Besides, Giovanni, you simply can't forget all the good work you did in Collaquila. Proof of which was Don Agostino's grief when you were removed.

"Bishop Pantaleone's detractors say he overlooked your indiscretion in order to advance his personal ambitions by promoting your sister's cause. In fact, your advancement was due recognition of an intellectual brilliance which could, should and will be put to the benefit of Our Holy Mother Church."

"So what you're saying is that there are lessons to be learned from suffering. *Παθήματα μαθήματα* as the Ancient Greeks put it: *we learn from the things we suffer.* And from its natural consequences, we grow in wisdom and stature and in favour with God and man."

"No, Giovanni, I was saying no such thing although I am flattered you should think so. However, what I saying is that if there had been no Lucrezia-driven crisis in your life, then something else would have cropped up. Just ask yourself this: was your decision to leave the priesthood influenced by disclosure of the less attractive features of her martyrdom? Would you have all the details of what occurred in the cellar made all the more sensational by your decision to quit?

Chapter Twenty Nine

Giovanni Bartolomeo was recalled from his Spiritual Retreat when Cataldo Lorenzo Pantaleone's days, as Bishop of Venafro, were numbered in months rather than in years.

Travelling via Frosinone and Ceprano from Subiaco, Michele il Brigante, chauffeur, entrepreneur and purveyor of village gossip, had catapulted Giovanni to the Bishop's residence in less than three hours. Without uttering a word.

Michele's uncharacteristic silence was the clearest of indications that he had no intention of commenting on the contradictions associated with the gossip he was spreading about Lucrezia Bartolomeo's death and Irma Pacitti's pregnancy.

He had no intention of undermining the credibility of the Borelli sisters regarding the part they played, not only in concealing the truth behind Lucrezia Bartolomeo's death but also the truth of what had happened on his bus in Montecassino. What his friends had said and done was for the benefit of all concerned.

"Bishop Pantaleone," said Michele breaking his silence, "has asked me to wait in the courtyard while he gives you time to pack your bags."

Giovanni was taken aback on learning of his fate from His Grace's part-time chauffeur. Michele's inopportune remarks left him bewildered and angry. It was unlike His Grace. Until that moment, he had never doubted the Bishop's loyalty or discretion. It grieved him deeply to have learned of his dismissal from the likes of Michele.

Eager for confrontation, Giovanni barged into the Bishop's private study. Before swords could be crossed, the Bishop cut him short. "Sit and be quiet. Say nothing you might regret for the rest of your life. Your ill-tempered, ill-mannered and insolent entry into your Bishop's presence will be overlooked. This time." Pantaleone gave Giovanni a withering look of disapproval before continuing. "You should know that Don Agostino is ill, drifting in and out of consciousness with alarming regularity. His housekeeper, for reasons best known to herself, did not contact me directly but asked your uncle to inform me of the situation.

"I got Michele to take me to Collaquila as soon he could. There, I'm sorry to say, I found that Don Agostino was unable to fulfil any of his priestly obligations. Before you ask, let me inform you that he has chronic lymphocytic leukaemia. In lay terms, cancer of the white blood cells. Self-evident symptoms of which are a severe loss of appetite and weight and progressive tiredness causing chronic fatigue. I am disappointed that you did not see fit to report any of these symptoms to me when you were in Collaquila."

Giovanni said nothing but reproached himself for having attributed Don Agostino's signs of fatigue to old age.

"In the meantime, for want of better, I have instructed Don Pietro to deputise for Don Agostino within the limits of his incompetence. His duties in the Santa Maria Maggiore are less than onerous given the time he spends on his farmstead."

"How bad is Don Agostino's condition, your Grace?" enquired Giovanni ignoring Bishop Pantaleone's disparaging remarks about Don Pietro.

"In point of fact, his illness is terminal."

"How long, Your Grace before he..."

"Hard to say. We have no idea when his blood cells became infected. His housekeeper thinks that they were infected by the Goumiers. Nonsense of course. Cancer is not contagious. However, if his Housekeeper is perchance correct, then, according to our Haematologist, the incubation period is roughly seven to eight years. Which means Don Agostino has about three months left. Six months at the most."

"I take it that Don Agostino has refused hospital treatment?"

"Not only that, he has refused to be treated by the local doctor. His Housekeeper informed me that Don Agostino can't and won't trust a Doctor who declared Staffieri dead after you had knocked him unconscious with a violence which would have done credit to your father.

"My personal Physician visits him every other morning because Don Agostino has refused to be treated in the Diocesan Hospice. He is adamant about wanting to die in Collaquila. And more to the point, he requests your reinstatement and so I've....."

"Of course I would ... " "Don't interrupt... decided to comply with his request. However, let me make one thing clear to you, young man: your stay in Collaquila, starting from today, will be for the duration of what's left of Don Agostino's life before he gives up the ghost. When the Good Lord sees fit to liberate him from his agony, you will return as my Secretary in double quick time. Is this absolutely clear?"

Giovanni nodded his head. He was humbled by Don Agostino's request and was more than happy to comply with the Bishop's decision to send him back to Collaquila. He believed his return to Collaquila was providential. As if it had been written in the stars. And a well-timed opportunity to eliminate any lingering doubts he still had about his vocation.

Given that it was a heaven-sent opportunity to savour his friendship during the few months that remained, re-joining Don Agostino was something he welcomed with all his heart.

Giovanni could also look forward to renewing acquaintance with the local worthies in Collaquila, in particular with the members of his clandestine Anniversary Committee. There would also be an opportunity of extending an olive branch to Raffaele Staffieri, Collaquila's Undertaker and Itinerant Butcher.

He wondered if the Brigadiere had finally got round to making his first arrest and if the children still ridiculed him when he was on patrol. Involuntarily, Giovanni began humming the words of the song the children sung to the tune of *My Darling Clementine*:

Our local Bobby, Our local Bobby,

Sings this song unto his wife:

We're a eating and a-drinking and a-pooping free for life.

What became of his career, after Don Agostino had been granted Eternal Rest, Giovanni would leave to Divine Providence as seen through the eyes of his Bishop.

Chapter Thirty

Parish Presbytery of San Sebastiano, Collaquila

In the early morning hours of Monday 26th of January 1953, ten months after his appointment as the acting-parish priest of Collaquila, Giovanni administered the Sacrament of Extreme Unction [1] to a semi-conscious Don Agostino.

"May the Lord help you by this holy anointing and His most holy mercy through the grace of the Holy Spirit, so that He may save you, free you from your sins and in His goodness raise you up."

While Giovanni was intoning the Latin words of the Sacrament and anointing Don Agostino's sensory orifices for sins he might have committed with his eyes, mouth and ears, the dying priest opened his eyes. On recognising Giovanni, Don Agostino Porrini whispered the words *Solomon's Heir*, nodded his head, smiled and closed his eyes for the last time.

By the time Staffieri delivered a hand-carved trapezoidal coffin from his repository, Emilia and her friends, Mangiabambini and La Cappriciosa, had washed Don Agostino's gaunt corpse from head to toe and dressed it in his best alb, black chasuble, matching stole, battered biretta and favourite open-toed sandals. Despite her hernia condition, the honour of lifting the skeletal body of Don Agostino and placing it in the padded silk interior of the coffin was left to Emilia, his housekeeper and friend for over fifty years.

Later that same morning, after Don Agostino's open coffin had been placed on two brass stands near the main altar's communion railings, the Sacristan was tolling the church bell. It was a signal to Collaquila's Faithful that Don Agostino was ready to receive their last respects.

Church of San Sebastiano, Collaquila, Tuesday, January 27th 1953

Giovanni Bartolomeo con-celebrated Don Agostino's Requiem Mass with his friend Monsignor Fiachre Fahy, teacher of Italian at the Irish College in Rome and Don Pietro Verrecchia, parish priest of Milignano. The church of San Sebastian was packed. Sitting alongside the Sindaco and the Brigadier were Giovanni's Uncle and Aunt and their chauffeur, Michele il Brigante.

Bishop Pantaleone was conspicuous by his absence. He was still in Paris, having gone there on the Feast of Stephen to congratulate Monsignor Roncalli on his appointment as Cardinal Patriarch of Venice.

Until the reading of the gospel, Matthew, Chapter Five, verses One to Twelve, Giovanni had managed to keep his emotions under control. He had chosen the former because it contained the Eight Beatitudes which would provide the main thrust of his homily to his dearly departed friend.

Giovanni stood beside the coffin in silent prayer. Placing his right hand over Don Agostino's brass nameplate, he bowed his head in what was to be a forlorn attempt to steady his nerve. However, what self-control he had mustered, vanished soon after he began his Funeral Oration.

"In the name of the Father and of the Son and of the Holy Ghost. Let us rejoice and be glad, for Don Agostino's reward is a well-earned communion with the Lord in heaven. My dear people, brothers and sisters, the light, the light.....the light has gone from our lives......from my life...." Giovanni's voice faltered and cracked. He could no longer contain his tears. The words Don Agostino had ever so modestly wished for his epitaph flashed

303

through his mind, shattering the last vestiges of composure he had been endeavouring to maintain: *A life blameless and free from sin.*

Many of the women present had been quietly grieving up to this point, but the distress shown by their Curate released their bridled emotions of sorrow and grief.

Don Pietro came to Giovanni's rescue. He headed for the pulpit while Monsignor Fahy ushered a sobbing Giovanni to the concelebrants' bench to the left of the narrow aisle which separated it from the three semi-circular altar steps.

From the pulpit, so beloved by Don Agostino, Don Pietro delivered an impromptu sermon based on the Eight Beatitudes and selective paraphrasing of the *De Profundis*, the commemorative Psalm to the dead.

"My dear brothers and sisters, Blessed indeed are the *Pure of heart for they shall see God.* Let us rejoice therefore that Don Agostino is surely this day in the presence of God. Let us rejoice, even more, that we have a man whom future generations here in Collaquila will remember as a priest who lived a life of self-sacrifice in the service of others.

"And which of us here present," placing a hand over his heart while his eyes swept from the congregation to Fiachre Fahy and back again, "would not wish to be accorded such an epitaph?

"My dear brothers and sisters, in today's gospel we heard the inspirational words of the Eight Beatitudes. And as Don Giovanni read each and every one of them, we contemplated on which of them best reflected the life of Don Agostino. But, my dear people let me say there is no need for any such selection when contemplating the life of Don Agostino.

"Why is this so, my dear brothers and sisters?" Once again Don Pietro's gaze swept from the congregation to Fiachre Fahy and back again, "Because the purpose of the Eight Beatitudes is to inspire us to live and behave in a certain way. In simple words, each of them carries a promise of salvation. Therefore they must be considered collectively and in Don Agostino's case, never in isolation."

Don Pietro paused for a few moments as he looked down on the hushed congregation with the words Bishop Pantaleone had used at Giovanni's ordination dinner flashing through his head: *All were silent and fixed their eyes in close attention.* "For many here today," Don Pietro resumed, "if not for all of us, Don Agostino will be remembered as having been a beacon of light and hope during those dark days when we were persecuted, scourged and scarred by those who were sent to liberate our villages from the occupying forces of German tyranny.

"Did not Don Agostino defend the defenceless from persecution, violence and death, when trying to bring peace where there was fury and calm when there was frenzy? When he defended others knowing the price he would have to pay for his courage? And as a result, did not Don Agostino himself become a victim of unspeakable violence and abuse? From which he carried literal and figurative scars as permanent reminders, if ever they were needed, to each and every one of us, of his torment and suffering? *Blessed indeed are the persecuted for they shall see God.*

"*If Thou, O Lord, hath kept a watch* .....on whatever little faults Don Agostino might have had …. his legendary thrift....his endearing and irascible disposition....his tendency to quote from the poetry of Horace....his love of cheese.....his predilection for a certain type of salame ...." There was a ripple of laughter from those who had encouraged Don Agostino's liking for *Caccio Cavallo* and *Salame Suppressato*, "....for his aversion to waste......then we ask you humbly, O Lord, to forgive these imperfections, sure in the knowledge that such wrongdoing could not possibly banish Don Agostino from the joy of your Eternal Light.

"Each and everyone here present today.........in this church dedicated to the martyr San Sebastiano..... holds, sustains and

305

believes that with *Thee O Lord there is merciful redemption.* And it is for this mercy on behalf of Don Agostino that we turn to You, O Lord. in supplication. *Our souls rely on Your Word and our souls have hope in the Lord.*

"My brothers and sisters let us Pray to the Lord in thanksgiving and for His mercy in granting Don Agostino the joy of eternal bliss in Thy Presence. In the name of the Father and of the Son and of the Holy Ghost. Amen."

When Don Pietro had finished delivering his consequential remarks from the pulpit, he headed for an ashen-faced Giovanni with a view to apologising for the inadequacy of his impromptu address. Before he could do so, Giovanni embraced Don Pietro and whispered thanks for his face-saving intervention.

Following words of encouragement from Fiachre Fahy, Giovanni resumed the Requiem Service, albeit his voice trembling like the leaves of an aspen in an Aeolian breeze [1].

As soon as Giovanni had retired to the sacristy with Don Pietro and Fiachre Fahy, Raffaele Staffieri, dressed in black from head to toe, sealed the interior zinc lining of the lid to the zinc lining of the casket with an amalgam of metallic phosphate and powdered glass. Having removed the excess paste with a sponge, Staffieri screwed the lid to the casket. This witnessed, the congregation left to stand in silence on the church steps.

While the bell tolled languidly, the coffin was borne from the church by Giovanni, Don Pietro, Fiachre Fahy, Ettore Bartolomeo, the Sindaco and the Brigadiere. They carried it down the crowded stairway to the piazza while villagers jostled to touch the coffin as it passed.

Parked in the Piazza, ready to receive Don Agostino's coffin was an open-hatched Gothic Hearse, recently re-sprayed with a glossy black lacquer smelling of formaldehyde.

Having been told to spare no expense for Don Agostino's funeral, Staffieri had refurbished the hearse and opted for four rather than two horses. The black horses were bedecked with enormous black plumes emerging from black leather blinkers attached to each ear. Preceding the horses would be the first of the two brass bands dressed in brand new funereal livery. Similarly attired, the second brass band would follow behind the mourners.

Giovanni had made it clear to Staffieri that the Funeral March to be played had to be Chopin's and not the march composed for Garibaldi's funeral. This was in accordance with the preferences of Don Agostino who would have wanted nothing to do with music dedicated to a man who referred to Pope *Pio Nono* as a cubic metre of dung. As far as Don Agostino was concerned, Garibaldi belonged, as *Pio Nono* himself had put it, *to the Synagogue of Satan, the last fruit of the serpent Lucifer and the legitimate descendant of Cain and Judas Iscariot.*

The cortège moved off slowly towards the Campo Santo to the rhythm of the drums, trombones, bullhorns and euphoniums playing the thirty-eight notes of the opening movement of Chopin's Funeral March. Both bands repeating the same phrases until the cemetery gates were reached, twenty minutes after leaving Piazza San Sebastiano.

Walking ahead of the second band were the mourners led by the Giovanni, wearing soutane, surplice and biretta and clasping a missal against his chest. He was flanked by two altar boys, each carrying a two-metre high ebony pole crowned with a brass crucifix.

Following behind Giovanni were the women of the village, led by Emilia, her arms linked with Mangiabambini and La Cappricciosa, heads covered by black lace mantillas. Bringing up the rear, were the men, each wearing broad black armbands and black straw hats supplied by the enterprising Staffieri.

When settling the substantial account, Giovanni met it in full without comment. He was sure Staffieri would never boast of having taken advantage of the son of the man who had outsmarted him seventeen years ago in Glasgow's Casa D'Italia.

To have done so would have been his own undoing and brought the wrath of Collaquila's women on his head.

Don Giovanni

Epilogue

Ambition in a man is such a powerful passion that no matter how it is achieved, he will never be satisfied. (Nicolò Machiavelli)

Following Don Agostino's funeral, Giovanni was not recalled to Venafro as his Bishop had threatened in January of the previous year. This welcome respite for Collaquila's acting parish priest had nothing to do with forgetfulness on the part of Bishop Pantaleone. It was due to the promotion of the latter's mentor, Monsignor Roncalli.

Following thirty-five years of diplomatic service as Papal Nuncio, first in Sofia, then in Istanbul and finally in Paris, Angelo Giuseppe Roncalli, at the age of seventy-two, was appointed Cardinal Patriarch of Venice. An appointment which he would assume on the 15th March 1953.

Leaving his Secretary to represent him at an inconsequential village funeral in Collaquila, Bishop Pantaleone had visited his mentor in Paris to congratulate him on his promotion to the Patriarchy of Venice.

In confidence, Cardinal Roncalli would inform him that Papa Pacelli was about to appoint him as Advisor to the most senior official in the Vatican's Secretariat for Extraordinary Affairs: Monsignor Giovanni Battista Enrico Antonio Maria Montini[1].

In Cardinal Roncalli's opinion, the advantages, of being attached to the entourage of someone who was most likely to be a future Pope, were inestimable. It never occurred to the next Patriarch of Venice that he himself could be the 260th successor to the Papacy when Papa Pacelli's eventful nineteen years' reign finally came to an end in 1958.

However, this possibility had crossed Cataldo Pantaleone's mind

309

from day one of his mentor's appointment as Patriarch of Venice. In his view, his friend Angelo was infinitely more *Electable to the Papacy[1]* than Monsignor Montini. He had no doubts that Cardinal Roncalli would follow in the footsteps of the Blessed Giuseppe Sarto who, as Patriarch of Venice, was elected to the Papacy fifty years ago as Pius X.

That Montini was not made a Cardinal by Papa Pacelli when Roncalli received the Red Hat, which came with his promotion, was a clear sign, as Pantaleone would have it, of how the wind was blowing in the Vatican corridors of power.

Nevertheless, needing a fall-back plan, Pantaleone felt he had nothing to lose by ingratiating himself with Monsignor Montini, just in case the latter jumped the queue in Papa Pacelli's next Consistory and beat him in the race for a Red Hat.

As Cardinal Cataldo Lorenzo Pantaleone, he saw no reason to doubt that he would be as *Electable to the Papacy* as any other Cardinal. And even more so when his friend and mentor became Pope.

But first things first. To keep his eye on the main opposition, he would make sure Giovanni succeeded him as Montini's adviser in the Vatican's Secretariat of State for Extraordinary Affairs.

APPENDIX ONE

Illustriousness AC Reverentissimo Domino Laurentio Pantaleoni Episcopo Venafri

Baldassari Hippolitus Roccaravindola Cardinalis Ponens Congregationis Rituum Sacrorum.

Quandoquidem ex quaestionibus a nostro Postulatore summa diligentia susceptis suspiciones quaedam a Serva Dei LUCRETIA BARTOLOMEO depelli non posse videntur, nobis satis constat de causa beatificationis non esse procedendum.

Nam res ita se habet:non solum de virgine fideli stupro violata necique turpiter demissa agitur, sed etiam de militis cuiusdam infidelis interfectore. Qua de re, utrum culpa Servae Dei LUCRETIAE BARTOLOMEO aliqua ex parte sit attribuenda an amitae eius an nesciocuique ignoto, in dubio ponitur.

Quae cum ita sint, nobis hoc certe persuasum est : si quid ab Advocato Diaboli afferatur argumentum quo manus Servae Dei LUCRETIAE BARTOLOMEO sanguine infectas esse demonstrentur, fieri omnino non potest ut exordia ipsa beatificationis suscipiantur; serva enim Dei in nullam talem suspicionem vocari debet.

Quoniam igitur Serva Dei LUCRETIA BARTOLOMEO hac culpa vel suspicione carere confirmata non est, (etiamsi martyrium eius minimo in dubio ponitur) de causa beatificationis desistendum protinus censemus.

De hac nostra sententia decedi non licet neve fiat nulla a quoquam in contrarium appellatio.

Datum Romae sub Signo Cardinalis Ponentis die X Februarii MCML11 .

Chapter Notes

Preface

Page 5 [1] **The Gustav Line,** *a German Military Line of Defence which ran from the Garigliano River in the Tyrranean West, through the Apennine Mountains, and into the Sangro River on the Adriatic Coast to the East.*

Page 6 [1] Monsignor Angelo Giuseppe Roncalli, elected Pope in 1958.

Chapter Two

Page 13 [1] Cinecittà, *a large film studio in Rome.. With an area of 400,000 square metres, it is the largest film studio in Europe and is considered to be the hub of Italian Cinema.*

[2] League of Nations, *an inter government organisation established after World War 1 in order to maintain world peace. It failed to prevent the invasion of Abyssinia by Italy in 1935 and failed to prevent the outbreak of World War 11 four years later.*

[3] AM lira, Allied Military Currency, *issued in Italy after the Allies landed in Sicily in 1943 and interchangeable with Italian lira. One hundred AM lire was valued at one US dollar*

Page 15 [1] Their affair was encouraged by her elderly husband, Sir William Hamilton who had nothing but respect and admiration for Nelson, who was revered as an English National Hero.

Page 19 [1] Five Boys, *solid chocolate bars made by JR Fry of Bristol until 1976.*

Page 20 [1] Paschal Candles, *candles blessed on Holy Saturday (day before Easter Sunday) and placed on the altar until Pentecost, representing the gift of the Holy Spirit.*

Page 21 [1] The Italian Expeditionary Corps, *Armata Italiana in Russia (ARMAR) also known as 8th Italian Army consisting of 250.000 sent to the Russian Front in 1941. Inadequately equipped for action during harsh Russian Winter, the Italian Army lost over 130,000 men during its defeat at the Battle of Stalingrad in 1943.*

Page 24 [1] University of Glasgow, *Fourth oldest university in the English-speaking world; founded in 1451.*

[2] Listen to your discerning heart; Don Pietro is referring to Chapter One Kings, verses 3 to 9, when Solomon asks God to give him a discerning heart to help him distinguish between right and wrong.

Chapter Three

Page 26 [1] The Evil-Eye, *a look or glance that is thought to be able to harm someone*

Page 27 [1] Hector Powe Tailors, *established in London's Regent Street in 1910. By 1925, it had shops in Glasgow, Edinburgh and Manchester.*

Page 29 [1] Sacristy, *a room in a Church where a priest prepares for a service and where vestments and articles of worship are kept. These are laid out as and when required by an unpaid volunteer called a Sacristan who, as often as not, also assumes the duties of bell-ringer.*

[2] Pax Romana, *was a long period of relative peacefulness and minimal expansion by the Roman Military Forces of the Roman Empire.*

Page 31 [1] Piazzale Loreto, *where the dead bodies of Benito Mussolini and his mistress Clara Petacci were strung up following their capture and execution in Dongo, a commune in the Province of Como, Region of Lombardy.*

Chapter Four

Page 35 [1] The Pope is the nominal Bishop of Kilfenora and Parish Priest of Liscannor under a Papal Dictate dating from 1883.

[2] Bloody Maxwell, *after the Easter Rising of 1916 in Dublin, the British Commander, Sir John Maxwell, arbitrarily ordered the execution of Republican Commanders and Sympathisers (Sinn Feinners) despite advice from the British Prime Minister Herbert Asquith.*

Chapter Five

Page 37 [1] Giuseppe Garibaldi, *born in Nice (formerly Nizza) in 1807 and died on the Sardinian Island of Caprera in 1882; a heroic figure in the Wars of Unification in mid-nineteenth century Italy. Today, he is seen by many Italians as a criminal who sowed death and destruction while annexing the former Catholic Bourbon Kingdom of The Two Sicilies in an undeclared war on behalf of the recently constituted Kingdom of Italy (declared in 1861) and headed by Vittorio Emmanuelle 11, the former King of Sardinia. Considerable funding for Garibaldi's anti-papal military campaigns came from admirers based in the General Headquarters of Scottish Freemasons in Edinburgh.* **(Garibaldi Biscuits are also called Nice Biscuits)**

Page 38 [1] German V1 Rockets, *contained propaganda leaflets which were fired into front-line Allied troops in Italy.*

Page 39 [1] The Osservatore Romano, *a daily newspaper of the Vatican City State which carries the Pope's discourses, reports on the activities of the Holy See and on events taking place in the Church worldwide.*

[2] Palazzo Giacomo Bartolomeo da Brescia, *demolished in 1936 to make way for Via della Conciliazione which linked St Peter's Square to Castel Sant' Angelo.*

Chapter Six

Page 43 [1] Faldstool is a portable folding chair, used by a bishop when not occupying the throne in his own cathedral or when officiating in a church other than his own;

Page 48 [1] Battle of Enderta, *took place, during the Second Italo-Abyssinian War (1935-1939), in February 1935 when the Italian Army, despite heavy losses, captured Amba Aradam.*

Page 51 [1] Mammone, *a legendary brigand who supported the Neapolitan Bourbons against their French counterparts. Mammone was a cannibalistic monster who is said to have murdered five hundred men and women with the greatest refinements of cruelty, and who wore at his belt the skull of one of them, out of which he used to drink human blood at mealtimes*

Page 52 [1] The Oil of Catechumens, *is intended to help strengthen the person about to be ordained, and prepare them for the probable struggles of priesthood. Generally speaking, a Catechumen was a person receiving instruction in preparation for receipt of a sacrament.*

Page 53 [1] The Royal Pygmy, *refers to Vittorio Emanuele 111. The 5ft tall monarch reigned inconspicuously from 1900 to the year of his abdication in 1946.*

Chapter Seven

Page 57 [1] Armistice, 8th September 1943. Following hard on the resignation of Mussolini, the new Italian Prime Minister, Marshall Badoglio, to avoid further harm on the nation, signed an agreement to cease all hostility against the overwhelming power of Anglo-American Allies which had landed in Southern Italy.

Page 61 [1] Stronzo, vulgar and offensive word meaning, shithead, ass-hole, bastard and prick.

Page 63 [1] Quintus Horatius Flaccus (65BC-8BC), *better known as Horace. A leading Roman lyric poet during time of Emperor Augustus. Also wrote elegant and caustic Satires and Epistles.*

Page 65 [1] Mandorle Ricci, rough sugar coated almonds, first produced by the historic Pasticciera Carosella in Agnone (Region of Molise). The author's maternal grandmother was the younger daughter of its founder.

Chapter Eight

Page 67 [1] Publius Vergilius Maro, usually called Virgil, wrote the Aeneid which tells the story of Aeneas, the legendary hero of the Trojan War who travelled to Italy where he became the ancestor of the Romans.

Page 69 [1] Let's drink from the joyful cups, Libiamo ne' lieti calici is from a famous duet (with chorus) in Verdi's Opera, *La Traviata.*

Page 70 [1]Galeazzo Ciano, Mussolini's son-in-law. Italian Foreign Minister from 1936 to 1943 and thereafter Italian Ambassador to the Holy See until he was executed by order of Mussolini at the insistence of the Germans with a year of his appointment to the latter.

Page 73 [1] Henkell, a German sparkling wine. Hitler's Foreign Secretary, Von Ribbentrop, married Anna Henkell the daughter of a wealthy Wiesbaden wine-producer in1920. As a result, Hitler referred to the former as his Champagne Salesman. Von Ribbentrop was the first high-ranking Nazi to be hanged following the Nuremberg Trials constituted by the International Military Tribunal (1945-1946).

Page 74 [1] *"The farmer who hanged himself on the expectation of plenty",* from Shakespeare's *Macbeth,* Porter Scene, Act Two, Scene Three.

[2] In Ancient Roman Times, Venafro developed a renowned reputation for the production of Olive Oil. The Roman Poet, Horace, sang its praises as follows: *That corner of the world to me more than any other smiles, where the honey gives way to that of Hymettus and the olive competes with that of the green berry from Venafro.* When the Romans brought Christianity to the Apennine Plains, a bishopric for Venafro was established in the 5th century.

Chapter Nine

Page 77 [1] Jaun Fangio (1911-1995). was an Argentine Racing Driver and World Champion in 1951 and from 1954 to 1957

Page 84 [1] Giovanni 'Gianni' Agnelli, 1921-2003, known as L'Avvocato (the Lawyer), was the principal shareholder of FIAT Motors (Fattoria Italiana Automobilistica Torino/Italian Automobile Factory of Turin). Closely associated with Juventus Football Club of Turin.

Chapter Eleven

Page 94 [1] Mare Nostrum, *Latin form for* Our Sea*, was the Ancient*

Roman name for the Mediterranean Sea. The term was originally used by Romans when referring to the Tyrrhenian Sea following the conquest of Sicily, Sardinia and Corsica during the Punic Wars with Carthage.

Page 96 [1] General Luigi Cadorna (1850-1928), *following the disastrous Battle of Caporetto, in which 250,000 Italian soldiers perished, he was dismissed for incompetence at the insistence of British and the French Commands and replaced by the legendary, General Armando Diaz.*

Page 98 [1] Kristallnacht, *The Night of the Broken Glass, a pogrom against Jews throughout Nazi Germany on 9th November 1938, when windows of Jewish shops, buildings and Synagogues were smashed by SA Paramilitaries and Civilians.*

Page 99 [1] OVRA, Organisation for Vigilance and Repression, the Secret Police during the Mussolini Regime, and the Italian precursor of the German Gestapo. Assigned to stop anti-fascist activities and was headed by Arturo Bocchini.

[2] Arthur Neville Chamberlain (1869-1940), was Prime Minister of the United Kingdom from May 1937 to May 1940 when he was succeeded by Winston Churchill. Best remembered for his policy of Appeasement and the signing of the Munich Agreement in 1938 which conceded the German speaking Sudetenland Region of Czechoslovakia to Hitler's Germany.

Chapter Twelve

Page 101 [1] St Sebastian, *an early third-century martyr during the persecution of Christians by the Roman Emperor Diocletian. Left for dead by Imperial Archers, was nursed back to health by a Christian Widow. When the Emperor discovered he was still alive, he ordered him to be beaten to death and dumped into a sewer.*

Chapter Fourteen

Page 114 [1] *"Let me have men about me that are fat....Yon Cassius has a lean and hungry look. He thinks too much. Such men are dangerous. Shakespeare's 'Julius Caesar', Act One, Scene Two.*

[2] The Fear of Death perturbs me, *Timor mors peturbat me, a Latin*

phrase commonly found in medieval Scottish and English poetry.

Page 116 [1] SPQR, *is an initialism of Senatus Populusque Romanus i.e. The Roman State and People. It is also the official emblem of the current Municipality of Rome.*

Page 118 [1] V-F-N-C-L, *obscene expletive, Va Fa'n Culo i.e. Go fuck yourself.*

Page 120 [1]An Phoblacht, *was founded in 1906 as the official organ of the non-sectarian Republican and Separatist Members of the Belfast Dungannon Clubs.*

Page 124 [1] Eamon de Valera (1882-1975), *a prominent statesman and political leader in 20th century Ireland.*

[2] WASPS, *White, Anglo-Saxon and Protestant.*

Chapter Sixteen

Page 134[1] Farinata, Manente degli Uberti (1212-1264) *better known as Farinata degli Uberti because of his platinum blond hair; belonged to one of the most ancient and important Florentine families.*

Page 135 [1] Haile Selassie (1892-1975), Emperor of Ethiopia (historically known as Abyssinia). At the League of Nations in 1936 he condemned Italy for tts use of chemical weapons during the Second Italo-Ethiopian War (1935-1939). In 1973, famine in Ethiopia let to his removal in the year of his death.

Page 141 [1] Square Nimbus or Halo, used by artists when depicting living Saints in paintings and frescoes.

Page 142 [1] The Marshall Plan, also known as the European Recovery Programme was a United States initiative to provide aid to Western Europe following the devastations of World War Two.

Page 145 [1] *Lasciate ogni spernza voi ch'entrate, Abandon all Hope Ye who enter. Words written over the Gates of Hell in Dante's Divine Comedy*

Chapter Seventeen

Page 147 [1] In 1934, Cole Porter wrote the musical *Anything Goes.*

Its most famous song, *You're the Tops* contains no reference to Mussolini: The verse which contains the line "You're a Mussolini, You're a Mrs Sweeney" was written by Sir PJ Wodehouse. in an anglicised version of the song in question.

[2] Giovinezza. The official hymn of the Italian National Fascist Party, Regime and Army and the unofficial national anthem of Italy from 1924 to 1943.

Page 147 [1] Giacomo Matteotti (1895-1924), *Secretary of Italian Socialist Party and Member of Parliament; having accused Mussolini of using violence to win the 1924 General Election, he was subsequently assassinated by Fascist Loyalists.*

Chapter Eighteen

Page 160 [1] The Battle of Ambi Alagi, *was the first in a series of battles during the First Italo -Ethiopian War in which 30,000 Italian troops were annihilated.*

Page 163 [1] Le Droit de Jambage, *the right of a feudal Lord to have sexual intercourse with any of his or her dependents.*

Chapter Nineteen

Page 167 [1] De Senectute. *On Old Age, is an essay written by Cicero in 44 BC on the subject of ageing and death.*

Page 172 [1] Blackshirts, *Camicie Nere in Italian, members of the armed squads of Italian Fascists under Mussolini who wore black shirts as part of their uniform. Their function was to attack and destroy organisations which opposed the Fascist Regime, inter alia, Socialists, Communists, Republicans, Catholics and Trade Unionists.*

Chapter Twenty

Page 180 [1] Sarzana, *Province of La Trapezia, Region of Liguria (Genova). In 1921 Sarzana was the scene of fighting between the population and Mussolini's Fascist squads. During these riots, a group of Carabinieri and ordinary citizens opposed and pushed back some 300 armed Fascists who had come to devastate the town, resulting in eighteen dead and about thirty injured .*

Page 181 [1] *The Piave Front,* where two battles near the River Piave were fought between 10 November and 25 December 1917, and 15-23 June 1918, respectively. The Austro-Hungarian army, supported by German units, tried to bring about the final collapse of Italy. Both offensives were repulsed, marking a turning point in World War I on the Italian front.

Page 182 [1] Cavaleria Rusticana, *an Opera by Pietro Mascagni(1863-1945), famous for its drinking song: Viva il vino ch'è sincero, che ci allieta ogni pensiero e che annega l'umor nero e nell'ebrezza tenera, Long live good wine which cheers our thoughts and banishes ill-temper with tender intoxication.*

[2] Herman Goering (1893-1946), *German political and military leader and a powerful member of the Nazi Party. Created the Gestapo and was Commander-in-Chief of the Luftwaffe (Air Force).*

[3] Kesselring. *Generalfeldmarschall Albert Kesselring's military career spanned both World Wars. He was Nazi Germany's most skilful and most highly decorated soldier. He was nicknamed 'Smiling Albert' by the Allies and 'Uncle Albert' by his troops. Responsible for construction of the Gustav Line.*

Page 187 [1] The Miracle of Bolsena. *It occurred in 1263 when a consecrated host allegedly began to bleed onto the small cloth upon which the host and chalice rest during the Canon of the Mass. The appearance of blood was seen as a miracle to affirm the Roman Catholic doctrine of Transubstantiation, which states that the bread and wine become the Body and Blood of Christ the moment of Consecration during the Mass.*

Chapter Twenty One

Page 190 [1]The Black North. *An expression used to describe Northern Ireland. It refers to the majority presence of Protestants in the six counties that comprises Northern Ireland.*

Page 194 [1] PFN, *Partito Fascista Nationale, National Fascist Party*

Page 204 [1] Goldsmith, Oliver, *an Irish 18th-century playwright and poet, best known for his pastoral poem, 'The Deserted Village'. Scotland's answer to Goldsmith was Robert Burns. 'Nursing his wrath to keep it warm' is a quotation from the latter's epic poem, 'Tam O'Shanter.*

Chapter Twenty Two

Page 210 [1] The Mysteries of the Rosary, *are meditations on episodes in the life and death of Jesus from the Annunciation to the Ascension and beyond, known as the Joyful (or Joyous) Mysteries, the Sorrowful Mysteries, and the Glorious Mysteries.*

Page 212 [1]Santa Scolastica. *St Scolastica, born in Italy (Nursia) in the 9th century. She was the twin sister of St Benedict founder of the Benedictine Order of Monks.*

Page 216 [1]John McCormack, *born 1884, died 1945, was an Irish tenor famous for his operatic repertoire. Renowned for his diction and breath control*

.[2] Gigli Beniamino, *born 1890, died 1957. Italian tenor and actor. Considered to be one the most famous operatic singers of the 20th century*

[3] Rigoletto, *an Italian opera by Giuseppe Verdi. Despite serious problems with the Austrian censors who had control over northern Italian theatres at the time, the Opera had a triumphant premiere in Venice's La Fenice Theatre in 1851.*

[4] Titta Ruffo, *born 1877, died 1953. Italian operatic baritone. Known as The Voice of a Lion and is remembered for his glorious baritone sound.*

[5] Fortune favours the Brave, *Audentes fortuna iuvat, Virgil's Aeneid, X, 284.*

Page 219 [1] The Flying Fortresses. *The Boeing B-17 Flying Fortress is a four-engine heavy bomber developed in the 1930s for the United States Army Air Corps*

Page 220 [1] Placito Cassinese or Placito Capuano, *is the first in a number of acts, known collectively as the Placiti Cassinesi, written in the tenth century in which the Benedictine Order reclaimed their lands from squatters who had occupied them after the Montecassino Abbey had been abandoned following its destruction by the Saracens.*

Page 221 [1] Navigatio Sancti Brendani Abbatis, *the Voyage of St Brendan the Abbot. St Brendan, born 484, died 577. One of*

Ireland's earliest saints. Renowned for his legendary navigational voyages in search of 'The Island of the Blessed'

Chapter Twenty Three

Page 225 [1]Incunabulum, plural inconabula, *an early book printed from wooden blocks prior to invention of Gutenberg's Printing Press.*

[2]The Bramante Cloister and The Loggia del Paradiso in Abbey of Montecassino. *See illustration.*

Page 226 [1] Clonmacnoise Monastery, *founded in 548, is located on the banks of the River Shannon . Its strategic position helped it to become a major centre of religion, learning and trade by the ninth century.*

Page 227 [1] The March on Rome, *the insurrection by which Mussolini came to power in 1922. The March of Fascist Supporters marked the beginning of Fascist Rule and the end of the preceding parliamentary regimes of Socialists and Liberals.*

Chapter Twenty Four

Page 232 [1] Beatrice and Dante, *a reference to the famous painting by Henry Holiday (Walker Gallery, Liverpool), in which Dante looks longingly at Beatrice who is deliberately ignoring him.*

Chapter Twenty Five

page 239 [1] The Lateran Pact (1929), *an agreement between the Papacy and the Kingdom of Italy which recognised the Vatican City as a Sovereign State and the status of Rome as the nation's capital, in dispute since 1870 when the armies of King Vittorio Emanuele took possession of the city.*

[2]Santa Marinella, *Rome's historic beach on its northern coastline.*

[3] Feast of Holy Souls or All Souls Day *commemorates the souls of Christians and or Deceased Relatives on November 2nd. The day which follows is known as All Saints Day.*

Page 241 [1] Bèla Ferenc Dezsò Blaskò (1882-1956), *better known as Bela Lugosi, was a Hungarian-American actor famous for portraying Count Dracula in the 1931 film and in various other horror roles.*

Page 243 [1] Stock Medicinale, a brandy marketed originally as 'Stock Brandy Medicinale' in Trieste 1884 by Lionello Stock and from 1955 as 'Brandy Stock 84'. Its great popularity in the United Kingdom gave vent to the expression : Drinking Brandy for medicinal purposes.

[2] Pluralis Maestatis, *The Royal We or Majestic Plural, is the use of a plural pronoun by a single person of high rank such as a sovereign or religious leader*

Page 250 [1] Topolino, *from the Italian name for Mickey Mouse, an Italian digest-size Disney Comic book. It first appeared in 1932 and is a magazine Published today by Panini Comics.*

Page 251 [1] Valeria Messalina (20-48), *was the third wife of the Roman Emperor Claudius, a paternal cousin of Emperor Nero, a second-cousin of Emperor Caligula and a great-grandniece of Emperor Augustus. Was reputed to have an insatiable sexual appetite. According to Roman Historian, Pliny the Elder, she took part in all-night sex competition with a prostitute which lasted 24 hours and won with a score of 25 partners.*

Chapter Twenty Six

Page 261 [1]Soup-takers. *During the Irish Famine or other times of great hunger and poverty, soup kitchens were set up around the country by Anglican Landlords. However, in order to obtain this life-saving nourishment, Irish Catholics had either to renounce their religion or anglicise their names.*

Page 263 [1] Betty Grable, Elizabeth Ruth Grable (1916–1973), *was an American actress, pin-up girl, dancer, and singer. Her 42 movies during the 1930s and 1940s grossed more than $100 million.*

Page 271 [1] Craic, Irish word for enjoyment in a Public House when mixed with alcohol and music.

Chapter Twenty Seven

Page 272 [1]The Mezzogiorno, *the southern part of Italy, including*

Sicily and Sardinia.

Page 274 [1]*When Mussolini came to power in 1922, the myth was born of fascist efficiency, with the train as its symbol. Party Propaganda turned the ramshackle Italian Railway System into one that was the envy of Europe featuring train times that were mythically dependable and punctual.*

Chapter Twenty Eight

Page 286 [1] Devil's Advocate, *in the Roman Catholic Church, an official appointed to present arguments against a proposed canonization or beatification.*

Page 297 [1] *This quotation was attributed to St Augustine when it should have been attributed to Shakespeare's, 'Measure for Measure', Act One Scene Two.*

Chapter Thirty

Page 302 [1] Extreme Unction, the sacramental anointing of a person in immediate danger of death. The term was discarded in 1972 with the establishment of a more general sacrament: The Anointing of the Sick.

Page 306 [1] Samuel Taylor Coleridge, *Songs of the Pixies, 'On leaves of aspen trees, We tremble to the breeze, Veiled from the grosser ken of mortal sight'.*

The Epilogue

Page 309 [1] Monsignor Montini. *He was made a cardinal by Papa Roncalli in1958 and elected Pope in June 1963, taking the name of Pope Paul V1.*

Page 310 [1] *Electable to the Papacy i.e. Papabile. A Cardinal most likely to be elected Pope.*

Printed in Great Britain
by Amazon

15675430R00187